It was quite an eye-opener to learn that there are so many plants with edible leaves. A word of caution though, there is often a reason that rare leaves and fruits are rare. Be careful to note any that require special preparation; pay attention to how those who eat and enjoy them prepare the leaves.

Some 20+ years ago I learned that this book's author was about to retire. I urged him to come to Florida to volunteer at ECHO, which he did!

I was concerned to learn that this incredibly unique book was about to go out of print. ECHO then offered to reprint the book, which you have in your hands right now.

Martin Price

Edible Leaves of the Tropics

Third Edition

Edible Leaves of the Tropics
Third Edition

by

Franklin W. Martin

Ruth M. Ruberté

Laura S. Meitzner

ECHO : North Fort Myers, Florida

The original edition of this book is available in Spanish (*Hojas Comestibles del Trópico*, 245 pp.) by special order on microfiche or paper from:
National Technical Information Service (NTIS)
5285 Port Royal Rd.
Springfield, VA 22161
USA
phone (703) 487-4650
fax (703) 321-8547
http://www.ntis.gov
NTIS order number PB84-112549

Edible Leaves of the Tropics, Third Edition
© 1998 by Educational Concerns for Hunger Organization, Inc.
All rights reserved
Published by ECHO
Printed in the United States of America

ISBN 0-9653360-1-8

To purchase this book or for more information contact:
ECHO
17430 Durrance Road
North Fort Myers, FL 33917-2239
USA
Telephone (941) 543-3246
Fax (941) 543-5317
Electronic mail ECHO@echonet.org
Web site http://www.echonet.org

Contents

Foreword

Under tropical conditions, green leaves are everywhere, providing that soil and water conditions are not limiting. Leaves can be considered highly organized factories which convert the local raw materials of carbon dioxide, water, and minerals into food. Plants are the beginning of the food chain, and on them depends the life of other terrestrial organisms. Humans, as an example of an advanced or predator species on the food chain, would be sorely pressed in the absence of green leaves.

Green leaves in the tropics serve as direct food sources for people under the most civilized circumstances. The important species are grown and preserved on both home and commercial scales. In remote areas, green leaves from wild plants are used as regular and important items of the diet. In times of food shortage, green leaves provide nutritious and readily available sources of food. Yet, these usages hardly touch on the potentials that exist in most environments. The green factories are underutilized and neglected, or depreciated and destroyed.

Among the reasons for such neglect are ignorance and prejudice. Both conditions are hard to cure. Many people living in cities have not had the opportunity to try wild herbs and other green leaves. Special knowledge of the plants' uses is often held by a few wise members of a tribe or society, and it is not always passed down to the younger generations. In the interests of marketing, only a limited number of species are propagated on a scale sufficient to permit economy of handling operations. Furthermore, as dependence on market products increases, wild or weedy plants become despised. As pressures on the land increase, there is a growing danger of extermination of minor species. In many cases, experimentation ceases. Without doubt, some local usages have already disappeared, not even leaving written records.

Lost in this historical process are the techniques for discovering new vegetables. Surely usages were revealed only through experimentation. There must always have been those who looked for, cooked, and ate new leaves for the excitement of discovery. In the process, the poisonous species were discovered, the irritating types avoided, and the obnoxious ones rejected. In isolated areas and in emergencies, interests may be maintained or restimulated. During a civil war in Nigeria, for example, starvation stimulated new experimentation in the bush, the results of which may be lost again rapidly.

Nevertheless, a new breed of explorers has arisen: those whose tastes are adventurous, those who are disenchanted with the bland products of the supermarkets, those who still feel the primordial urge to plant. Those whose pocketbooks are thin can benefit from green leaves easily grown at home. Finally, there are the few who recognize that the vegetables we emphasize now are but a part of a larger, and mostly still available heritage, a heritage with potentials still not fully realized.

It is to the lovers of edible green leaves that we dedicate this book.

Franklin W. Martin and Ruth M. Ruberté

Notes on the Third Edition and ECHO

Edible leaves hold great potential for improving the lives of people who lack sufficient high-quality food on a regular or seasonal basis. Green leaves add essential and often scarce nutrients and variety to the diet, and many species are locally marketable. Perennial vegetables can be a dependable food source requiring very little care. For these reasons, the edible properties of a wide variety of leaves deserve attention among people seeking to help those who are hungry.

A third edition has been published by ECHO so this resource can again be available to communities who can benefit from using leaves as food. The additions in the text are based on ECHO's experience with many of the plants mentioned, both in Florida and in correspondence with many people who have experimented with them in a tremendous range of soils, climates, and cultures worldwide. In this global laboratory, several little-known species have distinguished themselves as first-rate leafy vegetables for their productivity, nutritive value, ability to thrive in poor growing conditions, and other qualities. These species are noted in the text. This edition is intended for use by gardeners and agricultural development practitioners as well as botanists, so a list of germplasm suppliers has been included. Wherever possible, scientific names have been updated. Many localized species were not found in current databases or references used for correction, however, so some errors may persist or have occurred in the process of revision.

Since the original publication of this book, several key resources of great use to those interested in this topic have been published. These are noted in the Introduction and Bibliography sections, and the reader is encouraged to access those materials. This book serves as an overview, but individuals may now find many regional publications which specify a range of greens available and consumed locally.

I extend special thanks to Jim Richard for his tireless and optimistic work in revising the appendix. Christi Sobel designed the artwork for the cover. It is also a pleasure to thank Herb Perry, Matt Stonecypher, Ruth Bartels, Ann Elyse Merritt, Beth Gutheil, and Jen Heller for invaluable assistance in preparing this edition.

Laura S. Meitzner

ECHO is a nonprofit, Christian organization which serves as a resource for people who work in agricultural development in the tropics. Missionaries, Peace Corps volunteers, national extension agents, students, scientists, and many others in 140 countries participate in ECHO's overseas network. ECHO publishes the quarterly technical bulletin *ECHO Development Notes*, which discusses ideas and plants for growing food under difficult conditions; maintains an active seedbank of promising tropical plants, available for small-scale trial by members of ECHO's network; answers technical questions on a wide variety of agricultural topics; hosts an Agricultural Missions Conference each year in November; and tests plants and techniques on a demonstration farm in North Fort Myers, Florida. Write for information about educational tours of the farm. Most of ECHO's publications, seeds, and services are free to people working in developing countries.

Preface to the Third Edition

Edible Tropical Leaves, a Few Reflections

The first edition of this book was conceived in 1971 and published in 1975. A total of 13,000 copies, in English or Spanish, were printed in two editions. Since that time the U.S. Office of Technical Information has distributed photocopies and microfiche copies. Obviously the book has been useful, and there is a suggestion that the book may continue to be useful. At this moment, as a new printing is underway, it is useful to think over the field of edible leaves, and to ask what is new, what has changed, what needs more emphasis, and what can be better said today.

The position of green leaves as food has not changed in the tropics. Leaves are widely used as food, and because they are easily available, they are often considered poor people's food, and held in disdain. However, from a nutritional point of view, the leafy vegetables of the tropics are more valuable than the preferred and commonly available temperate vegetables, head lettuce and cabbage. Except in very limited circumstances, the most valuable of the many tropical species are not playing the role that should be open to them.

The reasons for this are not difficult to assess. They include the overwhelming, inundating influence of Western urban culture together with the implication that all parts of this culture are superior. As a corollary, native cultures and their practices are often considered inferior, a patent absurdity. A second major problem is the nature of the tropical leafy vegetables. Most are not annuals, and most do not lend themselves to the intensive, row-type agricultural technology of modern vegetable production, nor the convenient forms of handling and transport now common. Their important characteristics of continuous production and thus year-round availability at the household level become disadvantages in their marketing. These vegetables, grown near the home, are used logically in small amounts harvested very near the time of actual use. Still another factor limiting use is the poor distribution of these vegetables precisely in the areas where they are most needed, and a failure to understand and to appreciate their values, even when they are present.

The appropriate action in the face of these obstacles is continued, constant efforts to put the vegetables and the information into the hands that most need them. The task of reaching out and accomplishing this front-line task is formidable and never-ending.

Increased experience on my part suggests that of the thousands of leafy vegetables available throughout the tropics, relatively few are great winners, and these should be emphasized first. Emphasis on the ten species below might be one way to make progress. In addition, there are perhaps 25 other quite valuable species frequently available. The rest of the species, 4000 or more, can be thought of as supplementary or emergency foods, but they, too, would be of great value in preventing vitamin A deficiency and blindness in children.

Annuals/Perennials Grown as Annuals	Perennials
Amaranth (*Amaranthus* spp.)	Moringa (*Moringa oleifera*)
Quail grass (*Celosia argentea*)	Katuk (*Sauropus androgynus*)
Sweet potato (*Ipomoea batatas*)	Chaya (*Cnidoscolus chayamansa*)
Water spinach (*Ipomoea aquatica*)	Edible hibiscus (*Abelmoschus manihot*)
Watercress (*Nasturtium officinale*)	Belembe (*Xanthosoma brasiliense*)

In the previous treatment, chaya (*Cnidoscolus chayamansa*) was not sufficiently emphasized for its many values as a leafy vegetable. Now, after sufficient experience with the type that is free of stinging hairs, it is obvious that this is one of the most efficient producers of useful food among the tropical vegetables. It is easy to grow, highly productive, highly nutritive, and tastes good. On the other hand, I now consider that the value of the leaves of cassava (*Manihot esculenta*) was overrated. It has now been seen that tannins of the leaf combine with protein, reducing its potential nutritive value. In fact, it is now increasingly clear that what we know of nutritional values of all vegetables is not enough, for the real value of the vegetable can only be determined by very careful tests based on its use in the diet, just as the values of vitamins were determined. This kind of work may not be done for a large group of tropical leafy crops, and for the most part our judgments of nutritional value will be made on the basis of conventional analyses. Since leaves often contain antinutrients as well, the truth is that we do not really have sufficient evidence of their relative values as food.

There is a growing movement of proponents of natural foods to use vegetables raw. I believe this is a mistake. Cooking in general reduces bacterial and fungal contaminants, tends to wash off any pesticides, and changes the nature of some antinutrients. In general, leaves are safer to eat after cooking. There is a real question in my mind if stir-frying is a sufficient technique for cooking leaves. In third world countries where contamination might be common, it is always safer to boil vegetables of all kinds.

I am also concerned with the safety of leafy vegetables grown under a system of intensive culture. The use of nitrogen fertilizer will increase the succulent nature and tenderness of the vegetable but will also increase the nitrate concentration. High nitrates are tolerated by adults, but are poisonous to babies.

The previous advice to use leafy vegetables in moderate quantities, about a half cup of cooked leaves per day, and to vary the species used in the diet still seems to me to be very good advice. As good as leaves are as foods, and there is no class of vegetables of higher food value, diets for humans are not just leaves. But, in some cases, leaves might be the critical and missing element of great value to some people. I am still enthusiastic about edible tropical leaves.

Franklin W. Martin

List of Illustrations

(Note: The photographs in Figures 1, 2, 4, 6, 7, 12, and 30 are by Karen Lugtigheid.)

List of Tables

CHAPTER I

The Place of Green Leaves in the Diet

Green leaves are not equally appreciated in all parts of the tropics and thus play a varied role in the diets of distinct peoples. East and West Africans make frequent use of green vegetables. In parts of Latin America, green leaves are considered food for animals, although local or weedy species may be added to the cookpot in times of food shortage or in remote regions. In the temperate zone, lettuce is an essential item in salads and is eaten uncooked. Crucifers of many kinds are also well known and used worldwide. The place of green vegetables in the diet is largely a matter of culture, training, and habit.

The role of green leaves in the diet may also be considered by noting how the green food is used. Probably the most common use in all parts of the world is as a boiled vegetable. Such usage is very sound as potential pathogens are thus eliminated, sometimes poisonous or irritating substances are neutralized, and spoilage is brought to a halt. Nevertheless, this technique reduces the leaf to a limp and soggy mass, which may not always be appetizing. Some nutrients may be destroyed by heating while others may be leached out. As a general rule, cooking should be as brief as possible. Some leaves may contain mucilaginous substances, which are often, but not always, appreciated. Frying leaves in oil or enveloped in batter preserves some of their unique characteristics and maintains their texture.

Raw vegetables add novel touches and serve to vary and make interesting the meal. Many green leaves may be eaten raw, but some knowledge and judgment must be applied. *Xanthosoma brasiliense* leaves contain irritating calcium oxalate crystals, easily removed by boiling. Leaves of cassava (*Manihot esculenta*) contain dangerous hydrocyanic glycosides, which are inactivated by cooking.

The drying of green leaves and their preservation as powder is a common practice in Africa and elsewhere. Although some of the food value is lost in the drying process, this method permits storage of easily perishable leaves, making them convenient for use in the kitchen or into the dry season when greens are scarce. Drying merits more investigation, for it is a simple technique that can be widely used throughout the tropics, especially using easily constructed and efficient solar dryers.

Nutritional Aspects

Many diets of the tropical zones are based on starchy staples supplemented, when possible, by foods high in protein. Green-leaved vegetables offer enrichment to such diets and are useful as regulators of the digestive tract. Leaves are the most physiologically active parts of the living plant, and as such are usually rich in vitamins and minerals. Their carbohydrate content is usually insignificant. Although leaves are often not rich sources of protein, some contain sufficient to supplement an otherwise inadequate starchy diet. Greens also contain high amounts of important antioxidants, which serve a protective function against certain diseases. Finally, leaves offer non-nutritional benefits, such as making other foods more appealing, providing a dependable source of food for the family, and adding to household income.

1

Green leaves have a role in preventing or treating the malnourishment present in many tropical areas where leaves grow abundantly, often with little effort in their cultivation. Three considerations in addition to taste preferences ought to influence the choice of foods for a normal diet: the caloric needs, the protein requirement, and the need for vitamins and minerals. Leafy vegetables are particularly important with respect to the latter requirement, adding vitamins and minerals quite out of proportion to their weight. Indeed, no other class of edible plants is equally rich in these nutrients. The diet should include modest amounts of green leaves every day.

Vitamin A deficiency is one of the most widespread nutritional problems, and green leafy vegetables often have been prescribed to supply this nutrient in deficient diets. Vitamin A is generally found in rich quantities in leaves in the form of provitamin A carotenoids, which the body converts to vitamin A. Improved analytical capabilities have shown, however, that the carotenoids are less abundant than older methods indicated. Recent studies also suggest that they have a lower bioavailability than was previously believed (De Pee 1996). This may be due in large part to the placement of the carotenoids in the leaf matrix structure and other dietary components, such as fiber, chlorophyll, and non-provitamin A carotenoids, which can limit absorption. Beta-carotene in leaves is embedded in cell chloroplasts, which must be disrupted for the nutrient to be made available. Some preparations which rupture the cells or remove these impediments, such as the preparation of leaf concentrate (Kennedy 1993), may make the vitamin more available. It is likely that the beta-carotene in non-photosynthetic plant parts, such as mangoes, sweet potatoes, and pumpkins, can be more readily freed from its matrix for absorption by the body. Carotenoids are somewhat resistant to the effects of cooking. There is much ongoing research on this topic (De Pee 1996; West and Poortvliet 1993).

Vitamin C is often present in appreciable amounts in leaves, but tends to be destroyed by heat. Riboflavin occurs in abundance and thiamine is also present in reasonable quantities. The B vitamins are partially soluble in water, and can be lost if the cooking water is discarded (which is necessary in the case of some leaves). Many studies point to the very rapid post-harvest deterioration of vitamins, so as a rule it is best to eat leaves freshly picked, store them cool and moist or wrapped in plastic, and cook them as quickly as possible.

The minerals of importance in green leaves are iron, calcium, and phosphorous. Some doubt exists, however, of the availability of these minerals to the human body. Calcium, for example, when present as an oxalate, is not soluble and thus is not taken up in the digestive tract. A study of iron in 46 lines of amaranth revealed that as little as 6-12% of total iron was bioavailable (Rangarajan 1997).

The protein of green leaves varies considerably. That of some green leaves approaches a significant level. Highest protein contents of leaves are found in certain shrubby species including *Poinsettia*, *Gnetum*, and *Moringa* (Terra 1966). Knowledge of the protein contents of important tropical green leaves can be useful in balancing the diet. However, the protein may combine with tannins on cooking so that it is not available; for example, the leaves of cassava have extremely high protein content, in contrast to the low-protein edible roots, but the leaves' high tannin content limits their usefulness as a protein source. A study of four wild species of *Amaranthus* found that the highest protein concentrations (22.8-27.8%) were found in leaves at the

2

preflowering stage; the study found that, of the major antinutrients, only nitrates exceeded safe levels (Wesche-Ebeling *et al*. 1995). The amino acids of green-leaved vegetables also vary. As sources of the usually short sulphur-bearing amino acids methionine and cystine, *Moringa oleifera*, grown for edible leaves, shoots, young fruits, and roots, is incomparable.

Green leaves are sources of several substances which guard against disease, including the antioxidant vitamins C and E and beta-carotene. These are believed to block some of the cellular damage done in the body by free radical molecules, which can lead to cancers and heart disease.

There are many resources available for current and detailed information on the composition of a variety of vegetables and other foods (http://www.crop.cri.nz/ foodinfo/infoods/infoods.htm; West and Poortvliet 1993). Persons seeking to address problems of malnourishment may consult those resources to determine the relative nutrient value of crops which may be grown to improve nutritional status. However, an examination of the quantitative studies available shows that leafy vegetables are extremely variable, and their food value depends on species, variety, growing conditions, age, harvest timing, post-harvest handling, and preparation. Growing conditions cause vitamin and mineral levels to vary widely within a species, even within individual plants. In general, healthy leaves cut in the preflowering stage provide the highest quality foods. The best sources of green leaves will likely be those which are naturally prolific in the local growing conditions. These may be cultivated annuals; in other settings, weedy species or perennial vegetables will be most appropriate. Trying a wide variety of leafy vegetables is the best way to determine which ones are preferred, as well as discover the appeal of new flavors.

One more point should be mentioned regarding the place of green leaves in the diet. Many of these foods taste good. Those who appreciate the flavors of a few green leaves will find enchantment in the wider range of edible leaves available.

Classification of Green-Leaved Vegetables

The bewildering diversity of nature and the need to simplify it for our limited minds may well be the source of the urge to classify. Edible green leaves occur in such abundance that some classification is necessary and contributes to the orderly treatment of these plants. Classification permits the rapid choice of particular leaves for special purposes. It also serves to satisfy a sense of orderliness.

But how to classify? In this book, green leaves are classified principally by conventional taxonomy into families. To any student of botany this classification is meaningful. From the family one can often obtain a rough idea of the nature of the plant and at times of the characteristics of the leaf. Nevertheless, the conventional taxonomic system is a bulky apparatus for those unfamiliar with taxonomy. Other classifications are useful in further characterizing the plant, and are used in developing the chapters, and in the descriptions later.

When green-leaved vegetables are classified by plant type (herbaceous, viny, shrubby, arboreous, annual, or perennial), useful information is immediately conveyed. Useful appended information may suggest season of production of edible leaves, effects of daylength on flowering and seeding, and physiological limitations.

3

Such information is indispensable to the gardener.

Green leaves are also used in a variety of ways that make easy classification possible. *Salad* vegetables are those that are normally uncooked as a side dish. However, if used principally to decorate the food, and not necessarily eaten, they may be considered *garnishes*. Some may be used to *wrap* food for cooking and are then eaten or removed. Small quantities pickled or sweetened when used to contrast with other foods are called *relish*. When the leaf is cooked and eaten as a side dish, it is called *spinach*, but if it is mixed in stew or with other vegetables, it is a *pot herb*. When the leaf imparts a desired flavor to the dish, it is a *spice* or a *condiment*. However, when the cooked dish is taken as a beverage, it is a *tea*. Leaves may also be soaked in water to give an *infusion*, used as tea or for medicinal purposes. Some green leaves have many different uses.

Green leaves may be classified into those of commerce, those more suited to home gardens, and those that grow wild. The classification into commonly available and exotic species also has practical value. Importance can be measured many ways, by economic value, by frequency of use, or by contribution to the diet. Each method of classification adds useful information to the description and understanding of the species.

Use of Green Leaves Throughout the Tropics

Whether or not green leaves are accepted in the diet is largely a matter of education and experience. These particular cultural and dietary phenomena are largely related to geography. Oomen and Grubben (1978) estimate the following figures for average daily consumption of leaves in grams per person: humid regions of Africa and Asia, 20-24; drier regions in Africa and Asia, 15; and Latin America, 6-8.

Green leaves are an accepted part of the normal diet in tropical Africa. The knowledge of the various species is widespread and systematically passed on through the home. Cultivated and wild species, their seasons, uses, and tastes are well known (see Abbiw 1990). Many species are marketed or bartered, and are even carried long distances to sell. The number of species used in Africa is large, perhaps 500. It is interesting to note that many of these are introduced species. The people of Africa have experimented with the edible qualities of newly introduced plants, and there are probably few that have not been tested. In Africa the green leaf is generally cooked into a stew that is eaten with a staple starchy food. The stew offers many of the nutritional qualities not available in the starchy staple.

In the Orient the situation is somewhat different, where heavy population pressures and frequent starvation have forced a systematic study of the edible qualities of all plants. The discoveries have often proven not only edible but also nutritious. A highly skilled and sophisticated treatment of new edible greens has developed with time into a unique form of cookery. Now green-leaved plants are eaten not only to fill the diet but also to add variety and to please the taste.

In Southeast Asia, from India to the Philippines there is an enormous diversity of plant materials, which is almost matched by the diversification of languages and peoples. It is highly probable that an equally energetic process of exploration for edible leaves has occurred. Many trees, including those of the forest,

are known for their edible leaves. A wide variety of other fruits and vegetables are used also as a source of leaves. The attitude appears to have been, "If it is green, try to eat it." Probably many of the uses of wild species have not yet been recorded. Unfortunately, while this area is rich in leaves known to be edible, many are not utilized due to tradition or prejudice, often resulting in unnecessary malnutrition.

On the other hand, green leaves are not now an important item in the diet of the peoples of Central and South America. In fact, the edible nature of the green leaves of many native and introduced plants is largely unknown except to the initiated few. It is uncertain whether this relative lack of interest in leaves is a very recent development or whether it also characterized the original peoples of the area. Records are not extensive enough to be sure, but native North Americans did eat leaves and recognize edible and poisonous species. Bye (1981) and Booth *et al.* (1993) discuss the current uses of indigenous, introduced, and weedy greens by traditional peoples in Central America, indicating a highly seasonal use of leaves during land clearing before planting maize. It can be presumed that many uses of green leaves have died out in reaction to the views of those who depreciated local customs.

In the treatments of wild and domesticated edible plants of tropical America, few edible greens are mentioned. Most of those that have come to the attention of economic botanists are introduced plants. Nevertheless, a few special items merit attention as being Latin American in origin, including the leaves of *Arracacia xanthorrhiza* and *Pereskia bleo*, and an assortment of palm cabbages. The following sources of green leaves in South America are of particular nutritive value: *Amaranthus tricolor* L., *Chenopodium berlandieri* Maq., *Malva parviflora* L., *Crotalaria longirostrata* Hook. & Arn., and *Cucurbita pepo* L. Among the few uses of greens in South America, the use of cassava leaves was a widespread and logical practice related to that principal staple. However, the custom of eating such leaves is not universal, and in Latin America today green leaves are frequently scorned.

Sources of Information on Edible Leaves

Surprisingly little has been written on tropical edible leaves, considering their importance in the diet. The published information available, often repetitive and seldom complete, has generally been hidden in more general publications concerning tropical gardening or useful plants. Recent years, however, have seen an increase in the efforts to investigate the role of greens in the diet. Both the classic references and newer publications on nutrition are of value. The best single source of information which can be recommended for the principal species is Ochse and Bakhuizen van den Brink (1931). Seeds and plant materials may be difficult to find, although some species are offered in commercial seed catalogs; some local and regional seedbanks also now include leaf species. Facciola (1990) is the essential resource for the gardener seeking information on varieties and looking for planting materials. The present authors obtained and tested some of the leaves included in this text only with much difficulty, and others were not tested at all. In most cases, the serious student will not find any single source that gives more information than that presented here, but major review papers are mentioned in the text describing particular vegetables. Some of the better general sources are below. Full references are in the bibliography.

Vegetables of the Dutch East Indies (Ochse and Bakhuizen van den Brink 1931). One of the richest sources of green-leaved vegetables is Indonesia. As a crossroads of Southeast Asia, practically all edible plants of the surrounding regions have been introduced and many have become part of the diet. This volume is one of the authoritative works in this field. First published in 1891, it was translated to English in 1931. Principally pot herbs and side dishes are covered, but tubers, bulbs, rhizomes, and spices are also mentioned. The problem may be obtaining a copy; it has become a collectors' item, difficult to even borrow.

Tropical Leaf Vegetables in Human Nutrition (Oomen and Grubben 1978). For the health promoter in tropical countries, we know of no more practical handbook to assist in evaluating, growing, and using leaves in nutrition programs. The authors offer a practical perspective on the nutritive value and usages of greens and describe the cultivation of major crops (hot and cool season annuals and perennials). Ideas for nutrition education and several detailed recipes from six countries are helpful to the field worker. There are excellent pictures on every page. *The Leaves We Eat* (Bailey 1992) is also full of useful information and fantastic photographs.

Cornucopia: A Source Book of Edible Plants (Facciola 1990). This is an indispensable guide to further information and germplasm sources for over 3000 species, including over 800 species with edible leaves and leafy shoots. Extensive, detailed varietal descriptions are included for common crops, but little-known and localized species are also included. Common names, listings of edible portions, and thorough indices make this resource even more valuable. In the past it was extremely difficult to locate planting materials of many plants discussed here--not anymore.

Tropical Crops, Dicotyledons (Purseglove 1968). The text of this remarkable and useful publication is arranged by families. Most of the principal crop plants of the tropics are treated, but emphasis is definitely on plantation crops. Information on greens is usually quite brief, and except for a few principal species, cannot easily be located. Frequently the only mention of an edible green is a reference such as "used for pot herbs." Nevertheless, because of its high quality and extensive coverage of tropical plants, it is a reference of considerable value in the library.

Handbook of Tropical and Subtropical Horticulture (Mortensen and Bullard 1964), is an extremely condensed treatment summarizing many other sources. Tropical greens are treated briefly, not nearly as adequately as they merit.

Fundamentos Botánicos de los Cultivos Tropicales (Leon 1968). For the Spanish-speaker this book is a particularly valuable source of information on the edible species of South and Central America. Only the principal species are covered. Most are illustrated by hand drawings. This book has a good regional flavor.

Tropical Vegetables: Vegetable Growing in the Tropics and Subtropics, Especially of Indigenous Vegetables (Terra 1966) is particularly valuable as a comprehensive list of major and minor vegetables. As is the case when many items are included, the textual information is often quite brief. However, most of the principal species are well treated.

Growing Native Vegetables in Nigeria (Epenhuijsen 1974). Uses, cultural requirements, harvesting, seed production, and pests and diseases of a wide variety of local plants are discussed.

Vegetable Production in Southeast Asia (Knott and Deanon 1967). Probably

the best text on tropical vegetables, it is particularly useful for its chapters on principles of production. Many unusual vegetables are treated here, including some of the better edible greens.

The Samaka Guide to Homesite Farming (Samaka Service Center 1962). An integrated approach to subsistence on a small (600-1000 meter) lot in the Philippines is presented in this publication. Native and introduced vegetables including edible leaves are described, along with practical suggestions for use. The book is enriched by its folksy style, hand-drawn illustrations and earthy suggestions. In addition to its value for gardening, it merits a place in the library for its unusual nature.

An Inventory of Tropical Vegetables (Martin, Doku, and Ruberté 1991). This is a listing of principal and minor vegetables, especially complete with respect to the edible plants of tropical America. Plants are considered by family, with good indices for scientific and common names. Major vegetables have short descriptions, while the hundreds of minor species receive a single line with names, growth habit, origin, edible parts, and whether cultivated or wild. As this is the present authors' own work, species with edible leaves are always mentioned. This is available from ECHO.

Useful Plants of the Philippines (Brown 1951). These encyclopedic volumes rival those of Burkill as sources of information on plants from Southeast Asia. However, while a good source of general descriptions and an excellent source of information on medicinal uses, the food uses of green leaves are often overlooked. This is particularly true of important economic species used for other purposes, but of which the leaves can be eaten.

The Food Plants of the Philippines (Wester 1921). Although old and based in large part on two even older treatments, this continues to serve as a useful source of information on native edible plants of the Philippines. Many of the 444 species described are not available from other areas. Their names, characteristics, edible parts, and methods of use are well presented. Cultural information is sometimes given, together with geographical distribution. Comments on the relative importance of the species are particularly useful.

List of Foods Used in Africa (Claude 1967). Nearly 4000 items are included in this comprehensive, well-documented, paperback publication. Foods are classified into 20 groups, of which more than half are entirely of plant origin. Because of the large number of species listed the information is held at a minimum, and consists chiefly of names, areas where eaten, parts eaten, frequency of consumption, and references. More than 400 exact references include practically every relevant publication in English and French and can provide additional information on species of interest. Group 7 consists of vegetables. Over 1000 are listed, and of at least half of these the leaves are eaten. Especially useful is the frequency of consumption scale by which the relative importance of each species can be judged. Unfortunately, the family to which the species belongs is not listed, nor is the method of preparation given. Occasional footnotes clarify some of these points. Many of the minor species listed in this volume have not been dealt with in the present treatment.

Fruits and Vegetables in West Africa (Tindall 1965). Considerable information is provided on a variety of native and introduced green leaf vegetables of West Africa. Details of cultivation are included. The treatment is practical.

A Dictionary of the Economic Products of the Malay Peninsula (Burkill 1935)

is one of the best sources for information on any economic plant of the tropics. The encyclopedic tendency of this two-volume work prevents detailed treatment of most species. A very large number of plants with edible leaves or shoots are mentioned, including those used for minor purposes, such as for condiments or relishes. Plants are listed by their scientific names arranged alphabetically. An easy book to use, it is made much more valuable by marginal notes that quickly guide the reader to the information desired. The wide range of information given on local usages makes for entertaining reading.

CHAPTER II

The Principal Edible Green Leaf Herbs of the Tropics

A quick glance at the appendix of this volume should suffice to show that the number of species bearing edible green leaves in the tropics is very large. Most of the listed species are not well known, not well distributed, and have a limited potential. Only a few have become world travelers, and it is only from these that sufficient information is available.

Among the characteristics of the better species included in this chapter are availability throughout the tropics, ease of cultivation, relatively long periods of production or relatively high amounts produced, and acceptable flavors. All of these are cultivated plants that normally grow better when systematically cared for, although most also occur wild at times or survive well when abandoned. The species mentioned here constitute a select group that should satisfy every taste.

Aizoaceae

Tetragonia tetragonioides (Pallas) Kuntze (New Zealand spinach) is a vigorous, rapidly growing prostrate herb that appears to be widely adapted in both temperate and tropical climates. It is native to New Zealand but has been widely introduced and now is often found weedy, especially on beaches and in sandy areas. It has become an important spinach in many tropical areas because it can be grown where temperatures are too high for temperate zone spinach (*Spinacia oleracea* L., Chenopodiaceae). Nevertheless, it too has its temperature limits, and should be considered a subtropical or upland herb. In the Philippines it grows best at elevations of 600 meters or more, and it is found even at 2800 meters in Ecuador.

The species is distinguished by its thick, fleshy, spreading stems; its succulent, alternate, short-petioled, deltoid leaves; small, inconspicuous, petalless flowers borne in leaf axils in small numbers; and a dry, hard, horned fruit. It is usually described as an annual, but may persist as a perennial. Under appropriate conditions, it can survive for many years; old plants can be used for new cuttings.

Young leaves and about 8 cm of stem are eaten as a spinach dish, rich in iron and a very good source of calcium and phosphorous. When other greens are not available, the shoots serve well uncooked in salads, where they are especially noted for their crispness. This practice is not recommended because of the saponin content.

Plantings can be established either from cuttings, which root very easily in damp sand, or from the large brownish fruits. The seeds germinate very irregularly. Soaking them in water for 24 hours is useful. Initially the seedlings are too succulent to transplant easily. A sandy soil is especially desirable in the case of this plant. On such a soil the plant will spread rapidly, and the drier surface assures less rot of the prostrate stems. Nevertheless, good fertility, especially nitrogen fertilization, promote an abundance of succulent growth. Because of the dense growth habit of this species, a few plants suffice for a family. Due to its drought resistance and immunity to most insects, the planting needs very little care. As it is easy to grow, and nutritious as well, New Zealand spinach merits a spot in any tropical vegetable garden.

9

Amaranthaceae

Amaranthus tricolor L., *A. paniculatus* L., *A. caudatus* L., and *A. cruentus* L. (edible amaranth, Chinese spinach, love-lies-bleeding, bush greens) are a few examples of the many cultivated species of this genus, well known chiefly for their edible seeds in Mexico and Central America, but equally useful as pot herbs. The amaranths are of the few genera of plants domesticated in both Old and New World tropics. The leaves of many wild species are equally edible. These species probably arose in close association with the cultivated species. Generally the wild species are considered to have hybridized frequently with the cultivated and thus produced a series of intermediate types. However, some of the species are separated by rather strong reproductive barriers.

Amaranthus species are distributed throughout the temperate zone and the tropics. The best types for use as spinach or salads, however, are cultivated in Southeast Asia and West Africa. There are many varieties and the plant in such areas is widespread and greatly appreciated. The variety 'Calalou' has demonstrated exceptional vigor in many sites; while this quality may endear it to the gardener, it demonstrates the weed potential of a prolific seed producer.

The species are all herbaceous, short-lived annuals (Fig. 1). They are upright and branch sparsely. The leaves are relatively small (5-10 cm in length) but quite variable among varieties. Some varieties are purplish with betalain. The flowers are small, and are borne in abundance in terminal or axillary spikes. The life span of these species is rather short. Small edible seeds are borne in large numbers. The flowers are not edible. The leaves, their petioles, and the young tips are sometimes used in salads. This is a dubious practice as the oxalic acid content of some species is uncomfortably high (1-2%). Boiling produces a very acceptable spinach. Vitamins A and C, calcium, and iron are found in good quantity.

The amaranths are generally propagated from seeds. They germinate irregularly, a characteristic that facilitates the weedy nature of the genus. They are not exceptionally sensitive to season and thus may be planted any time. The young seedlings 5-8 cm high are transplanted 8-15 cm apart. Delayed transplanting reduces yields. Tender plants need some protection from hard rains. The soil should be very fertile, preferably with added manure, compost, or nitrogenous fertilizer. Plants grow very rapidly and thus require ample water. Some species can tolerate drought, but of course produce little edible material under such conditions. Leaves and tender shoots can be harvested at any time. It has been shown that yields are best when the upper portions are cut routinely at 2-3 week intervals. Eventually the plants begin to flower and develop fewer leaves. Frequent cutting delays the onset of flowering and thus prolongs the effective life of the plant. Close spacing (23 x 23 cm) stimulates height of plants and increases yield per unit area.

Amaranth leaves are particularly attractive to leaf-chewing insects. These may decimate a planting in a very short time. A useful practice is to cover the bed with a fine screen to eliminate insects. Insecticides are also used for this purpose, a risky and debatable practice when harvests are made so frequently.

Because of their high nitrogen requirement and attraction to insects, the edible amaranths are more difficult to grow than many other green-leaved vegetables.

10

Nevertheless, because of their succulent nature and excellent flavor, the amaranths are considered one of the better sources of edible greens.

Celosia argentea L. (quail grass) is one of the many edible species of this widespread tropical genus. The cultivated variety *cristata* is grown in the temperate zone as the summer annual cockscomb. Although now widely scattered through the tropics, it is of Asiatic origin. It is often seen growing uncultivated. The edible species are most commonly used in Southeast Asia and West Africa. Some species (*C. trigonal* L.) have medicinal uses, and even the edible-leaved species are slightly diuretic. The plants normally require somewhat rich conditions for maximum development, but some forms are weedy and produce even on dry bare land.

Quail grass (Fig. 2) is among the most promising greens for poor or variable growing conditions, with wide tolerance to both dry and humid conditions and few pest or disease problems. The plants are vigorous annuals that grow rapidly from seed. They are upright with alternate leaves and few branches until near flowering time. Flowers are borne in dense heads that yield large numbers of edible seeds. Fallen seed can establish the plant in an area of the garden. The flowers are often brilliantly colored, and even the green foliage may contain large amounts of betalain pigments. In some areas it is cultivated for its ornamental value as well as its leaves.

The leaves, young stems, and young inflorescences are eaten as pot herbs. Steamed leaves are not acceptable. Much of the pigment is lost on boiling, producing dark, ugly cooking water which must be tossed. Nevertheless, leaves retain a pleasant green color. They soften up readily and should not be overcooked. Texture is soft, and the flavor is very mild and spinach-like. Bitterness is entirely lacking.

Alternanthera sissoo (Brazilian or sissoo spinach) is a perennial which spreads to cover the ground and is very popular in Brazil for home gardens due to its dependable production and assistance in weed control. It prefers well-drained soils with high organic content. Viable seed is not produced; plants are propagated easily by cuttings. Frequent harvest of the 15-25 cm shoots promotes optimum yields. This plant suffers severe insect attack on the leaves in some areas.

Araceae

Xanthosoma brasiliense (Deaf.) Engler (Tanier spinach, Tahitian taro, belembe) probably has its origin in the river valleys of Brazil, but was distributed throughout tropical South America, and was cultivated for its leaves in pre-Columbian times. Since then it has been taken to all parts of the tropics, and frequently has replaced *Colocasia* in usage of leaves. It is not well known, but is very much appreciated for its delicious leaves by those who do know it.

The plant develops from a rather insignificant corm which, unlike the corms of most *Xanthosoma*s, never becomes very starchy. These corms off-shoot readily so that a normal plant consists of a colony of small corms clustered around the mother corm. The species is a perennial capable of growth throughout the year. Under favorable conditions, it may reach a height of 80 cm, but more normally is about 50 cm tall. The leaves are sagittate (arrowhead-shaped) to trilobed, glabrous, dark green, fairly smooth, and succulent (see cover). They are produced singly in rapid flushes of growth. The petioles are long and succulent. No above-ground stem is produced.

Leaves and stems are eaten. Some people prefer the very tender young leaves, but once one is accustomed to the stronger flavor of older leaves, they are then preferred. Only aging and diseased leaves need be rejected. The upper portion of the petioles is also sufficiently tender to be eaten, but the very lowest parts are tough without excessive cooking. Corms are edible, but because they are small and not very starchy, they are seldom used as foods.

The leaves may be harvested for food at any time. For commercial purposes, whole, mature leaves and petioles are cut from the plant and bundled together. For home use, frequently all leaves are cut, and then sorted in the kitchen to eliminate unsuitable leaves or portions of leaves. The leaves wilt promptly if not protected by water sprays or by plastic bags. They may be stored several days in a household refrigerator before use.

Although the leaves are said to be used in salads, the authors find that the calcium oxalate crystals are usually too irritating to use the leaves raw. Before cooking, the leaves and stems are cut into bite-sized pieces. They are boiled 10-15 minutes, until the stems are soft. Overboiling results in a pasty dish, and should be avoided. The softened preparation is served with salt, light seasoning, or butter. Because of its excellent flavor, it is preferred as a spinach over all other greens.

From a nutritional standpoint, this spinach is worthwhile particularly for its calcium, phosphorous, and vitamins A and C. The protein content is only 3 percent.

Propagation is by replanting the offshoot corms. The center corm is sometimes large enough to be cut into 2 or 3 pieces for propagation. Any season of the year is suitable for planting, but other requirements must be met. The soil requirements are rather exacting. A loam or clay soil is quite suitable, but sandy soils are not tolerated. The soil must be maintained at a high level of fertility. Organic material in the soil is particularly important. Nitrogen requirements are high. Furthermore, the plants require large amounts of water and even tolerate occasional flooding. During dry conditions the older leaves die back rapidly. The plants grow best in full sunlight or very light shade.

Suitable leaves for harvesting are produced in 2-3 weeks, but about 6 weeks are required to bring leaves to a mature state. Harvests of single leaves can be made each week, or of all the leaves every 6-8 weeks. Refertilization should be frequent. Plantings lose vigor with time, and transplanting is thus desirable every 1 or 2 years.

Few pests or diseases are found. Vigorously growing plants often develop symptoms of virus. Because of vegetative propagation, virus diseases have probably accumulated, but these are tolerated. Occasionally root and tuber rots occur, but these, too, seldom cause serious concern. Leaf spots are common, but principally affect the older leaves. Precautions against diseases are generally not necessary, but production on a commercial scale would undoubtedly reveal new problems.

Xanthosoma spp. (tanier, tannia, yautia) are plants closely related to the taros and dasheens, but without peltate leaves (Fig. 3). The various species are difficult to classify, especially from vegetative characteristics, and indeed may be closely related. The taniers are of New World origin. They were cultivated and widely distributed in pre-Columbian times. By now taniers have been introduced to all parts of the tropics, but are particularly well known in Africa.

Superficially, plants of the genus *Xanthosoma* are quite similar to plants of

12

Colocasia (taro, dasheen). In addition to the difference mentioned above, the plants produce fewer leaves but these are often larger, with a much stouter petiole. They are usually arrowhead-shaped. A few species produce above-ground stems. The typical spiked and sheathed flowers are rarely seen.

Xanthosoma species are grown chiefly for their starchy corms. The principal corm is large, spherical to ovate, and usually quite acrid. The lateral corms are borne in abundance from the base of the principal corm. The starch grain is large and not easily digested. However, the leaves make excellent greens if carefully prepared. This means using chiefly the younger leaves (unfolded is preferred), and peeling the petioles. Oxalic acid and calcium oxalate occur in abundance in leaves, stems, and some corms. The use of baking soda to neutralize the oxalic acid is recommended. Leaves are frequently stewed in native dishes.

Taniers are propagated from the large central corm. This can be cut into several pieces, preserving at least one eye in each. The soil should be rich and deep. Heavy clays are well tolerated. Much water is required through the relatively long season of growth (8-11 months). Some mechanical aid in harvesting of the tubers is desirable. The leaves, however, may be harvested at any season. Plantings are relatively free of pests and diseases.

Among twenty-two varieties of taniers tested, differences were encountered in the cooking time necessary to reach tenderness, the color of the cooking water, the appearance and attractiveness of the cooked leaf, and flavor. The calcium oxalate crystals persisted more in some than in other varieties. The range in quality led us to rate varieties from unacceptable to excellent. The Puerto Rican varieties judged excellent were Dominicana and Inglesa.

Because of the availability of the superior species, *X. brasiliense,* the taniers are not recommended as a leaf vegetable for the home garden. Where the species are grown for their corms, however, the leaves may be used as a by-product.

Colocasia esculenta (L.) Schott consists of two well-defined varieties. That with an elongated corm is called taro and is generally grown by paddy culture. However, upland (non-paddy) varieties are also common. The botanical form *globulifera* known as dasheen or malanga is set apart by various characteristics. Cultural techniques are generally upland. Taros and dasheens were well distributed from the Pacific Islands to Egypt in pre-Columbian times, and are now widely grown throughout the tropics as staple crops.

Taros and dasheens are grown principally for their large edible, starchy corms from which the leaf petioles spring; there is no above-ground stem. The leaves are large, mostly peltate, and rather succulent. They are short-lived. New corms form readily at the base of the old. The taro corm is fibrous and has a spongy texture. It is difficult to cut. Taros are therefore often beaten after cooking to free the starch materials and to make the partially fermented dish, poi. Dasheen corms, on the other hand, are much more crisp, cut easily, and are more often used just as a boiled vegetable. There are many varieties which differ in details and are well known for their particular virtues.

All taros and dasheens contain quantities of oxalic acid crystals. When the leaves and petioles are not too acrid, they are frequently eaten. Among 74 taros of the Pacific described by Whitner, *et al.* (1939), 5 varieties are grown principally for

13

their leaves and 7 belong to a non-acrid group of which the leaves are often eaten. The most common methods of eating the blade or the petiole are as a side dish (sometimes pickled), in a stew, or as a green wrap for baked foods. The leaves and petioles of dasheen are generally more acrid, and are cooked with baking soda or fat meat to counteract the oxalic acid. On preparation of petioles the skin is often removed; this is not necessary if the leaves are small. The unfurled leaves are eaten before the crop is harvested, and are especially delicious.

A further use for taros and dasheens is as a blanched shoot vegetable. The corms are placed in the dark where they eventually sprout. The blanched shoots make one of the most tender of vegetables.

In the West Indies a stew, calalou, is often made from dasheen leaves. The recipe for this delightful dish is given below in one of its early forms:

Ingredients	Quantity
Young dasheen leaves	Enough for four persons
Okra	Ten or twelve pods
Bananas (almost green)	One (cut in bits)
Roselle (Sorrel)	Handful
Ham (or other meat with fat)	One pound
Peppers	One or two small bird peppers
Rosemary	A very little (to taste)
Cloves	A very little (to taste)
Nutmeg	A very little (to taste)
Cinnamon	A very little (to taste)

Take as many young dasheen leaves as will make the amount of plainly prepared dasheen desired. Wash the leaves and take out the midrib and largest veins. Have only enough boiling water as is absolutely necessary. Put in the meat chosen and the dasheen leaves. After half an hour, add all the other ingredients, with spices to taste and sufficient peppers to make the dish quite hot. Cook until all the ingredients except the salt meat are quite soft, then take out the meat. Stir well with a swizzle stick or egg beater. Guard against burning by having a slow fire or an asbestos mat under the casserole. Cooking time is about two and a half hours.

The following may be substituted in the place of the ham mentioned, the total quantity always being one pound: salt pork (1 lb.); or crab meat (3/4 lb.) and 1/4 lb. salt pork; or frog legs (3/4 lb.) and 1/4 lb. salt pork. Any of the above ingredients may be omitted except the dasheen, the bananas, one meat and fat, the peppers, and the roselle. If roselle is not procurable, the juice of a lime may be substituted.

Dasheen makes the principal constituent of the dish, which resembles a puree of spinach in color and consistency. It is served over hot boiled rice in the proportions of half rice and half calalou.

The starch grains of taro and dasheens are very small, making the starch very digestible. As a baby food, particularly in the form of poi, taro is said to be non-allergenic. The protein content is fairly high in some varieties but is low in sulfur-bearing amino acids, methionine and cystine. On the other hand, the food value of the leaves is generally considered high.

Paddy-type taros are normally grown in submerged beds where a steady flow of water is maintained. Fertilizers or rotted plant materials are incorporated in the soil. The plants are propagated either from the small side shoots or from the upper portion of the corm of the principal shoot. The propagules are planted in the mud 30-45 cm apart. The paddy is gradually flooded as the new leaves form Periodically the beds are drained for weed control and for fertilizing. Harvest takes place from 11 to 15 months after planting by pulling or prying out the corms. They are trimmed on top and bottom, washed, and marketed. The leaves, on the other hand, may be harvested at any time during the long growing season. Light harvesting of leaves does not substantially affect the yield of tubers.

The culture of upland taros and dasheens is quite similar. The same types of propagating materials are used. The soil should be exceptionally rich and almost continuously well-watered. These plants tolerate poor drainage but cannot stand very much dry weather. Harvesting is done after 11 months. Some mechanical assistance, such as a moldboard plow, is desirable to remove the tubers. As with taros, leaves and petioles may be harvested at any season.

Basellaceae

Basella alba L. (Malabar or Ceylon spinach, libato), is a very succulent trailing or climbing perennial vine that apparently originated in India or Indonesia, but which has now spread throughout the tropical world, and is even used in the temperate zone as an annual. It is one of the better of the tropical spinaches, and is widely adapted to a variety of soils and climates. A short review of this species and its characteristics has been presented by Winters (1963). Malabar spinach is particularly abundant and appreciated in India, Malaysia, and the Philippines, but it is also seen throughout tropical Africa, the Caribbean, and tropical South America.

The little-known family Basellaceae, consisting of only 4 genera, shares many of the characteristics of the Chenopodiaceae. *Basella* consists of only one species, but two specific names are often applied. The green form is known as *B. alba*, while the foliage of *B. rubra* is deep red like the foliage of the table beet. On germination of the seed, the cotyledons are large, fleshy, and continue to grow for some weeks. The foliage and thick tender stems are glabrous. The leaves are almost circular to ovate, alternate, and short-petioled (Fig. 4). They are thick, rugose, succulent, and colored from green to purple. The flowers, borne on axillary spikes or branching peduncles, are bisexual and inconspicuous. The fruits are fleshy and purplish black. The juice is sometimes used as a dye.

The succulent young and mature leaves and stems are eaten. Inflorescences, unless very young, are tough and should be avoided. The most common method of cooking is as a pot herb, mixed with stew or other vegetables. However, the young plants also make excellent cooked greens. On cooking, the green form retains its fresh green color. The red form loses much pigment to the water, and is less attractive. The odor of the cooked leaves is strong. The leaves themselves have a mild flavor or are almost tasteless. The stems may be somewhat bitter, but not objectionably so. The stems in particular become somewhat gelatinous or mucilaginous, especially if over-cooked. The green leaves can also be used uncooked in salads as an acceptable lettuce

15

substitute. Malabar spinach is a good source of vitamins A and C, calcium, and iron. Protein content is low as compared to that of other leaves.

Malabar spinach is a perennial that extends itself with time. When it runs over a light soil, it can develop new roots at the nodes, and thus continue indefinitely. If given supports on which to climb, it can develop a superstructure, but it is not a strong climber. After two or more years, individual plants, if not well cared for, tend to die back. With fertilization, hedges may be maintained for long periods, and production is continuous. It is very susceptible to damage by root-knot nematodes

Although *Basella* is tolerant of many soils, a sandy loam appears to be most suitable. In such soils the seeds can be sown directly. They germinate within a few days. Or, the vines may be established directly from stem cuttings. These need a little shade on transplanting, but root readily. Plants are spaced at about one meter. *Basella* can thrive under only moderate fertility, but it is quite responsive to added nitrogen.

The first harvest can be taken as little as four weeks after planting, but this stunts the plants. After about three months, the established planting may be pruned every week or so to produce an edible crop. The leaves and about 7-13 cm of stem are harvested. *Basella* vines branch readily, and frequent harvest is desirable to maintain the planting within bounds. During the season of most intense flowering (short days of winter), the leaves tend to be small, and the new growth occurs chiefly as new flowering clusters. Excess pruning may help at this stage to maintain the production of new green shoots. Plantings remain remarkably free of insects and disease problems, and need little attention besides adequate watering and harvest.

Compositae

Gynura crepioides (Okinawa spinach) is a fast-growing, perennial ornamental low shrub native to Indonesia. It is noteworthy for its good production with very little maintenance and its distinctive pine-like flavor of the leaves. The leaves are dark green on the top surface and purple on the underside. Tender leaf shoots and young leaves are marketed, and are generally eaten mixed with other greens, imparting their flavor to the dish. It is propagated by cuttings.

Convolvulaceae

The sweet potato, *Ipomoea batatas* (L.) Lam., originated in the New World, although the site of origin and the manner in which it originated are still unknown. Distributed as far as New Guinea and New Zealand before the time of Columbus, the sweet potato was an important crop related to the colonization and welfare of the islands of the Pacific. Its range has since been extended so that the species is known throughout both temperate and tropical zones. Propagated vegetatively, the sweet potato is represented by thousands of varieties, but is seldom seen in the wild state.

Sweet potato is normally a trailing vine, although climbing forms resembling typical morning glories are known. Although a perennial, its succulent nature restricts its cultivation to short growing seasons of 3-5 months. Unlike many roots and tubers, it begins to store starch at a very early stage, making early harvests possible. It is one of the most efficient plants to capture the energy of the sun as calories.

Sweet potatoes are grown principally for their starchy roots. However, the edible leaves and stem tips are well known. Often considered poor people's food, sweet potato foliage has a rich protein content that helps fill the nutritional gap left by eating principally the protein-poor tubers. In West Africa, sweet potato greens are particularly important, and varieties have been developed that are used only for the leaves. These are especially rich in calcium.

In a laboratory study of their cooking qualities, 44 varieties of sweet potato were found to differ in their general appearance, flavor, and amount of bitterness. Many varieties have a resinous flavor that is not objectionable unless quite strong. Because of anthocyanin content and other phenolics, the cooking water is often unpleasantly colored. It should always be discarded. Raw leaves are said to contain some HCN, and therefore thorough cooking is desirable. Accounts of vomiting and purging associated with eating the young tops might be related to the presence of poisonous substances commonly found in other species (*I. purga* Hayne) which are sometimes used medicinally.

Because it is so easy to culture, and because the species yields edible roots as well as leaves, sweet potato merits a place in the tropical garden. Leaves and tubers can be produced year-round, and plants resist climatic extremes. Most soils are suitable, but richness of organic material or nitrogen promotes lush growth of leaves.

Ipomoea aquatica Forssk. (kangkong, water spinach) is an important green leaf vegetable crop in Taiwan, Malaysia, Indonesia, and Southeast Asia. It must have been domesticated centuries ago, probably in China, and has been introduced sporadically throughout the tropics and semitropics, but has not become popular elsewhere. Wild forms have become established in many areas of the tropics, where they are occasionally put to use. Its cultivation is restricted in Florida due to concern over its weed potential, but this plant is widely appreciated in much of Asia and is an excellent producer of edible green leaves. An account of water spinach, its cultivation and importance, has been given by Edie and Ho (1969). Several varieties are known, but the most important distinction is between upland (dry) and paddy (swamp) forms.

The species is a trailing vine that spreads rapidly by rooting at the nodes. Vertical branches arise from the leaf axils. It is quite glabrous, with sagittate, alternate leaves. The foliage is somewhat succulent, particularly so in the case of the wetland form, and has a pleasant light green color. A white flower is produced, followed by a four-seeded pod.

Practically all parts of the young plant are eaten. Older stems, especially of plants cultivated on dry land, contain considerable fiber. Cultural methods emphasize the production of young, succulent tips. These can be eaten fresh in salads. The flavor is agreeable. More frequently, they are cooked as a spinach. Cooking in oil is also very common. The flavor is bland, and something should be added to enhance it. The leaves maintain much of their green color, but the yellowish stems are not attractive. The protein content of the leaves is high, making this species one of the best green-leaved foods. In addition, it is a good source of vitamin A, iron, calcium, and phosphorus.

In South China where the culture of water spinach is most advanced, two types of culture are common. Particular varieties are adapted to each set of cultural conditions. In the tropics some modifications of the Chinese techniques are desirable.

Varieties are planted either from seed or from cuttings. Seeds do not germinate well under water, but can be direct seeded. Plants are frequently grown in nursery beds for later transplanting. Cuttings can be over-wintered, but are generally taken from nursery beds. They are rooted directly in mud in the paddy method.

In both upland and paddy culture, large quantities of organic material are almost continuously added to the soil. This results in lush growth and very high yields (in the case of paddy culture, 45 metric tons per hectare). For upland culture the plants are spaced at 12 cm in raised beds. They require large amounts of water. Weeds are inevitably a problem. The entire plants can be harvested 60 days after planting or the vines are allowed to grow and may be trained to trellises. The latter technique permits a continuous harvest of leaves during the growing season, and is recommended for the home garden. In such cases harvest can begin 6 weeks after planting and can be continued at weekly intervals.

In paddy culture, long cuttings (30 cm) are planted in mud and kept moist. As the vines grow, the paddies are flooded to a depth of 15-20 cm, and a slow flow of water through the field is maintained. The water flow is stopped for purposes of fertilization. Weeds are well controlled by the flooded conditions of the field. Harvest begins after 30 days. When the succulent tips of the vines are removed, lateral and upright branches are encouraged. These are harvested every 7-10 days. Sustained harvesting encourages yields over a long period of time.

Plants switch to the flowering stage as the short days of winter approach. During flowering, less vegetative material is available for harvest, but heavy pruning and fertilization will counteract this tendency.

Under tropical conditions water spinach may be grown on a year-round basis. The plants are perennial and can continue several years. However, they tend to exhaust the fertility of their surroundings, and accumulate disease and insect problems. Because of the simplicity of propagation techniques, it is probably desirable to begin again from seeds once each year, and to plant in new areas.

Cruciferae

Nasturtium officinale R. Br. (watercress) is a European plant naturalized in the temperate zone of both hemispheres. It has been widely distributed within the tropics, where it often occurs as an aquatic weed. It is not extensively cultivated, except in an informal way, but excellent, long-standing plantings are seen in Hawaii.

Watercress is a perennial herb that lives for years, even in temperate climates. The angular, hollow, much-branched stems root freely at nodes below the water. The leaves are pinnately compound; leaflets are odd in number, and circular in outline. The frequent flowers are small, white, and inconspicuous. The pods are small, cylindrical, narrow, and curved.

The plant may be propagated from seeds. The seeds germinate rapidly if adequate soil moisture is maintained. However, watercress is more frequently cultivated by cuttings that, even when soft and succulent, root readily in sand or a container of water. It can be grown conveniently in streams or ditches where it spreads profusely, and yields very well. It favors humid soil, rich in organic material. Plants can also be grown on the soil surface, but watercress does not tolerate drying

out. A familiar cultural system is to grow the plants in paddies such as those used for taro. Normally, a minimum of water is used, but when necessary to control pests, the beds may be flooded. Typical yields of watercress are so excellent that the species outranks most other edible crops in the production per unit area of calories, protein, and other nutrients. It is high in vitamins A and C, and has a fair amount of vitamin D. Watercress is eaten raw in salads where it imparts a peppery flavor, or can be served as a cooked vegetable. In stews it is also a condiment. It is particularly good cooked with meat, and is a Chinese favorite. Watercress has high food value.

Precautions should be taken to ensure that the water from which the cress is taken is not polluted. If a doubt does exist, the greens should be cooked or thoroughly cleaned with an antiseptic solution. Washing alone will not make the plant safe to eat.

An almost sterile hybrid of *N. officinale* and *N. microphyllum* is also grown as a salad vegetable. Other species of *Nasturtium* also bear edible shoots and leaves.

Cucurbitaceae

Telfairia occidentalis Hook. f. (fluted gourd) is seldom seen outside of its habitat, tropical Africa, where it is well known, appreciated, and a frequent item of commerce. The closely related *T. pedata* (Sm.) Hook. (oyster nut) is also seen, which has a smaller fruit with less pronounced ribs; this species has high weed potential. Both species bear edible seeds, but the former is grown chiefly for its edible leaves. Because of its wide soil tolerance and highly productive nature, it merits wider trial.

Fluted gourd is a drought-resistant perennial vine, climbing to heights by tendrils. It is glabrous or almost so and tinted purplish by anthocyanin. The leaves are palmately divided into five or more segments (Fig. 5). The large fruits are characterized by thick, protruding ribs that give the wall added strength and durability. The seeds are large, up to 5 cm in diameter, and slightly flattened. The pulp is yellow to orange and relatively scant.

Fluted gourd can best be grown from seeds. These are often found to have germinated inside the fruit. When planted in the garden, such tender seedlings need a few days of shade and adequate watering. New vigorous plants are established readily. Stem cuttings can also be used for propagation. The vines are vigorous and climb rapidly. Therefore, they should be trained to a trellis that is not too high, but that permits easy access for harvest of vine tips. Many soils are tolerated, including those of low fertility, but the plant responds well to nitrogen fertilization.

Flowering begins the first year. Female flowers are not abundant. The fruits set readily and grow to a size of 50 kg in some cases. If the vines are grown principally for greens, it is wise to eliminate the fruits for they reduce the capacity for vegetative growth. The seeds are generally utilized somewhat before the fruit is fully ripe. They have a very high oil content and can be rendered to supply cooking oil. On roasting, the chestnut-sized seeds are said to resemble almonds in flavor.

Vine tips are harvested in lengths of about 50 cm and are bundled together for marketing. Although these can be taken any time of the year, they are most abundant in rainy seasons. Before using, the leaves and tender tips are removed from the tougher stem. The tendrils are usually too fibrous to eat. The usual method of cooking in Africa is in a stew, but the leaves make a very good cooked side dish.

They retain their dark green color on boiling.

Euphorbiaceae

Manihot esculenta Crantz (cassava, manioc, yuca, mandioca) is best known for its starchy edible roots, used as a staple food in many parts of the tropics, and as a source of tapioca, starch, and animal feed in the temperate zone. Although it has its origin in the tropics of Central and South America, cassava is now so well known in both tropical Africa and Asia that it is often locally thought of as indigenous. Not everyone who appreciates the tuberous roots, however, is acquainted with the edibility of the leaves.

Cassava is a large (up to 5 meters) and ungainly woody shrub of relatively short life span. It tends to branch irregularly and bears its large (20 cm long) lobed leaves near the tips of long branches. The leaves are short-lived (1-3 months) and are readily lost during drought or after insect attack. Inconspicuous, usually unisexual flowers are borne chiefly during the time of shortest days, and when pollinated give rise to trilobed capsules which burst on ripening. Leaves for consumption can be produced throughout the year if plants receive sufficient water to maintain their vegetative growth.

The portion eaten is generally the maturing leaves that are just reaching full size (Fig. 6). Although the younger leaves and a small portion of the stem may be consumed, it is advantageous to leave the growing point for further leaf production. Old leaves may be too tough and fibrous for consumption. Petioles, particularly when large, should be discarded.

Cassava leaves are not eaten raw, and indeed it is risky to do so. The leaves of all species contain harmful glycosides which easily release deadly hydrocyanic acid. Even leaves of sweet varieties that bear roots of low hydrogen cyanide content must be considered dangerous. To dispel the poison, the leaves are boiled at least 15 minutes. The leaves are generally cooked into a stew in Africa, and this then is eaten with the cooked starchy roots. However, the leaves can be cooked alone as a side dish or spinach. The many different ways cassava leaves are used in Africa are presented by Terra (1964).

The nutritive value of the cassava root is chiefly its caloric content. On a dry weight basis the protein is normally only one or two percent, and is particularly deficient in essential amino acids. In contrast to the starchy roots, the leaves of cassava contain sufficient protein to merit consideration in the diet. Protein content is highest in young leaves. The amino acid content is unbalanced, especially in the case of methionine. This essential amino acid is present only at a level of 60-80 percent of that desired. Levels of tryptophan are only marginal. On the other hand, the level of lysine is quite high in comparison to that of other plant proteins. Cassava leaves also contain appreciable quantities of B vitamins, phosphorous, and iron.

It is possible that large quantities of leaves in the diet might cause health problems. During cooking, the enzymes which release hydrocyanic acid from the glycosides are inactivated, and the resulting product is usually considered nontoxic. Some evidence suggests, however, that the glycosides themselves are poisonous, and that conditions such as goiter may result from long-term habitual consumption.

20

Cassava plants can be grown as a hedge for the yard or garden. Some varieties are upright whereas others are bushy. The bushy habit can be promoted by harvesting shoot tips as well as leaves for food. Close planting, heavy fertilization, and monthly harvesting of shoots should provide year-round leaf production.

Methods of cultivating cassava are well known. Woody cuttings of about 30 cm are planted in the soil oriented upright, or with a slant, or are buried in shallow trenches. Such cuttings root readily and establish plants within two months. Growth requirements are not exacting. Almost any soil is tolerated, and in fact, cassava is frequently planted on the poorest of soils. Cassava also withstands drought, dropping its leaves, but recuperating after rainfall. Nevertheless, for leaf production, the plants benefit from high nitrogen in the soil and from adequate rain or irrigation.

Cassava is rather resistant to insects, but two particular problems may cause loss. During the dry season, populations of red spider mites often develop and can defoliate the plants. These almost disappear when seasonal rains begin; they may also be controlled with miticide. Several species of flies often kill the tender growing point of the stem, causing proliferation of new branches. Systemic insecticides are very effective in ridding a planting of these flies, but their possibly harmful residues have not yet been fully studied. In Africa a principal disease is mosaic, which can be avoided by the use of resistant varieties. A troublesome leaf spot is known, which may make the production of edible leaves difficult. If precautions are taken, cassava can be considered a good tropical green leaf vegetable as it is one of the easiest to grow and most prolific. In addition, the roots are equally useful.

Sauropus androgynus (L.) Merr. (katuk) is a common cultivated shrub, rarely wild, found from India to Malaysia. It is little known outside of its native areas, but merits wider attention as one of the most prolific, nutritious, and appetizing of the green-leaved vegetables. In trials in Sarawak this species has outyielded all other sources of green leaves. Its vigor, long life, year-round production, and ability to recuperate after planting recommend it as a source of edible greens.

The plant is an awkward-appearing shrub with long, upright main stems that tend to fall over with time due to their own weight. There is little tendency to branch. Pruning generally results in rapid production of one or more new upright shoots to replace those which are lost. Lateral branches appear to be compound leaves, but bear flowers along their undersides. The fruits, about 1 cm in diameter, open and let drop their seeds at maturity (Fig. 7).

The tender tips, the young leaves, flowers, and the small fruits are used for food. These represent a very small portion of the entire plant. Older leaves can be stripped from the stems for cooking. The young leaves and tips, eaten raw in salads or lightly stir-fried as "tropical asparagus," have a strong, characteristic odor. They are more frequently cooked and have a distinctive, agreeable nutlike flavor. The leaves and stems tend to retain their dark green color and a firm texture. Roots and leaves are sometimes used medicinally. The plant is used to color preserves. The protein content of the leaves is good, from about 6 to 10 percent. It has been reported that excess consumption of leaves causes pain of the limbs or lung damage.

Sauropus can be propagated from seeds, which are borne in abundance and germinate readily. Under conditions of adequate fertility, seedlings grow very rapidly. Cuttings root well if placed in appropriate conditions. Somewhat woody cuttings 20-

30 cm long are used. Plants can tolerate very heavy soils and heavy rainfall, but grow much better if attention is paid to good fertility and drainage. Because of their perennial nature, fertilizer in the form of mulch is preferred. The most usual and convenient way to grow katuk is as a hedge. Plants are established at intervals of 10 cm or more, and rapidly develop a strong hedge of edible leaf materials. The plants grow very straight without branching and need frequent pruning to maintain them at hedge height. Katuk is frequently referred to as a low shrub, probably because it is maintained low, but its natural tendencies are to grow very high indeed. Diseases and insects are seldom a problem. No special treatments are necessary.

Malvaceae

Hibiscus species are native to the Old and New Worlds, and have been widely scattered by people. The young leaves and even mature leaves particularly of the African, but also of the Australian species are often used for food. For purposes of this presentation, only the most important food-bearing species are mentioned, but others are included in the appendix. These are *H. sabdariffa* L. (roselle, Jamaica sorrel), *H. acetosella* Welw. ex Fic. (false roselle), and *H. cannabinus* L. (kenaf). They are plants of African origin possibly domesticated in the Sudan but well distributed throughout tropical Africa. The first two species serve as a commercial source of fibers. Roselle, however, is better known as a vegetable of high quality. The forms used for fibers are distinct from those used as food, but all are edible. Roselle has been adequately treated in a review with kenaf and other *Hibiscus* species by Wilson and Menzel (1964).

A description of these species is difficult, for each consists of numerous disparate varieties. The principal food-producing form of roselle is a woody annual herb that is much branched, with glabrous or almost glabrous foliage. The fibrous forms are more erect. The leaves are green, and vary from entire to palmately divided. The stems are deep red. The attractive flowers, yellow with red center, are borne solitarily in the axils of the leaves, and the red, acidic calyx of these becomes enlarged and succulent. Plants of *H. acetosella* are very similar to some of those of roselle. It occurs in two main forms, one with bronze-green leaves and yellow flowers, and the other with entirely red foliage and usually pink flowers. The calyx is small, not fleshy, and not eaten. These species have the advantage over kenaf of resisting nematodes.

Kenaf, on the other hand, is a very woody, green-leaved shrub that grows to heights with little or no branching. It is chiefly used as a fiber source and has been extensively bred for that purpose. It is highly susceptible to root-knot nematodes.

Most varieties of roselle and kenaf are very susceptible to the length of day (photoperiod) although the latter is probably more sensitive than the former. Plants of even 15 cm can be induced to bloom by daylengths of 9, 10, or 11 hours. The sensitivity of particular varieties varies. Roselle is often used as a laboratory example of photoperiodic effects because of this sensitivity. Thus, time of planting exercises a profound effect on morphology of the plant.

Practically all parts of roselle are edible. The species is appreciated for the fleshy bases of the buds. These, when cooked, form a colorful sauce not unlike that

22

of cranberries. The colorant is widely used in the preparation of jams, jellies, and other products. The seeds are eaten toasted, and in fact, the plant may have been domesticated for its edible seeds. The leaves and the tender shoots are sometimes eaten raw in salads, but are usually cooked, becoming somewhat mucilaginous, and reminiscent in texture and taste of rhubarb. The acid flavor is seldom excessive, and is easy to learn to enjoy. It is distinctive and lingering.

The leaves of *H. acetosella* are used in much the same way as those of roselle but they tend to be more sour. Upon cooking, much of the anthocyanin coloring is lost, and the cooked dish may not be attractive.

Leaves and shoots of glabrous forms of kenaf are equally edible and are cooked as spinach in Africa and India. Removing the shoot of kenaf changes the growth habit, however, and makes the plant less useful for fiber. In Africa, where these species are so appreciated, the leaves of another closely related vegetable, okra (*Abelmoschus esculentus* (L.) Moench), are eaten in the same fashion.

All the edible *Hibiscus* species are propagated by seeds, which are produced in abundance. These can be sown directly if the soil is properly prepared. Because of the long tap roots of roselle, a particularly deep, loose soil is desirable. *Hibiscus* species are fairly tolerant of distinctive soil types but require good drainage and benefit from mulching and fertilization. The nematode-susceptible varieties grow poorly and produce little in infested sandy soils.

Plants grown for fiber are seeded in ridges at very close spacing. Individual plants of roselle may grow to a very large size, and thus need spacing distances of a meter or more. Roselle plants grow slowly in contrast to those of kenaf. To obtain maximum size, they are therefore seeded early in the rainy season when daylengths are increasing.

Because of their reddish color and normal tendency to branch, false roselle plants may be grown as a colorful, temporary hedge. It is generally poor when served on its own, but a few leaves cooked in other dishes and raw in salads or as sour snacks help this plant earn its spot in the home garden. Pruning the hedge to shape and harvesting the leaves are the same operation. Under such conditions the amount of edible material produced in a small space is quite large.

The useful life span of the plants of both roselle and kenaf is brought to a close by flowering during short days. Seeds are borne in abundance. For its many uses, roselle merits a place in the home garden, and contributes to a variety of dishes.

Tiliaceae

Corchorus olitorius L. (bush okra, jute mallow) is probably the most important source of edible green leaves in a genus known for such species. Authors differ in opinion as to the origin of the species. It is most likely from Africa but was introduced at a very early date to India and China. It is still seldom seen and little appreciated in the New World. Bush okra is grown in some regions principally for its commercial fiber jute, and thus competes with the better-known jute source *C. capsullaris* L. It occurs wild in Africa and Asia, probably as an escape from cultivation, especially in open, damp areas. It is of major importance as a fiber in Bengal, but as a food from the Middle East to tropical Africa. The fibers are used in

coarse twine, cloth, and burlap bags.

Jute mallow is a vigorous, annual, upright, branching, glabrous (or almost so), slightly woody herb. Leaves are narrow and serrate, about 5-13 cm in length. Flowers are small, yellow-petioled, and borne in small clusters in the leaf axils. The cylindrical capsules of 2-5 cm are produced in large numbers, especially during the short days. Many varieties are known. The vegetable types are smaller than the fiber types, and are more branched, but the leaves and shoots of all varieties are edible.

The plant is propagated only from its seeds, which can be sown at any time of the year. Steeping seeds for ten seconds in just-boiled water may aid their germination. The usual practice is to sow in excess and thin the plants to spacing desired. With time the plants reach more than a meter of height and 50 cm in diameter. Closer spacing may be desirable, especially in order to provide abundant greens from small plants. Plants tolerate wide extremes of soil and are considered easy to grow. They profit from spring rains but are also drought resistant. Organic soils can reduce nematode damage to this species. In some climates, branching is excessive, flowering occurs early, and the lifetime of the plant is too short for convenient gardening. On the other hand, a first edible crop may be had as little as 4 weeks after planting. In Egypt, the first cutting is made after 2 1/2 months and subsequent cuttings are made each month.

The edible shoot tips and leaves are always eaten cooked. Their edible qualities are widely known but particularly appreciated in West Africa. There the shoots and leaves are combined in stews to be eaten with starchy paste. In India the shoots are cooked with rice. They are considered a tonic. The leaves may be dried and retained for future use, either as a tea or a cooked vegetable.

Corchorus requires little cooking for it rapidly softens and becomes mucilaginous, a characteristic unappealing to many persons but sought-after in West Africa. The flavor is very good. Varieties are said to differ in their cooking qualities and flavor. The protein content, particularly of older leaves, is excellent. Other edible species of *Corchorus* are mentioned in the appendix.

CHAPTER III

Some Vegetables, Ornamental Plants, and Fruits
with Edible Leaves

Edible green leaves can be found almost everywhere. It is difficult to imagine a place, except the ocean, the polar ice caps, and the barest deserts, where edible leaves cannot be found. Probably the majority of the species of flowering plants have not been tested thoroughly for edibility of leaves. With proper treatment, many leaves that might be poisonous or irritating are perfectly safe. Thus, in the tropics, edible leaves are always in abundance.

Frequently the common plants around us bear edible green leaves. These plants, whether used as sources of other foods, for ornamenting our homes, or for shelter and shade, are overlooked for their values as sources of green leaves. While we spend extravagant amounts in the supermarket for fresh greens brought from long distances, potential food is wasted around us, or is thrown out with the garden clippings. With a knowledge of the edible green leaves of common plants around us, there may be no need of searching for greens outside of one's own backyard. Furthermore, these common green leaves vary in taste, and afford new thrills to the gourmet, when eaten raw or when cooked.

Vegetables

Common garden vegetables grown for other purposes often bear edible green leaves that can be harvested with minimum damage to the plant.

Zea mays L. (corn, Gramineae) is of course grown for its edible seeds, eaten in their immature form on the spike, or in a variety of products after maturation. However, other parts of the plant are also edible. The young ears can be eaten raw, cob and all, or used as a salad ingredient. The tassel, while still enveloped in the leaves, is tender, delicious, and highly nutritious. The leaves are produced in sequence with each young leaf enveloped by the next older. These young developing leaves (Fig. 8) are extremely tender and delicious, and are edible either raw or cooked. Removing of the edible leaves of corn usually destroys the growing tip. Thus corn can be thought of as an emergency or luxurious source of edible green leaves.

Allium cepa L. (onion, Liliaceae) is not normally valued for its mature green leaves, although the leaves of young onions are often appreciated. The leaves of older onions are also edible but apt to be too strong for consumption raw. Cooking modifies the irritating substances, and makes of onion leaves a flavorful pot herb that can be taken alone, but is particularly good when combined with meat dishes. In addition to onion, other species of *Allium* are frequently grown. Chives (*A. schoenoprasum* L.) are, of course, grown as a leaf-producing vegetable, but leaves of other species, including those wild, are equally edible. It might be wise to always cook any except very young onion leaves.

Zingiber officinale Roscoe (ginger, Zingiberaceae) and other wild and cultivated *Zingiber* species produce edible, slightly spicy shoots. The shoot consists principally of the succulent young leaves folded around one another. On cutting and

cooking, these separate like the leaf bases that form palm cabbage.

The family Leguminosae is particularly rich in species with edible green leaves. Those of practically all the edible species of beans, for example, are edible. The amateur should be cautioned, however, that the family also includes species with poisonous leaves. Legumes should be identified before their leaves are eaten.

Among the better-known tropical vegetables, the pigeon pea (*Cajanus cajan* (L.) Huth) is known for its small flavorful seeds shelled fresh from the pod or cooked when dry. The leaves as well as the young shoots and pods are eaten cooked. The protein content of the leaves is high, making this a particularly desirable species. The plants can produce even under extremely difficult conditions, including very poor soils and times of drought. The cooked leaves have a strong spicy odor, somewhat too much fiber, and a new flavor not agreeable to everyone.

Vicia faba L. (broad bean, fava bean) is a species usually grown only at high elevations in the tropics. This useful vegetable, the seeds of which are edible green and mature, is also used as a green-leaf source. The related species *V. abyssinica* Steud. is used in the same fashion.

Vigna unguiculata (L.) Walp. (cowpea) is commonly cultivated throughout the tropics. Its edible ripe seeds are an important vegetable over wide areas. The long pods of some are especially tender and delicious. The young leaves are also quite suitable as cooked greens. The leaves of other *Vigna* species are also edible. On cooking they lose much of their color and soften excessively. The cooking odor is quite strong but the flavor of the finished dish is mild.

Pisum sativum L. (garden pea) is widely grown in the temperate zone, where it is used for both its green immature seeds and its dried seeds. The pea is not a tropical plant, and grows well only at cool sites at high locations in the tropics. The young leaves are quite edible and worthy of further trial.

The common garden bean or snap bean (*Phaseolus vulgaris* L.) is almost always grown for its edible immature pods or dried seeds. Many varieties are grown throughout the tropics, and suitable types are available not only for the highlands, but also for the coastal plains. Beans grow rapidly and provide a crop within a very short time. There is no real need to grow beans for their leaves, but the young leaves are edible and can constitute an interesting new dish to the sated gardener.

The leaves of many other beans are edible, including those of *Phaseolus coccineus* L., the scarlet runner bean; *P. lunatus* L., lima bean; and *Vigna radiata* (L.) R. Wilczek (*P. aureus* Roxb.), the mungbean. The cooked leaves of the winged bean, *Psophocarpus tetragonolobus* (L.) DC, are surprisingly delicious, with appealing texture and an excellent flavor of their own.

Glycine max (L.) Merr. (soybean) is not well known in most parts of the tropics. Its real success has been as a dried bean in temperate zones, and it merits special attention by virtue of its high oil and protein content. Its protein has a very high quality. Varieties have been developed for the tropics, the immature pods of which are cooked as a green vegetable. It is not widely known that the young leaves are equally edible. Many other less common edible legumes with edible leaves are listed in the appendix.

Abelmoschus esculentus (L.) Moench (okra, Malvaceae) is widely grown for the edible and mucilaginous pods. It is a vegetable particularly important in West

Africa. By continuously harvesting, the plants can be kept producing for many months. Like many of the related *Hibiscus* species, the young leaves are eaten. They have an agreeable sour flavor. The popular Indonesian species *A. manihot* L. (edible hibiscus) is used exclusively for its leaves (Fig. 9), cooked alone, added to soups, or used as a substitute for lettuce. It can be planted each year from cuttings. When given normal care including weeding, periodic pruning, and normal fertility of the garden, it will outyield most crops and give much more for the effort than most other green-leaved vegetables. A shrub which grows to two meters, it shows a wide variation in leaf form, from large ovate with 5-9 lobes to very deeply lobed leaves resembling cassava, and colored sulfur yellow to dark green. The underside of the leaves may have white crystals which are readily washed off. The leaves have been ranked in Hawaii as very high in nutritive value. It is very susceptible to nematodes.

The ferny leaves of the carrot, *Daucus carota* L. (Umbelliferae), are perfectly edible, distinctive in flavor, and a welcome change in the diet. Young leaves, raw or steamed, are eaten with rice in the East Indies. There is no reason that once carrots have been purchased with tender edible leaves that these should be discarded in favor of the roots. However, young leaves cause dermatitis in sensitive persons. The carrot is not well suited in lowlands of the tropics but some varieties do well at higher elevations with cooler temperatures.

It is unfortunate that most people discard the leaves of the radish, *Raphanus sativus* L. (Cruciferae). The bristly leaves of this small salad vegetable are flavorful and have met with enthusiastic acceptance in several regions where their use has been encouraged in local recipes from tacos to soups. Where radishes are grown, the leaves should not be wasted. Other crucifers with edible leaves are discussed later.

To many people it will come as a surprise that the leaves of the solanaceous vegetables are also edible. The foliage of the potato (*Solanum tuberosum* L., Solanaceae) contains a poisonous alkaloid, and throughout the literature are frequent references to the poisonous leaves. Nevertheless, the young leaves of potato are sometimes eaten. Their protein content is twice that of the tuber. Another alkaloid-bearing species of the same family is *Nicotiana tabacum* L. (tobacco). The young leaves of this common plant, grown in both temperate and tropical zones, are also edible. Some caution should be exercised in eating leaves of plants that yield alkaloids. The amounts normally used for a cooked dish should not be harmful. Cooking questionable vegetables and discarding the cooking water is always desirable.

Other valuable solanaceous vegetables useful for edible green leaves are the peppers. The leaves of *Capsicum annuum* L. (green pepper) retain their texture well on cooking and have a mild flavor with slight bitterness that is reminiscent of the green fruit. Leaves of *Capsicum frutescens* L. (tabasco pepper) give off a pungent aroma when they are cooked. Sufficient pungency remains in the firm cooked leaves to add a special appeal. In Malaysia the leaves of the weed *Lycium chinense* L. are eaten, particularly with pork.

Solanum melongena L. (eggplant) yields a fruit well known in the tropics and used in many kinds of dishes. As is frequently the case, the leaves, which are seldom used but are perfectly edible, are more nutritious than the fruits. The leaves retain their texture on cooking. The fine leaf hairs are irritating to many people. The cooking water retains a spinach-like odor, but the leaves are not very flavorful.

Sechium edule (Jacq.) Sw. (chayote, Cucurbitaceae) is frequently grown throughout the tropics for its pear-shaped fruits, which are eaten boiled or baked as a vegetable. It is less well known that this perennial vine has a starchy tuber, up to 5 kg in weight, edible raw or cooked. The tender young leaves and stem tips are valuable green vegetables. The foliage contains fair amounts of iron, carotene, thiamin, riboflavin, and niacin. The tendrils are fibrous and should be discarded before cooking.

The various species of *Cucurbita* (*C. moschata* (Duchesne) Poiret, *C. maxima* Duchesne, and *C. pepo* L.), collectively yielding pumpkin and squashes, are rich sources of varied food materials. The fruits can be eaten at practically any stage from the flower until maturity, although the optimum stage for edibility varies. Squashes are not common in many parts of the tropics. The popular varieties in the temperate zone are seldom adequate for tropical lowlands. However, locally adapted varieties, often with many poor characteristics but good adaptation, can be found. The butternut squash is usually successful in warm climates. The young leaves of all species and varieties are edible.

Field and Plantation Crops

Field and plantation crops used for non-food purposes sometimes also produce edible leaves. For example, the common source of animal feed, alfalfa (*Medicago sativa* L., Leguminosae) is also a source of edible leaves and shoot tips. These have the advantage of being rich in methionine, an essential amino acid often in short supply in other plant foods. Alfalfa leaves are eaten in India. The dried, powdered leaves are now being promoted as a health tea. Ignorance and prejudice make alfalfa an unknown food crop for humans in most areas.

The oil crop sesame (*Sesamum indicum* L., Pedaliaceae), of African origin but now cultivated chiefly in India, Asia, and South America as a source of cooking oil, is also a source of edible leaves. The plant is an erect annual herb raised from seed. The leaves are quite hairy, which for most persons produces an uncomfortable feeling in the mouth. Nevertheless, the young leaves of this and of several related species are regularly eaten.

Another oil and nut crop of commercial importance, the peanut (*Arachis hypogaea* L., Leguminosae) of tropical South America but now grown throughout the tropics and temperate zones, is frequently utilized as forage, hay, or silage. However, the young leaves and tips are equally suitable as a cooked green vegetable.

Ornamentals

In addition to herbs commonly found in gardens, many of the ornamental shrubs planted around the house are valuable sources of edible green leaves. The edibility of these leaves is seldom known to the gardener, and thus in time of scarcity or starvation, the knowledge of these edible leaves would be especially useful.

Ardisia is not too common a shrub but it has been widely distributed from India. Leaves of a number of species are edible, including the most common *A. solanacea* Roxb. (Myrsinaceae). Many other species also bear edible leaves. These

are eaten raw as well as cooked. The rather small flowers are followed by attractive berries. Propagation is possible by air layering when seeds are not available.

Some *Bougainvillea*s (Nyctaginaceae) are used as sources of edible green leaves in West Africa. It is not known whether all species are edible.

Cassia alata L. (ringworm senna, Leguminosae) is a rather small shrubby example of its genus from the West Indies and South America (Fig. 10). The leaves contain chrysophonic acid and are widely used in treating skin diseases. The flowers are rather unusual in that they occur in dense, erect spikes, and are covered until maturity with yellow, petal-like bracts. It is a vigorous, floriferous water-loving species that responds to pruning by more vigorous flowering. The leaves are long and pinnately compound. The bush is normally propagated from seed. Only the youngest leaves are used as food.

Catharanthus roseus (L.) G. Don f. (Apocynaceae), commonly known as Madagascar periwinkle, is a very attractive, freely blooming, slightly woody species commonly seen in tropical gardens. It is propagated by cuttings or from seeds. The young leaves are used as a vegetable, but older leaves contain a poisonous alkaloid.

Hibiscus rosa-sinensis L. (Malvaceae) is the most common of the tropical ornamental *Hibiscus*, and indeed one of the best-known ornamentals of the tropics. Known as Chinese Hibiscus, it has been hybridized to produce many beautiful new forms. The unimproved types are extremely vigorous, and are often propagated by thrusting large stakes directly into the ground. Varieties that root with difficulty are often rooted with the help of hormone treatments, or are grafted on vigorous stocks. The leaves of many species of *Hibiscus* are edible. Because this species is so common, so vigorous, and is often used as an ornamental hedge, it should be a particularly valuable emergency source of edible greens.

The family Euphorbiaceae is known not only for its poisonous species, but also as a family with leaves which are rich in protein. All gardeners should be aware of any poisonous properties and take appropriate precautions. The white milky latex of many species may be irritating, and contact with skin should be avoided. The following ornamental species all belong to this important family.

Acalypha species such as *A. hispida* B. Wm. f. (chenille) and *A. wilkesiana* Muell. Arg. (copperleaf) are edible-leaved shrubs that thrive in full sunlight and develop rich anthocyanin coloration. The leaves are frequently variegated. Especially useful in foundation and hedge plantings, these East Indian and Pacific Island plants are now very common throughout the tropics. They are propagated from cuttings.

Codiaeum variegatum (L.) Blume is the common garden croton from Southeast Asia that is common to all tropical areas. It is highly regarded in the garden for its brilliant variegated leaves, year-round attractiveness, resistance to pests, and ease of culture. It is a plant with supposedly medicinal purposes, and is used especially to bathe the mother after childbirth. Young leaves, especially of yellow varieties, have a mild, nut-like flavor, but palatability varies with variety.

Euphorbia (Poinsettia) pulcherrima Willd. ex Klotzsch, the common poinsettia (Fig. 11) so much appreciated for its bright red foliage at Christmas time, is poisonous in the natural state. The latex from leaves or stems may irritate and blister sensitive skin. It causes eye inflammation and should not be swallowed. It is sufficiently caustic to remove hair from the body, but is mixed with oil for this

29

purpose. Nevertheless, the young leaves of this easy-to-grow ornamental are not only edible, but highly nutritious. They are never eaten raw. Native to tropical America, the poinsettia is widely distributed and well known. It grows rapidly from woody cuttings. Because of its lax habit, it can be improved by the pruning resulting from harvest. The warnings must be given that gathering leaves may lead to dermatitis, and this plant is poisonous and so should be kept from children who are apt to chew it.

Jatropha curcas L. (Barbados nut, physic nut) is well known, well distributed, and grown not only for ornament but also for the oil of the seeds. The dark green foliage is attractive, and the species is well adapted to poor and dry soils. The poisonous qualities of seeds and oil are well known, and yet the young foliage is cooked and eaten in Indonesia.

Closely related to *Jatropha* is *Cnidoscolus chayamansa* McVaugh (chaya, tree spinach), popular in Mexico and Central America and introduced into Florida (Fig. 12). This vigorous shrub yields flavorful edible young leaves and thick, tender shoot tips which are boiled as a spinach. Chaya contains hydrocyanic glycosides, so leaves must be cooked; the toxicity is eliminated after a few minutes of boiling. The leaves are rich in protein, calcium, iron, carotene, riboflavin, niacin, and ascorbic acid. The presence of stinging hairs in some varieties makes the use of gloves desirable when harvesting their leaves, but the stinging property disappears on cooking. A Belizean variety without stinging hairs is available from ECHO and is recommended.

Chaya is an extremely promising species for its high nutritional value, exceptional drought tolerance, and productivity even in very poor growing conditions. An attractive perennial shrub, it produces abundant quantities of large, dark green leaves. Chaya thrives on a wide range of soils in both hot, rainy climates and areas with occasional drought. It prefers good drainage, but can survive some waterlogging. Leaves are larger and more tender when grown in partial shade. Frequent harvesting keeps the new shoots within easy reach, but the entire plant may also be coppiced and allowed to regrow. Chaya grows very quickly, especially at higher temperatures, and resprouts well after cutting. It is virtually pest-free and has low weed potential, as it is propagated only by cuttings and does not generally produce seed. As a year-round source of high-quality food in a wide range of conditions, it is one of the most important edible-leaved plants for the tropics.

The common castor bean, *Ricinus communis* L., is often grown as an ornamental, although its height and rapid growth do not fit it for the typical garden. The oil from the poisonous seeds is used for many purposes, and the plant is therefore grown commercially. The young leaves, while edible, contain the poisonous alkaloid ricin, and therefore must be boiled sufficiently in at least two changes of water to render them safe. The water, of course, should be discarded.

Fruit Trees

Throughout the tropics there are a very large number of trees that bear edible fruits. It is not difficult to make a list of 300 species, and in addition many more of minor importance are found in restricted areas. Nevertheless, the majority of the fruits and nuts of the tropics come from a very limited number of species. These species found throughout the tropics are those that merit special attention here.

The leaves of citrus fruits (Rutaceae) often contain essential oils and flavonoids that impart characteristic pungent odors and tastes. These leaves are not eaten. Several minor species of the family do produce edible leaves (see appendix).

The leaves of the banana (*Musa* sp. and hybrids, Musaceae), once they have emerged from the pseudostem, toughen up rapidly and are more suitable for wrapping foods than to be eaten themselves. Nevertheless, within the pseudostem the developing leaves are much more tender, and can be eaten either raw or cooked. This portion is often called the heart. To extract the heart the trunk can easily be opened with a sharp machete. In addition to the heart, the flower bud of the banana can be eaten after boiling. The soft portions near the base of the flower bracts are eaten as are those of the bracts of globe artichokes.

Fruit-bearing trees of the family Anacardiaceae also bear edible leaves. *Anacardium occidentale* L., for example, is the source of the cashew nut and of the cashew apple, the fleshy peduncle of the true fruit. It is a species especially adapted to poor soils and dry areas. Although native to Brazil, it is widely planted throughout the tropical world, frequently in coastal areas, as a source of nuts for the international trade. Since the shell of the nut contains an irritating oil similar in structure and effects to that of poison ivy, the raw nuts should not be bitten into until they are roasted. The young leaves (Fig. 13) are commonly cooked in Southeast Asia but are too astringent for regular use.

Mangoes (*Mangifera indica* L.), now so displaced from their native habitats in India and Southeast Asia, are found everywhere throughout the tropics. Most mangoes perform best in a moderately dry climate. Nevertheless, tolerance to rain varies, and some varieties thrive and produce even under rain forest conditions. The fruits, which are usually seasonal, have sometimes been described as the peaches of the tropics. They are incomparable in flavor. Mango is an evergreen tree. New leaves are produced in several vigorous flushes of growth each year, usually beginning with the rainy season. These young leaves are frequently rose-colored or bronzed with anthocyanin. On cooking them, the anthocyanin is boiled out, leaving the leaves pale green. The cooked leaves tend to hold their shape and texture, and present an attractive appearance. The flavor is more or less resinous, and will not agree with every palate. The leaves of distinct varieties vary in their suitability. Some study to determine the best varieties as sources of edible leaves would be desirable.

A number of species of *Spondias* bear edible fruits, and it is probable that leaves of all species are edible. Young leaves of *S. cytherea* Sonn. (ambarella) are eaten raw or cooked. The leaves of *S. purpurea* L. (red mombin) are eaten raw, and those of *S. pinnata* Kurz (amra) are cooked. The fruit-bearing *Spondias* species vary in size. The leaves are typically pinnately compound. The fruits are borne in clusters, and vary in length from 2.5 to 8 cm. Most are rather sourish, but sweet, improved varieties have been developed. *Spondias* is propagated by seeds or from large cuttings. However, the better varieties are best multiplied by budding.

Leaves of the soursop (*Annona muricata* L., Annonaceae) are edible. This and its many relatives are mostly small trees, some adapted to dry and others to wet forests. Their soft, spine-covered fruits yield a pulp that varies from quite sour to agreeably sweet. The young fruit may also be cooked as a vegetable. *Annona* species are easy to grow, usually from seed. A few improved varieties and hybrids have been

developed. On cooking the soursop leaf, a good texture is retained. The cook pot emits a rich odor. Cooked leaves are slightly bitter, and do not have much flavor.

One of the rarest of tropical fruits in the western hemisphere, the durian (*Durio zibethinus* Murray, Bombacaceae) of Southeast Asia, is noted for its strong odor that appears pleasant enough to those who like the fruit but is extremely offensive to all others. The large fruit is covered with sharp, pyramidal spines. The soft pulp around the seeds is eaten raw or made into candies. This is a tall tree from which foliage cannot easily be taken (Fig. 14), but the young leaves of durian are sometimes eaten after cooking. Other species of *Durio* also bear edible fruits, and certainly the leaves of some of these must be edible.

It is not surprising that the fruit-bearing species of Euphorbiaceae also bear edible leaves, as this is so typical of many members of the family. One of the best known is the bignay (*Antidesma bunius* (L.) Sprengel) from Southeast Asia. The tree is large, evergreen, and bears clusters of berries which turn from green to white, to red, and finally to black as they mature. The fruits are small and large-seeded but can be used for jams and jellies. On cooking, the young leaves turn an unattractive brown but retain their texture. The flavor is slightly sour, but otherwise similar to artichoke.

Two species of *Phyllanthus*, another genus of Euphorbiaceae, bear edible fruits and leaves. The Otaheite gooseberry or grosella (*P. acidus* (L.) Skeels) produces large quantities of yellow, waxy, scalloped-edged fruits. When cooked, the fruits turn bright red due to the transformation of a leucoanthocyanin to its colored form. This is a small, rapidly growing tree that does well in dry areas. The tree is usually propagated from seed. Its cooked young leaves are neutral or mild in flavor, but somewhat fibrous. *P. emblica* L. (emblic) is not as common. The round, greenish, angled fruits are high in vitamin C. The leaves of this species, though edible, are very small. On cooking there is little odor, but the cooking water becomes an unappetizing suspension of yellowish particles. The flavor is extremely bitter and would appeal to very few people.

The common tamarind (*Tamarindus indica* L., Leguminosae) is a tropical tree from Africa now widely distributed, and particularly well known in India (Fig. 15). Wherever it is grown, the rusty-colored pods are harvested for the thick pulp found around the seeds. This is usually quite sour, due to the high content of tartaric acid. Sweet forms have been described. The pulp, when mixed with water and sugar, produces a pleasant drink not unlike lemonade. It is also widely used in confections, condiments, and chutneys. In addition to the pulp, the seeds are edible after toasting or boiling and removing the shell. They can also be made into a flour. The dried pulp is marketed for use in meat sauces and chutneys.

The tamarind is a handsome tree with hemispherical shape that grows best in dry areas. It is frequently seen along coasts, and in sandy soils, which suggests that it resists saline conditions. Trees are usually grown from seeds, but superior varieties are budded or grafted. Once cooked, the young leaves lose their color. The cooking odor is not pronounced. The flavor is agreeably sour and similar to that of the fruit. Thus, this type of leaf is best cooked with other, less flavorful vegetables. Both the leaves and flowers are eaten fresh in salads or cooked in curries, soups, and stews.

The family Moraceae furnishes several species with edible leaves. Many wild figs (*Ficus* sp.) bear edible leaves and shoots. Some species of *Artocarpus*, the genus

of breadfruit and jackfruit, yield young leaves that are good to eat. Perhaps the most important fruit species with edible leaves is the common mulberry, *Morus alba* L., a rapidly growing tree from China that is more common in temperate than in tropical zones. Nevertheless, there are varieties that perform well even at sea level in the humid tropics. Selected varieties bear very excellent fruits This and the variety *indica* are the sources of leaves traditionally grown as feed for silkworms in China. All parts of the tree have medicinal uses in China. The leaves are often used as cattle feed. The young leaves (Fig. 16) are edible and are consumed principally by nursing mothers. On cooking, the young leaves become very soft but retain their color. The flavor is mild. The fine pubescence may be slightly unpleasant.

The Rosaceae family includes a number of tropical fruits, but few species have leaves which are eaten. An exception is the raspberry, *Rubus rosaefolius* Smith, introduced from the Himalayas but now widely distributed and excessively weedy in some high rainfall areas. The foliage is light green, and the berry red on maturity, with little flavor. It is propagated chiefly by root suckers which are produced in abundance. Red young leaves of rose bushes (*Rosa* spp.) are edible raw or cooked.

Among the many fruits of the Sapotaceae, one of the best is the sapodilla or nispero (*Manilkara zapota* (L.) van Royen). It is very common in tropical America, especially Mexico and Central America, where it serves as a source of chicle for the manufacture of chewing gum. It is a handsome tree, planted as an ornamental because of its dense, deep-green foliage and an attractive symmetrical shape. The rust-colored fruit contains a soft, brownish pulp surrounding a few seeds. The seedlings are often grafted to propagate the excellent varieties that have been developed. The leaves contain a poisonous alkaloid; only the very young leaves are considered edible.

Papayas, *Carica papaya* L. (Caricaceae), are grown chiefly for their fruits. Although these are eaten ripe and fresh, the green fruits can be cooked as squash. Many other uses have been described. The interior of the stem is soft, and may be eaten raw. Dried leaves are used as a tobacco substitute, and can also be beaten in water to form a soap substitute. The leaves may be cooked as a green vegetable. They should not be eaten raw because of the possible danger from both the alkaloid carpaine and the enzyme papain. As a precaution, older leaves should be thoroughly boiled, changing the water at least twice. Younger leaves are not harmful. Flowers are also cooked and eaten, generally with the leaves.

Upon cooking, the leaves have a pleasant chartreuse color and retain their form and texture. The cooked leaves have a strong, bitter taste that is disagreeable to some people. In addition, they have a distinctive flavor reminiscent of asparagus. The tender petioles may be eaten, but are more bitter than the blades. Papaya leaves are more appropriately served in stews than as a separate dish.

Cultivation details need not be here, for the plant is well known. Seeds germinate in 3-4 weeks. Seedlings may be established in separate containers or directly in the field if protected. The plants grow rapidly and begin to bear fruit in less than a year. One or two leaves per plant harvested occasionally is not likely to interfere with fruit production. Since some plants are male, and therefore bear no fruits, these can be used for edible leaves. The growing tip should not be removed, for this will disfigure the plant. The plants can live for several years, but their continued growth will eventually place new leaves out of easy reach.

33

The leaves of coffee, *Coffea arabica* L. (Rubiaceae), are edible. On cooking, they have a strong brown color, a good texture, and a rather neutral flavor with only a touch of bitterness.

CHAPTER IV

Common Weeds with Edible Green Leaves

Weeds are often described as undesired plants, plants growing out of place, or plants which are a nuisance. They appear wherever the soil has been disturbed, grow rapidly, steal the fertility of the soil from desirable species, mature large quantities of seed, and are difficult to control. Both the definitions and characteristics of weeds emphasize that they are plants closely related to people. As is the case of so many human activities, weeds are ephemeral; they come and go as people disturb the soil. As people travelled and dominated the land, weedy species benefitted, and many weedy species are known now in both temperate and tropical zones.

Weeds are generally defined as herbaceous plants. Trees and shrubs are seldom weeds. Those that grow rapidly may be said to be weedy, but they lack an intimate relation to and dependence on human activities. Occasionally, transporting a species from one region to another permits weedy tendencies to manifest themselves, but weedy trees seldom become the plagues that annual plants can be.

Weeds probably evolved by a number of mechanisms. First, weeds are species adapted to naturally disturbed areas where fire, flood, drought, deforestation, or other activities have cleared the land. They constitute the pioneers in ecological succession. After weeds have covered the ground, more durable species are eventually established. As new species cover an area, the weedy species gradually disappear. Species of this sort are weedy because humans have established abnormal ecological situations which correspond to those that occur in nature. A second group of species are adapted more specifically to human activities, but are not necessarily involved in the ecological succession. Such species grow in disturbed soil; they follow the plow. They use the fertility added to the soil, whether in the cultivated field or the garbage dump. Then, to avoid extinction, they produce seed rapidly and disappear. Still a third group of species is associated with the domestication of wild plants. People carried many plants from the wild to their dwellings for convenient harvesting. Adaptation to the special environment grew with generations of use. The modified plants often hybridized with their wild relatives, and the hybrids showed new variations. Sometimes weedy species evolved which competed with related cultivated species. In some cases, the weedy species has continued even once the cultivated species has died out.

Because of their origin so close to human activities, many weeds have been discovered to be edible, and indeed are used locally as pot herbs throughout the world. Using weeds as food has a double advantage: something useful is achieved, and the weeds are removed from sites where they might compete with cultivated plants. In most areas of the world, weeds, during their season, offer the most available food, and that which is often most despised. It should be mentioned, however, that many weedy species are not only persistent, but are often obnoxious due to other qualities, including the presence of poisonous substances, irritating hairs or spines, or barbed seeds that are caught in the clothing. These adaptive qualities may be useful for the survival of weedy species, but also suggest to the amateur that caution should be exercised in testing the food values of unfamiliar species.

Acanthaceae

Justicia insularis T. And. is the best known of the various species of this genus cultivated or fetched from the wild in Africa for their edible leaves (see appendix). *J. quinque-angularis* Koenig and *J. precumbens* L. are eaten in India. *J. insularis* is a small herb (Fig. 17) that branches freely at the base, producing attractive clumps with dark green leaves. It is a slow-growing but definitely seasonal plant that dies back during the dry season after profuse flowering. The short-petioled, circular leaves are finely pubescent, as is the squarish stem. The species should make an attractive summer garden plant. The leaves and tender stems are eaten as a pot herb or spinach. They give off a strong but pleasant odor when cooked. The cooked leaves retain much of their dark green color. They are of good texture but tender. The hairs of the stem and leaves are a minor irritant in the mouth. The flavor is pronounced and likeable, but sometimes a little bitter. Stems are slightly fibrous and add little of value to the cooked dish. *Justicia* can best be grown from seeds, which germinate and grow slowly. The genus is common throughout the tropics and includes a few ornamental species. Some species have astringent characteristics and are used for local medicines. Most are herbaceous or only slightly woody. The edible species are very little known outside of their native regions, but merit some further trial.

A few of the clock vines (*Thunbergia* spp.) bear edible leaves. The species *T. alata* Bojer ex Sims is widely distributed and easily recognized by its yellow or orange flower with dark throat, and its winged stem. The leaves are eaten in the Congo (Fig. 18), but their edibility is practically unknown elsewhere.

Compositae

It is seldom well known that leaves of many weedy species of this family are edible. Some of the more tasty edible weeds are surprisingly common. Edible tropical species of *Lactuca* (lettuce) will be mentioned in a later chapter.

Bidens pilosa L. (Spanish needles, margarita) is a very common weed of tropical America that has spread throughout the tropics. Because of its needle-like seeds which readily adhere to clothing, it is easily transported. Moreover, for the same reason it is a nuisance wherever it grows. It is a difficult weed to eradicate because it grows as well in waste places as in cultivated fields, and re-establishes itself quickly, even in areas where it has been eradicated with chemicals. Perhaps it is its perverse nature that led Julia Morton (1962) to study it thoroughly for its possible worthwhile uses. As pointed out by Morton, this weed is valuable as a source of nectar for bees, in sparse amounts it is eaten in fodder, and it is eaten fresh by rabbits and chickens. The older foliage is somewhat purgative. It is also used medicinally for a variety of purposes. As a food plant, Spanish needles is used chiefly in Africa, but it is known and consumed also in tropical Asia.

The plant is herbaceous, annual, erect, branching, with opposite, serrate, compound leaves (Fig. 19). In addition, the stem is angular and finely pubescent. Where the stem touches the wet ground, roots can form at the nodes, and thus the plant can expand its area. This trait, and the ability to seed rapidly, leads to the formation of extensive weedy areas at times that appear more like seeded ground

cover. The flowers are abundant, with yellow disks (ray color varies). The black, long seeds stick to clothing by means of the remnants of the sepals.

Morton traced the utilization of the species as food through a thorough review of the literature. Peoples in widely scattered regions have used the plant to advantage as a boiled leaf and a tea. The young shoots are sometimes sold on the market in Malaysia. Morton has also investigated the characteristics of the leaf as a cooked vegetable. We have independently checked and confirmed her observations. The tender tops of the wild plant are normally taken. Older leaves have a more pungent odor, disagreeable to some people. Upon boiling, the greens retain their pleasant dark green color. They may be eaten as a vegetable dish, used cooked in salads (but not raw), or combined in a stew. The taste is strong but pleasant, and may leave an aftertaste. The leaves may also be dried, preserved, and cooked later.

Because of the assets of this species, its year-round availability, attractive appearance, and usually readily acceptable flavor, this species ranks as one of the best of the weed sources of edible greens.

Vernonia species (bitter leaf) occur throughout the tropics and bear edible leaves which are often used in local cooking. They vary from annual to perennial herbs, vines, and shrubs. There is sufficient variation among the edible species to make generalization difficult. The principal species *V. amygdalina* Del., with long, ovate, grayish leaves, is a popular leafy vegetable from South to West Africa. It is probably of very ancient origin and is both a cultivated plant and a spontaneous weed. The more cultivated races are almost free of bitterness. Other species occasionally used as food are either wild or weedy.

Because of the bitter taste common to all species, *Vernonia*s have found a wide usage in folk medicine. Most of their usages do not seem to stand up under trial, however. A glucoside has been found in the seeds of some species, and saponins account for the distinctive taste. Except in the case of the sweet varieties, the young leaves are usually not used in large quantities, but are rather more like a condiment, giving a bitter taste to other foods, particularly meats and soups. It is quite possible that the leaves of all species are edible; however, many would be too bitter for normal consumption. Leaves of *V. amygdalina* are partially debittered before use in Nigeria by macerating them in cold or hot water.

Convolvulaceae

This family, a large one of more than 1000 species, is widely distributed and well known, and many of the common weedy species have edible leaves. A few species can be distinguished as world travelers and are found throughout the tropics. Most of these have been tested and some found edible. Leaves of many of the inedible species are not poisonous, but their fine pubescence renders them unpleasant to the palate. The seeds of some species of the family contain hallucinogenic alkaloids, but so far these have not been shown to occur in the leaves. A full list of edible species mentioned in the literature is given in the appendix. However, some of these species are not widely extended nor weedy, and need not be mentioned here. Some of the better-known species follow.

The beach morning glory, *Ipomoea pes-caprae* (L.) R. Br., occurs on sandy

beaches throughout the tropics. Its succulent, glabrous, circular leaves with notched apex make it easy to recognize (Fig. 20). While a scraggling, running vine under circumstances of poor nutrition, it is capable of forming a handsome ground cover when well cared for. The large, pink flowers which open in the morning are attractive. The thick stems are similar to those of sweet potato, as is the flavor. The plant tolerates salt water, and may accumulate sufficient salt to give the leaves a salty taste. Although the herbage is sometimes fed to pigs and cows, it is said to taint the milk, and ultimately to cause illness if not fatality. In the Hawaiian islands this species is recognized to be useful only in times of famine. Regular consumption produces dizziness. The edibility of leaves of another and possibly related beach morning glory, *I. stolonifera* Poir, has apparently not been tested.

The moonflower, *Calonyction album* (L.) House, occurs wild in the tropics and is frequently planted as an ornamental in the temperate zone. Its flowers are large, showy, white, and fragrant. The species grows best in disturbed areas including roadsides and abandoned fields. The moonflower is a vigorous climber and needs an appropriate arbor to display the flowers and to permit collection of the young leaves. The plants, even when weedy, prefer wet areas, and are often found along riverbanks. The young leaves and the calyxes of the flower are cooked as a vegetable in Africa, India, and Indonesia or are used in vegetable soup in China. They may be used either fresh or dried. Contact with the plant may cause dermatitis.

Other common species with edible leaves that merit attention because they are easy to find include the cypress vine, *Quamoclit (Ipomoea) pinnata* Boyer, with its white or red salverform flowers; *Merremia umbellata* L., which produces yellow flowers; and *Ipomoea digitata* L., recognized by its deeply, palmately cut leaves. The latter species produces a tuberous root with purgative properties. *I. eriocarpa* R. Br. is used in India as a leaf vegetable. The possible edibility of leaves of the species most similar to the sweet potato, *I. triloba* L., *I. tiliacea* (Willd.) Choisy, and others merit investigation. Scattered reports in the literature prove very hard to verify.

Cucurbitaceae

Momordica charantia L. (balsam pear, cundeamor), is a widespread species known throughout the tropics and the subtropics where it is often weedy and not utilized, but which approaches a cultivated state in still other areas. The cultivated and semi-cultivated races have fruits which are large and attractive. As pointed out by Julia Morton (1967), it is edible, medicinal, and toxic.

Balsam pear is a vigorous tropical vine that grows from seed either as an annual or perennial. The rather thin stems are grooved and slightly pubescent. The leaves are deeply divided into 5 or 7 lobes (Fig. 21). The flowers are yellow, 2-5 cm in diameter, and somewhat attractive. As in the case of many cucurbits, both male and female flowers are produced. The spindle-shaped and somewhat spiny fruits develop rapidly. As they grow, they change from green to yellow to pale orange. The ripe fruit splits and twists, revealing the seeds surrounded by a red aril. The seeds are attractive to birds and thus are readily distributed.

Many parts of the plant are used as food or medicine. Children suck the sweet pulp from the seeds, although sometimes they are cautioned to not eat too

much. The immature fruits are sometimes boiled, without the seeds. The cultivated varieties are used in oriental cookery, before maturity, but they must be processed carefully to eliminate their bitterness. The tips of the vines are marketed in Southeast Asia, where they are generally cooked with vegetables, meat, or fish. The small fruit is also preserved in brine or pickled. On cooking, considerable bitterness is removed from the leaf. It may be necessary to change the cooking water. The leaves retain a good color and a firm texture with little of the bitterness of the uncooked foliage. The flavor is mild and unusual. The stems are mostly too tough to eat.

Probably much remains to be learned of the toxic qualities of balsam pear. The fresh juice from the foliage is a powerful emetic, probably removed or destroyed by cooking. Eating the ripe fruit has caused serious purging and vomiting, as well as death in extreme cases. The toxicology has been reviewed in Morton's paper.

Cruciferae

The leaves of most species of the mustard family are edible, but some are excessively pungent. The family is second only to Compositae as a source of cultivated green leaf vegetables. The most common species, chiefly of the genus *Brassica*, are familiar vegetables in the temperate zone, but grow only under special conditions in the tropics. The edible weedy species include native tropical species and temperate zone weeds which have been introduced and have become adapted. Edible parts include young shoots and tips, green pods, and sometimes ripened seeds. Most are eaten either raw in salads or cooked.

All of the cruciferous species share a common flower structure based on four sepals, four petals, and six stamens. The fruit is a dried capsule of one chamber.

Many of the edible species are listed in the appendix. Some are fleshy herbs found along the beach (sea rocket, *Cakile fusiformis* Greene); many are tolerant of dry conditions (*Brassica* species); others prefer moist places (*Lepidium virginicum* L.) or even running water (*Nasturtium officinale* R. Br.). Wild *Brassica* species are abundant and freely used, especially in Africa and India. Several species of *Lepidium* with edible leaves are known. Few countries are without examples of these pungent plants.

Gramineae

The grass family is one of the most important to people, not only directly as a source of grains, construction material (bamboo), and sugar, but also indirectly as forage and fodder for domesticated animals. Very few species, however, can be used as a source of edible green leaves. The rather fine, long leaves preclude such usage, for they are reinforced by supporting fibers that inhibit digestibility. In a few cases, especially with respect to the larger and more vigorous species, the developing leaves, either recently unfurled or still folded in the sheaths of older leaves, are eaten as at least an occasional food. Entire young plants from seed and the rapidly growing shoots from an underground rhizome are often eaten.

Perhaps the most spectacular of the edible grasses are the bamboos. The rapidly growing sprout or shoot of many species is edible. Others, while bitter, can be processed to an edible state. The shoot, however, cannot be considered a leaf and

need not be considered further here.

Among those species of which the unfolded leaf may be eaten are *Saccharum officinarum* L. (sugar cane) and *Zea mays* L. (corn), which was previously mentioned. A complete list including bamboos is found in the appendix.

Leguminosae

Many of the common weeds of the family Leguminosae bear edible leaves. Those mentioned here are only the most common. Probably the edible qualities of many other species of this large family remain to be discovered.

The jequirity bean, rosary pea, or jumbie bead, *Abrus precatorius* L., is a woody vine known chiefly as a source of red seeds, each with a black spot. These are often made into necklaces and sold to tourists throughout the tropics. The seed, however, is deadly poisonous, and death has occurred through ingestion of a single seed. The jumbie bead is a pestiferous weed, distributed by birds. It is found chiefly in abandoned fields, thickets, and fence rows. The very young leaves and shoots of this unlikely weed are sometimes eaten, or chewed raw for their licorice flavor.

Clitoria ternatea L. (butterfly pea, streaky bean) is a common, weedy vine sometimes grown as an ornamental for its blue and white flowers, and also used as a green manure crop; it is also a source of edible leaves. Under favorable conditions, the species is extremely weedy, and may cover foliage of all other plants with its vines. Of South American origin, it has become established throughout most of the tropics. The flowers are cooked with rice to color it. The seeds are quite poisonous.

Many species of *Crotalaria* produce edible leaves. In contrast, others are often poisonous, and kill slowly, even long after the leaves are eaten. Many of the species are used as green manure crops. Plants are herbaceous and slightly woody. Their flowers are yellow and usually attractive. By themselves they seldom form pure stands, but their weedy nature is suggested by the disturbed habitats where they are usually found.

Other genera containing edible weedy species irregularly distributed throughout the tropics include *Desmodium, Mucuna, Phaseolus, Tephrosia, Vicia,* and *Vigna*. Because leguminous plants are everywhere, further studies of the edibility of their leaves would appear justified. Nevertheless, extreme caution must be practiced, as this is one family that also contains a large number of poisonous species.

Malvaceae

Several species of the genus *Sida* (wireweed, escobilla) are used as green leaf sources. *Sida* is a genus well spread throughout the tropics, but particularly rich in species in Central America and the Caribbean. *S. alba* L. is used as a food in Central Africa. *S. rhombifolia* L. and *S. humilis* Willd. var. *moriflora* are common weeds that are cultivated in Central and South America for shoots and leaves. Without doubt many other species are edible, but are not recorded in the botanical literature. The various species differ from low herbs to semi-woody shrubs. The stems tend to be tough and wiry. One species in particular, *S. rhombifolia,* is grown in Africa for its fibers. According to the species, the flowers differ in size. They are usually yellow

40

or orange. A many-seeded capsule is produced. *Sida* is a rather prolific weed and constitutes a serious nuisance wherever it is found.

Urena lobata L. (cadillo, aramina) is a particularly obnoxious weed because of its small capsules with curved spines which adhere readily to clothing or animal fur. This African species is now well distributed throughout the tropics, and where it occurs abundantly, it is difficult to eradicate. Although an annual species, it is rather woody. In the upper parts of the Amazon river, the fibers are extracted and used chiefly in the construction of bags. With its large, pubescent leaves and white or pinkish flowers, it is an attractive plant when sufficiently small. The young leaves are edible. Several closely related species merit trial where they occur.

Piperaceae

Several common weedy species of value are found in this family. The small, succulent herb *Peperomia pellucida* (L.) Kunth is commonly found in very wet places, including greenhouse benches and flower pots (Fig. 22). It also grows well in the cracks of walls or in rocky areas. It is seldom obnoxious and in fact is even grown occasionally as an ornamental. The plant is used as a pot herb, or the leaves can be used in salads. In the West Indies the leaves are also brewed as a tea. Other less common species are probably also edible.

Few pepper species bear edible leaves. Exceptions are the herbaceous species *Piper umbellatum* L. (*Pothomorphe umbellata*) and *Piper stylosum* (also named *Heckeria*.) The species *P. betle* L. merits mention here because though not a weed, the species still exists in the wild, and its leaves are widely used as part of the betel quid that is chewed throughout Southeast Asia. Betel nut chewing, largely unknown to Westerners, is a vice still awaiting introduction.

Portulacaceae

Portulaca oleracea L. (purslane, verdolaga) is a common, spontaneous weed found throughout the tropics and the warmer parts of the temperate zone. Its wide adaptation is due to its high genetic flexibility that rapidly permits adaptation to new environments. All the many forms are edible. Nevertheless, the more succulent, selected forms are often distinguished as variety *sativa*. The variety *giganthes* is a large and vigorous form sometimes grown as an ornamental. Other species are less attractive, while probably all species are edible in an emergency. The species is extremely weedy, and indeed depends on human activity to provide a suitable environment. It thrives in newly disturbed areas and in cultivated fields. In more weedy areas it tends to die out by competition from other plants. Its highly succulent nature is maintained even under relatively dry conditions. It can withstand drought for long periods, and flourish after a slight rain. Of the 100 or more species, some are typically found only on beaches or salty flats. The related *Portulacaria afra* (L.) Jacq., sometimes known as elephant grass, is an upright, succulent ornamental herb.

Purslane is a vigorous, succulent, prostrate annual herb with glabrous foliage and obovate to spatulate leaves (Fig. 23). The plant creeps, and carpets the soil by rooting at the nodes. The bright yellow flowers appear almost sessile in the axils of

the leaves. They are up to 3 cm in diameter, especially in the ornamental forms. The fruit is a circumscissile capsule containing a large number of fine seeds. The leaves are dull green or tinged red with anthocyanin.

The leaves and tender shoots can be eaten raw and have a mild pleasant flavor. They are frequently used in salads. The leaves make a good food for chickens and for canaries. They are cooked as a spinach dish, mixed with rice, stew, or cooked meat dishes.

Although tolerant of many soils including those with extreme conditions, purslane favors sands or sandy loams. Since it is seldom cultivated, cultural instructions are difficult to give. When improved forms are obtained through French catalogs, the ideal site would be fairly rich in nitrogen, but free from weed competition. The young plants grow slowly at first due to the limited size of their seeds, but once established grow very rapidly and yield a crop every two weeks. Purslanes are usually thought of as a nuisance in the garden for they grow so readily, re-root when cut and left in the field, and distribute many thousands of seeds. Perhaps in the home garden the best solution is to eat them. Unfortunately, they are also highly attractive to various kinds of insects, which may be a curse or a blessing, depending on the viewpoint of the gardener.

In some soils purslane tends to accumulate excess nitrates and becomes poisonous to cattle. Purslane can also contain excessive amounts of oxalic acid and thus should not be eaten regularly in large quantities.

Talinum fruticosum (L.) Juss. (Surinam spinach, water leaf) is a weedy though widely cultivated species introduced from South America to many areas of the tropics. It is a small, slightly succulent, unobtrusive upright herb (Fig. 24) that branches readily, with obovate, spatula-shaped, glabrous leaves and a minimum of petiole. Small, white-petalled flowers are borne abundantly. *Talinum* reseeds itself or may be propagated from its abundant small seeds which germinate readily; it is also grown easily from cuttings, with woody stems preferred. Soil requirements are not stringent, of course, but fertile soil gives more rapid and succulent production.

Harvest can be made at any time, but it is better to let the plants reach about 30 cm and then cut the branches back to the main trunk. Well-pruned plants have a life expectancy of a year or more, and can produce regular crops at least every two weeks. The leaves and tender stems are chopped as salad. They have a slightly sour taste and a bitter, lingering aftertaste. On cooking, the inner basal portion of the leaf may turn brown, which is unattractive but not harmful. The cooking water is tinted pinkish by pigments extracted from the leaves. Cooked portions are excessively soft and mucilaginous, so overcooking should be avoided. The flavor is characteristic but mild; bitterness is absent. Older stems may have some fibers, but these constitute a very small part of the plant. This species, like purslane, contains too much oxalic acid (1-2%) to recommend its frequent consumption. The genus *Talinum* consists of over 50 species, some of which are used as food in Africa; others are ornamentals.

Solanaceae

The genus *Solanum* (nightshade) is a very large and varied one, including both weedy and non-weedy species as well as a number of well-known edible and

ornamental cultivars. Plants are herbs, shrubs, or even small trees, and some climbers. As a group they are easily recognized from their flowers with a characteristic cone of 5 anthers on very short filaments. The foliage is often spiny. The ripe fruit, a berry, is frequently eaten. On the other hand, leaves and fruits of many species are poisonous due principally to the presence of glycoalkaloids. Sometimes these disappear as the fruit ripens. The glycoalkaloids, if produced in quantity, can serve as precursors for cortisone and steroidal drugs. Others are used directly in both traditional and modern medicine. The commonly cultivated species are mentioned elsewhere. Here the principal weedy and wild species bearing edible leaves are briefly mentioned. These are sometimes cultivated sporadically.

S. nigrum L. (black nightshade) is an extremely variable species occurring throughout the temperate and tropical zones. The berries are often edible (morelle, wonderberry), but unripe fruits and leaves are often said to be poisonous. Var. *guineense* (*S. scabrum*, garden huckleberry), however, is grown for its leaves in West Africa. Plants are established from seed or cuttings. These weeds should not be eaten in quantity until the edible qualities of the available races are carefully established.

S. nodiflorum Jacq. (lumbush, popolo) is sometimes regarded as a variety of *S. nigrum*. It is more upright and bushy than most forms of the latter. Both the young leaves and the fruits are eaten. Both are somewhat bitter. Whether it should be regarded as a weed or cultivated species is difficult to say.

S. macrocarpon L. is another species that might be more cultivated than wild. It is perennial, glabrous, and shrubby. Originally from Africa but widely introduced into Southeast Asia, this species produces a small fruit similar to the eggplant. The fruits may be eaten when very small, often raw, but in many places the plant is grown chiefly for its edible leaves.

Solanum aethiopicum L. (mock tomato) is a herbaceous African species with glabrous edible leaves. The small red fruits are also eaten cooked. Other species with edible leaves are listed in the appendix. It is highly probable that the leaves of many other species will prove edible when systematically tested. *Solanum* species should, however, be tested with much caution. The alkaloids are quite powerful, and in some cases eating just a few leaves, cooked or not, can be disastrous.

In addition to the *Solanum* species, some weedy species of *Physalis* bear edible leaves. *Physalis* species are fairly well distributed in the tropics, especially of the Americas. They are distinguished from other members of the Solanaceae by the leafy bracts that enclose the fruit until maturity. Some bear edible fruit which is sometimes compared to the tomato, hence the name "husk tomato." One of the best of these is *P. peruviana* L. (goldenberry), a pleasant fruit with a poor aftertaste. It has been introduced from South America to Australia, where it has been completely naturalized. The fruits are widely appreciated by children where it is grown in West Africa. The leaves are sometimes eaten. Another species with both edible fruits and leaves is *P. angulata* L., distributed throughout the tropics, but used as a source of edible leaves in Central Africa.

Among the weedy species of the family Solanaceae, the *Datura* species are the most poisonous, and their culture in the garden is not recommended.

Sterculiaceae

A number of wild species in this family, mostly trees, are used as sources of edible leaves. Among the weedy species, the pantropical *Melochia corchorifolia* L. has a history of edible leaves, in India, for example. Another edible species of the East Indies is *M. umbellata* Stapt. Many species have highly pubescent leaves that are not really suitable when cooked. Leaves of the common West Indian annual *M. pyramidata* L. are said to be edible, yet in Costa Rica the species is associated with paralysis and death of cattle.

Typhaceae

The familiar cattails of wet places in the tropics and temperate zone are the sources of several kinds of food. The starchy tubers of most species are edible. The young inflorescence can be boiled as a vegetable. Young leaves or shoots are eaten, especially of *Typha angustifolia* L., a very widespread species. As in the case of many monocotyledons, the young leaves are first removed from the protective sheath of previous leaves while they are still tender, before they have become very green.

Umbelliferae

Leaves of quite a number of species of the family Umbelliferae are edible. Nevertheless, poisonous species are common, and extreme caution should be taken on eating leaves of a new species. Celery (*Apium graveolens* L.) is frequently found wild in cooler parts of the tropics. The leaves are good raw or cooked, but may be strong-flavored. An equally edible Indian species is *A. sowa*. Among the more weedy edible species are *Eryngium foetidum* L., common and easy to identify, and its relatives. Several species of *Hydrocotyle* should also be mentioned. Species of this family tend to have highly flavored leaves and some are used primarily for seasoning such as parsley (*Petroselinum crispum* (Miller) A. W. Hill).

Urticaceae

Many of the nettles of both the temperate and tropical zones are edible. Their edible qualities can hardly be appreciated when one thinks of the itching sensation caused by the hairs of many species. The family consists chiefly of herbs and shrubs, but also includes a few small trees. A family with many weeds, it is known best for the cultivated *Boehmeria nivea* (L.) Gaudich, the source of the fiber ramie. The young leaves of this species can be eaten.

The members of the family with edible young leaves are many. The genus *Urtica* is widely represented throughout the world. Young plants, shoots, and young leaves of the common weed *U. urens* are edible. The succulent and often attractive species of *Pilea* are often edible. *Fleurya aestuans* Gaudich, a noxious weed in the coffee groves of Puerto Rico, is eaten as a leafy vegetable in West Africa and Sri Lanka. The shrubby species with edible leaves include *Cudrania javanensis* Trecul. and *Laportea terminalis* Wight. Even the genus *Urera* that includes some of the most

painful and ugliest of the nettles, includes edible species. A list appears in the appendix but probably many less common weeds of the family bear edible leaves.

Zygophyllaceae

One of the most undesirable weeds of waste places that persists and even thrives in difficult locations where few other plants will grow, and where human, animal, and vehicular traffic beat it to the ground, is the puncture weed, *Tribulus terrestris* L. The plant is characterized by its sprawling tendency, its short, pinnately compound leaves, small but attractive yellow flowers, and especially by its capsule characterized by several sharp, straight spines that can puncture a shoe or a bicycle tire. It is a species often found in sandy areas, but by no means confined to such. It resists attempts to eradicate it, for the seeds can persist for long times in the soil, and germinate irregularly. Although often said to be poisonous (see later), the leaves and tender shoots are eaten in India and East Africa. The authors have eaten the leaves of the related *T. cistoides* L., and have seen the flowers of another species eaten by iguanas in the West Indies. Without doubt, however, this particular plant should never be planted for its edible leaves. Several related species are known in the tropics. Species of the related genus *Fagonia* are used for their leaves in the Sahara desert.

Other Weeds

Weeds are present everywhere agriculture is practiced. Many surveys of weeds and wild plants have been taken, and articles on their edibility are available. Duke (1992) surveys many of the most common edible ones; the bibliography includes many references, mostly to regions of North America, although many of the weeds can be found worldwide.

Table 1 summarizes a survey of the weeds of Puerto Rico. The list includes plants with leaves already described as edible and weedy species related to plants bearing edible leaves. No doubt the leaves of many of these species are equally edible, but in a few cases, such as the *Solanum* species, it might be somewhat risky to make the test. This brief survey is suggestive, however, of the richness of edible leaves that should occur in almost any tropical area.

Table 1. Edible weeds of Puerto Rico or weeds that have edible relatives

Family	Species
Acanthaceae	Thunbergia alata*
	T. fragrans-
Amarnathaceae	Achyranthes indice-
	Amaranthus dubius*
	A. spinosus*
Asclepiadaceae	Asclepias nivea-
Bataceae	Batis maritima*
Begoniaceae	Begonia decandra-
Boraginaceae	Cordia corymbosa-
	Tournefortia hirsutissima-
Bromeliaceae	Bromelia pinguin*
Capparidaceae	Cleome spinosa-
Chenopodiaceae	Chenopodium ambrosioides*
Compositae	Artemisia absinthium-
	Bidens pilosa*
	Centaurea cyanus-
	Daucus carota*
	Emilia sonchifolia*
	Lactuca intybacea*
	Pluchea odorata-
	Synedrella nodiflora*
	Vernonia cinerea*
	V. sericea-
Convolvulaceae	Calonyction album*
	Ipomoea pes-caprae*
	Ipomoea tiliaceae-
	Jacquemontia pentantha-
	Quamoclit (I.) pinnata*
Cruciferae	Brassica rapa*
	B. nigra*
	Lepidium virginicum-
Euphorbiaceae	Croton lobatus-
	Jatropha curcas*
Graminae	Bambusa vulgaris*
	Echinochloa colona*
	Eleusine indica*
	Setaria geniculata-
Geraniaceae	Impatiens balsamina*
Labiatae	Hyptis atrorubens-
	H. pectinata*
	Salvia serotina-
	Ocimum sanctum*
Leguminosae	Abrus precatorius*
	Clitoria ternatea*
	Crotalaria retusa*
	C. striata-
	Phaseolus adenanthes-
	Vigna repens-
Liliaceae	Aloe vulgaris-
	Smilax coriaceae-
Malvaceae	Sida carpinifolia-
	Urena spp.*
Nyctaginaceae	Pisonia aculeata-
Papaveraceae	Argemone mexicana*
Plantaginaceae	Plantago major*
Pontederiaceae	Eichhornia crassipes*
Polygonaceae	Polygonum portorricensis-
Portulacaceae	Portulaca oleracea*
Rosaceae	Rubus rosifolius*
Rubiaceae	Randia mitis-
Solanaceae	Physalis angulata*
	Solanum citratum-
	S. torvum-
Sterculiaceae	Melochia pyramidata*
	M. tomentosa-
	M. villosa-
Typhaceae	Typha angustifolia*
	T. fruticosa-
Umbelliferae	Eryngium foetidum*
	Hydrocotyle umbellata-
Urticaceae	Urera baccifera-
	Fleurya aestuans*
Verbenaceae	Stachytarpheta jamaicensis*
	Lantana camara*
	Lippia nodiflora*
Zingiberaceae	Zingiber zerumbet-
Zygophyllaceae	Tribulus cestoides*
	Kallstroemia maxima-

Edibility: * Edible
- Unknown

CHAPTER V

Tropical Trees With Edible Green Leaves

The deep emotions inspired by trees possibly result from their many uses and benefits to people. From trees the physical necessities of life are taken: wood for shelter and for cooking, bark and fiber to be pounded or to be woven into cloth, both sweet and starchy fruits, nuts, and rich sources of edible oils, liquids (not common) to be used as beverages with or without fermentation, or to be evaporated to yield sugar. In addition, trees fill aesthetic needs. They are often graceful and pleasing to the eye or give a sense of permanence by their sheer size. They often outlive humans, and because many grow so slowly, it is said that one must have faith to plant trees.

In spite of their abundance and their multiplicity of uses, trees are seldom thought of as sources of edible green leaves. In fact, very few trees of the temperate zone are utilized in that fashion. In some areas of the tropics, however, the edible qualities of the leaves of certain trees are much appreciated. It is common, for example, to see the gnarled living fence posts of various species that are so shaped because their leaves are continually removed for animal fodder. The harvesting of the edible crop maintains the form of the hedge. Some type of pruning of trees bearing edible leaves is always desirable to keep the leaves within easy reach.

Among the families of flowering plants, perhaps the most important with respect to edible-leaved trees are the Leguminosae and Euphorbiaceae. Both families, but especially the former, are sources of important and minor edible crop plants. However, both families also contain species with deadly poisons. Often enough, parts of a poisonous species are sometimes perfectly edible if properly prepared.

Leguminosae

Trees of the Leguminosae are well known, widely distributed, and probably available to almost anyone in the tropics. A description follows of some of the most important species with edible leaves.

The 65 or more species of *Erythrina* (coral trees) are widely distributed around the world, for they originated in America, Asia, or Australia. These common trees are known for their beauty, often of form but almost always of flowers, which are bright orange or red, and normally occur in upright clusters. In some cases, flowering before leafing creates a spectacular effect. Small birds seeking nectar often pollinate the flowers. Some of the smaller species can be successfully grown in pots. *Erythrina*s are usually propagated from seed, but some species can be grown from large, woody cuttings. These make colorful and long-lasting fenceposts. Both large and dwarf trees are often used for shade in plantings of coffee, bananas, vanilla, and black pepper. Many of the species are prickly. Few are useful for timber, but many uses have been recorded in folk medicine.

The leaves of coral trees are commonly used for fodder. It is not uncommon to see people harvesting the leaves along the fence rows in the tropics, often as not to feed them to rabbits. However, other animals eat the leaves also, and can keep the lower trunks of the trees pruned clean. The dwarf bucare, *E. berteroana* Urban (Fig.

47

25) is one of the easiest species to grow, and thus is often used to form retaining walls or hedges. The leaves are most commonly eaten cooked in stews with other foods, but it is not unusual for them to be eaten raw. A few of the edible species, their sources and uses, are listed below. Other species with edible leaves are listed in the appendix and without doubt other species remain to be tested.

E. berteroana Urban	C. America	Buds, young leaves and twigs, cooked
E. fusca Lour.	S.E. Asia	Young leaves, boiled or raw
E. poeppigiana Walp.	S. America	Flowers, in soups and salads
E. variegata L.	India-Indonesia	Young leaves, cooked, in salads, curries

In contrast, the orange or red seeds are poisonous. They contain the alkaloid hypophorine, which acts on the nervous system. Browsing animals are frequently killed from eating the seeds. Nevertheless, the seeds are often used in necklaces, and are sometimes made palatable by cooking, a risky practice. Pounded seeds of *E. variegata* are used as poultices for snakebites, and even for cancer.

Gliricidia sepium (Jacq.) Walp., often known as mother-of-cacao, is a small deciduous tree from tropical America commonly planted in fence rows or hedges (Fig. 26). In dry areas, it is used as a windbreak, and because it flowers fast as new leaves are produced, it is sometimes used as an ornamental tree. *Gliricidia* grows rapidly either from seed or from readily rooted cuttings. Fence posts take root and then last for many years. It is often used as a shade tree, not only for cacao, but also for vanilla and coffee. The tree fixes nitrogen efficiently, and thus serves also to fertilize the nursed crop. Because of its open structure and small size, this species does not compete so much with the shaded crop as do some other species.

The roots, bark, seeds and perhaps even the leaves are toxic and are used in home medicines and poisons. The poisonous qualities of the leaves are questionable. While recognized as nutritious for cattle, the leaves are said to poison horses, dogs, and rats. It is difficult to get an exact statement from the literature as to the effects of leaves on humans, but presumably they are edible, and are appreciated in some parts of the tropics. This is an important question that must be resolved before the leaves are eaten in quantity. It is quite possible that cooking removes or inactivates the poisonous alkaloid. The colorful flowers are also eaten, fried or boiled.

The genus *Cassia* (*Senna*) comprises about 600 species of herbs, shrubs, and trees throughout the tropics, also extending into temperate zones. Many of the species are of ornamental value. Among these are the lovely Rainbow Shower trees of Hawaii (*Cassia* hybrids), the well-known Golden Shower (*Cassia fistula* L.), other yellow-flowered species, and many others. A few species yield substances of more commercial value. The leaves and pods of several species (*C. angustifolia* Vahl. and *C. senna* L.) are dried and marketed as senna, a mild laxative. The purgative action is caused by emodin and other glycosides. The bark from *C. auriculata* L. is used in tanning. Several species are useful green manure crops. The seeds of *C. occidentalis* L., of American origin, are roasted as a coffee substitute. Finally, leaves of the beautiful *C. alata* L., already discussed, are used in the treatment of ringworm.

When the glucoside content is not too high, the leaves of various *Cassia* species are edible. A list of the principal species used as a source of green leaves is

given in the appendix. The leaves of *Cassia* species should always be eaten with caution, and judicious experimentation should be undertaken before the leaves of any tree are accepted as safe. A tea of some of the species is a strong purgative. Cooking removes some of the glucosides. Despite their purgative qualities, the leaves of even the more medicinal species are often cooked in small quantities with other dishes. They are considered a tonic, and without doubt exert a regulating influence.

The tropical herbaceous species *C. tora* L. is probably a more reliable source of edible leaves. Only the youngest leaves are used. Foliage is somewhat ill smelling, but this disappears on cooking. *C. siamea* Lam. leaves are poisonous, reportedly due to an alkaloid. This weedy tree should be recognized and its leaves avoided.

Sesbania grandiflora (L.) Poiret (agati, báculo) is a small, upright, and rapidly growing tree from Malaysia and India. It is widespread throughout the tropics, where it is appreciated for its exceptionally large flowers, usually white, but red in some varieties. Unfortunately, their smell is unpleasant. The tree begins to flower at only two years of age, when it is still small. It has finely pinnate leaves and a long, narrow seed pod, with small seeds separated by ingrowths of the pod walls. It is well adapted to both dry and moist regions.

The tree has many minor uses. Its wood is soft and white, but seldom used. The living tree is used as a nurse or shade tree, particularly for black pepper. The bark is bitter and is used medicinally, as an emetic, and in lesser doses, for treatment of stomach disorders. The tree is grown sometimes for its value as a green manure crop, and more often as a source of green leaves for cattle. It is sometimes planted in pastures for this purpose. The flowering shoot, flowers, pods, and young leaves are all used as greens. The flowers are often bitter, and are not appetizing to many people. The most common preparation is in stews or salads, but the leaves may also be used as a spinach. The utilization of leaves is widespread, from Africa to India, Indonesia, and some of the islands of the Pacific. At least two other species of *Sesbania* are used as sources of edible leaves (see appendix). Nevertheless, the young pods and the flowers are more appreciated as food than the leaves.

One of the most annoying of weedy trees throughout the tropics, particularly obnoxious in dry regions with well-drained soils, is *Leucaena leucocephala* (Lam.) De Wit. (zarcilla, tantan, lead tree). The tree grows very rapidly from seed, is very aggressive, blooms at a very young stage (Fig. 27), and produces large quantities of seeds. The seeds germinate irregularly so that it is very difficult to eliminate the species from a garden. Cut trees regrow rapidly and soon dominate other cultivated or wild plants. Areas where the tree is particularly prevalent include the Hawaiian and Virgin Islands. Its origin, however, is the New World. In spite of its weedy nature, this species is often planted for a variety of purposes. It is used as a source of charcoal, in which the plantings are recut each 6-7 years. As in the case of other legumes, it replenishes the nitrogen of exhausted tropical soils. It serves as a shade crop and a hedge plant.

Although often used as a forage plant, the foliage contains the alkaloid mimosine, which causes poor weight gains, infertility, and hair loss in non-ruminants. It can be fatal to rabbits and pigs. Even sheep, goats, and cattle in some areas may be adversely affected when the diet contains excessive quantities. Mimosine is concentrated in the young leaves and seeds and may be increased in response to high

temperatures and water stress. Breeding and selection for low-mimosine varieties have proven difficult. *Leucaena*'s shiny brown seeds are attractive and thus are often used in necklaces. They must be first softened by boiling. The full grown but unripened seeds are dried and eaten uncooked. Seeds are ground into a coffee substitute in the Philippines. Ripe seeds are also eaten parched. Habitual consumption results in loss of hair. As a food for humans, the young pods are most commonly used; tender leafy shoots too are occasionally used in stews. Flowers are less commonly eaten with rice.

The genus *Bauhinia*, of almost 200 species from the tropics of both hemispheres, is best known for its attractive trees and woody vines that bear large open flowers with a striking superficial resemblance to orchids. From this has come the name "poor man's orchid." The leaves of many consist of two roundish lobes or partially joined leaflets resembling a cloven hoof, hence the name "pata de vaca" (cow's foot). A number of species are prized for their flowers, including *B. variegata* L., *B. purpurea* L., *B. pauletia* Pers., *B. petiolata* (Mutis) Triana, and *B. monandra*. Colors of the flowers range from pure white through delicate rose and lavender, to dark reds and purples. Usually long, flat pods are borne in profusion, and the rather large and attractive seeds are sometimes used in necklaces. The *Bauhinia* species have minor medicinal uses, or are occasionally used for fibers for rope, and in some cases, as very good sources of tannins for preparing leather. A few of the larger species yield wood used in agricultural implements. Many of the species are partially sterile. Among these, the Hong Kong *Bauhinia* is believed to be the most beautiful, with large, spectacular flowers. Experimental hybrids have been produced, and thus the beauty of these species may be enhanced by judicious breeding.

The leaves, flower buds, flowers, young shoots, and young pods of some species are often eaten as vegetables. The flower buds are sometimes pickled. The young cooked leaves are sour or have unusual flavors and are used as condiments. Probably leaves of all of the species are edible at least as animal feed. Among the species used for human consumption are the common ornamentals *B. variegata* L. and *B. purpurea* L. Other species with edible leaves are listed in the appendix. In contrast to legumes of other genera, none of the *Bauhinia* species are known to be poisonous.

Trees of the genus *Pterocarpus* are found in both Old and New Worlds, and have been widely introduced as handsome shade trees. Many are good sources of timber, and others are valuable for their tannins and dyes. The pods of these species are distinctive in that they are flat, often discoidal, and contain a single seed. Young leaves, flower buds, and flowers of a number of species are frequently eaten as vegetables. The edible species include the common roadside tree *P. indicus* Willd., a source of a valuable reddish timber, and *P. angolensis* DC., known throughout Central Africa. The fruits and the leaves of *P. santalinoides* L'Her. ex DC. are roasted and eaten in times of scarcity. Several other species are also utilized, and others remain to be tested.

Before leaving the Leguminosae, a few other genera, the trees of which yield edible green leaves, should be mentioned. These include *Acacia, Afzelia, Albizia, Ceratonia, Cynometra, Delonix, Parkia,* and *Pithecellobium.* A few species that also bear edible fruits were mentioned in an earlier chapter.

Euphorbiaceae

In spite of its size (8000 species) and diversity (herbs, shrubs, and trees), the family Euphorbiaceae is not a major source of edible plants. Many of its species are, in fact, poisonous, and a certain amount of caution is therefore appropriate in dealing with plants of this family. The species are well scattered through the tropics and the temperate zone, and some examples are probably known to everyone. Some of the economic species with edible leaves (*Manihot, Acalypha, Ricinus, Codiaeum,* and *Euphorbia pulcherrima*) have been previously mentioned. Here only the trees will be treated, and most of these are not very common.

The genus *Bridelia* is represented by trees, shrubs, and a few vines found throughout the tropics. They are little known in most areas and have few economic uses, except in tanning and folk medicine. *B. micrantha* (Hochst.) Baillon is known for its edible fruit in Central Africa. *B. scleroneura* Mill. Arg. is known chiefly in the Congo of Africa, where it is used as a source of leaves. One wonders how many more species of this genus might be equally edible.

The genus *Claoxylon* is less well known for it occurs only from Madagascar to the islands of the Pacific. Several different species are used as vegetable or condiments in one form or another. The young branches of *C. longifolium* Miq., a small tree, are sold in the markets from Malaysia to the Pacific as a fresh vegetable. The leaves of *C. polot* Merr. are purgative in nature, but nevertheless used as a condiment in sauces in Indonesia. One species is more generally distributed throughout central Africa, *C. oleraceum* O. Prain. It is well known in its particular habitat as a source of edible green leaves.

The genus *Glochidion* is rather small, and of Asiatic origin. These trees are little known outside of their native habitat, and have little value except for tannins and cheap lumber. Several bear attractive flowers but have seldom been introduced from their native habitats. Several species serve as sources of edible leaves, including *G. borneense* Boerl. Only the youngest leaves of *G. rubrum* Blume, a shrub, are eaten; the others contain too much tannin. Another tree, *G. blancoi* Lowe, is valued for its young leaves and shoots in the Philippine Islands.

Among the even lesser-known edible-leaved plants of the Euphorbiaceae are species of the genera *Hymenocardia, Maesobotrya, Microdemus, Pterococcus,* and still others (see appendix). These include not only trees but shrubs and woody vines.

Other Families

Many families of trees, even some large ones, do not include species with edible leaves. Often the trees that are edible are not only little known, but are also poorly distributed or unknown outside of their native regions. The task of introduction is thus still unfinished, and without doubt many trees remain to be made known to the world of horticulture. Some of the more interesting are included here.

Two species of the family Bombacaceae, a small family of large trees, are widely utilized for a diverse number of products. One of these, *Adansonia digitata* L. (baobab) is a large tree with an enormous trunk characteristic of the savannahs of Africa. The seeds do not germinate very well, and young trees are seldom seen.

Thus, in some areas the trees are believed by local people to have originated at their present size. In pot culture in the greenhouse some germination of carefully tended seeds is seen after one year.

Many parts of the baobab tree find a special use. The short, wide trunk is composed of a soft wood of no value for timber, but useful as wood pulp. The inner bark is fibrous, and has been used for ropes; the bark is pounded into a soft, white paper, or a fabric used for mats. The flower is large and exquisite (Fig. 28), but sometimes not seen among the mass of foliage. The fruit hangs from a long stem and has been responsible for the name, the "dead rat tree." The pulp around the seeds consists chiefly of tartaric and citric acid. It is eaten fresh, sometimes cooked into a porridge or made into a drink. The seeds are acid, and are sucked on. When cooked they taste like almonds, and contain about 12 percent oil. The seeds are also dried, ground, and used as a substitute for coffee, or as a meal in times of scarcity. The tender roots of the tree are used as a stewed vegetable. The pollen is made into glue.

The leaf of the baobab is palmately divided into 5 to 7 segments and may be downy or smooth. The young leaves and shoots serve as cooked greens, in soups, and as a condiment with other foods. The leaves or tea made from them are considered useful in reducing perspiration. Both fresh and dried leaves are commonly marketed. Leaves are obtained by continuously lopping off the new branches from smooth-leaved trees grown especially for this purpose. Downy-leaved trees are allowed to grow for fruit production and other uses.

The second economically important species of the Bombacaceae is the ceiba (*Ceiba pentandra* (L.) Gaertner, the silk-cotton tree). It is a tree widespread throughout the tropics, well known for its large trunk, flaring buttresses, height of up to 30 meters, and large horizontal branches. The tree grows best in forest conditions with heavy rainfall, generally at low elevations. The kapok of commerce comes from this species. It is the floss derived from the wall of the large seed capsule. The chief uses for this material are associated with its buoyancy and insulating properties. It can also be spun into thread and woven into cloth. Ceiba is an important plantation crop tree. Other uses are also common. The soft wood, for example, is used for dugout canoes. Cuttings are used as living fenceposts. The buttresses are cut up for doors, tables, etc. Very young, unripe pods are cooked as a vegetable in Indonesia. The seeds are also edible either fresh, germinated, or after pressing the oil, are used as a cattle feed. The leaves also have many uses, for example, in a hair lotion and as medicine for coughs. The young leaves are cooked as a vegetable or dried for later cooking. The leaves of young trees are eaten by cattle.

The fig of temperate and subtropical regions is only one example of a very large and diversified genus (*Ficus*, family Moraceae) of shrubs and trees that occurs throughout the tropics. Some figs are especially noted for their aerial roots which grow into new trunks and account for the spreading tendency of the banyans. In other species, however, the roots serve chiefly as props for the long branches. Most species produce abundant latex which has been used as birdlime (a sticky substance placed on branches to catch birds), and as inferior rubber. The fruits of many figs are edible although none match in quality those of *F. carica* L., the fig of commerce. Some figs have very bad odors, but the fruits can be eaten if cooked green. There are about 20 species with edible fruits. The leaves of figs are not only frequently used as food, but

are also smoked, along with opium, or chewed with betel nut. Young stem tips of *F. alba* Reina are used in salads in Indonesia. The leaves of this species are also used as horse feed. This is a rapidly growing shrubby species of possible ornamental value. The large leaves of *F. benghalensis* L. are used as platters and also as elephant feed. Very young leaves of the rubber tree, *F. elastica* Roxb. ex Hornem., are eaten in salads. The leaves of at least a dozen other Asian species are edible, and at least five African species bear edible leaves (see appendix).

The family Gnetaceae is a strange source indeed for trees with edible leaves. The principal genus *Gnetum* contains about 30 species, most from Southeast Asia. The trees and woody vines bear small fruits that are single-seeded, and somewhat fleshy. The fruits are sometimes sweet and edible, or in other species the starchy nuts themselves are eaten. The seeds of some species are covered with irritating spicules. Some of the species are occasionally cultivated, and merit more attention as a source of nuts. Best known of the species is *G. gnemon* L., an attractive tree reaching a height of about 9 meters. The leaves are opposite, dark green, and shiny. The red fruits, about 2.5 cm long, occur in clusters and are eaten raw though they are tough. The seeds are eaten roasted, boiled or fried. The leaves are not used everywhere where the tree is grown, but in some regions they constitute a much-prized and nutritive spinach dish. The young flowers and fruits are also eaten. All require cooking to eliminate their irritating substances.

The little-known family Salvadoraceae contains one species of merit, *Salvadora persica* L., known also as toothbrush tree or the mustard tree (as referred to in the Bible), although completely unrelated to the Cruciferae. This tree found from West to East Africa is appreciated for the pungent odor of its leaves. The leaves are eaten raw in salads and as antidotes against poison. The berries are small and red, and though sweet, are also pungent. They are dried like raisins and marketed.

Quisqualis indica L. (Combretaceae), the rangoon creeper, is a fairly well-known and widely distributed shrub appreciated for its showy and fragrant flowers. As with others of its genus, it is a plant of the Old World tropics. Several related species are used for medicinal purposes. The fruits of this species are dried and sold medicinally in Indonesia. They are dangerous, and can cause unconsciousness and even death. The fresh fruits are used as a vermifuge when half ripe. The leaves are used in a variety of ways, as a lotion for boils and a potent brew for headaches. It is the young leaves and stems, however, that are eaten, principally in Indonesia, as either a raw or steamed vegetable. The proper stage to gather them is before the bronzing associated with anthocyanins in the young leaves disappears.

Pisonia alba Span. (Nyctaginaceae) is sometimes called tree lettuce. It is a common tree in India and Indonesia, growing wild but also cultivated in gardens. The leaves of the female tree are bright yellow green, and are favored over the darker leaves of the male as a food. Since the trees are propagated by cuttings, the male is seldom seen. The leaves are eaten with rice or boiled as spinach. Other species of *Pisonia* are common in the tropics but some have strong emetic properties and should be avoided. All *Pisonia* species are fast-growing trees with soft wood. The base of the tree is often enlarged grotesquely.

Morinda citrifolia L. (Rubiaceae) is a small tree (Fig. 29) grown widely throughout the tropics which does especially well in dry, well-drained areas, including

almost barren lava rock of volcanic islands. A few variegated leaf forms are used for ornament. It is also notable for its large, elliptic shiny leaves. Known as the noni (in Hawaii) or Indian mulberry, the white fruit has a very unpleasant odor when ripe, and is used as a famine food. The Burmese cook the young fruits for curries, or it is eaten raw. A common source of folk medicines, it also yields dyes, timber, and affords shade for coffee and support for pepper. The older leaves are used as wrappers but the young are cooked as a vegetable.

The neem or margos tree, *Azadirachta indica* A. Juss. (Meliaceae) is common wild and cultivated in India, where it is prized for its many uses. It is now widely distributed in the tropics. It produces timber, lamp oil from the seed, medicinal bark from the trunk and roots, a sweet sap used for toddy, and leaves for insecticidal purposes and for fodder. The somewhat bitter leaves and flowers are added to cooked foods as flavoring and for their supposed value as tonic. The young leaves contain 11.6 percent protein. The neem tree should not be confused with the chinaberry tree, *Melia azedarach* L., all parts of which can cause human and animal poisoning.

Moringa oleifera Lam. (moringa, horseradish tree, reseda, Moringaceae) is one of the most promising leafy vegetables for a range of climates and soils in the warm tropics, valued for its many edible parts and exceptionally nutritious leaves. It is a small tree (Fig. 30) introduced to all parts of the tropics from eastern India, and very widely grown not only for its edible parts but also as an ornamental. The family is small, little known, and distinctive. Other species include *M. peregrina* (Forsk.) Fiori, used in West Africa as a condiment and for other purposes. *M. stenopetala* (known as "cabbage tree" in Africa), native to Ethiopia, may be superior to *M. oleifera* in many ways: it is more drought tolerant, bushier, larger-seeded, and the leaves are both larger and better tasting. It is reportedly slower to bloom and sets less seed than *M. oleifera*. Unfortunately, seed of *M. stenopetala* is difficult to locate.

The *M. oleifera* tree seldom reaches 8 meters in height, but it can grow up to 5 meters in its first year. It is characterized by a corky bark that yields a gum of minor value. The mature tree can attain a trunk diameter of 25 cm, but would be of little use at that size. A better system is to maintain the trees as a hedge, with plants about a meter apart. The hedge should be trimmed regularly not only to maintain its shape but also to provide the crop of edible leaves. Foliage is feathery or fernlike due to the finely tripinnate division of the leaves. Leaves are easily stripped for use; in many areas of Africa, people have found *Moringa* leaves, which are produced in abundance through most of the year, easy to preserve by drying in the sun for when vegetables are scarce at the end of the dry season. Mulching and fertilizing improve the production and quality of the leaves. The tree has the potential to flower throughout the entire year; the white flowers are abundant, quite showy, and attractive to bees. The seed capsules are up to 45 cm long, triangular in cross-section and split into three parts at maturity. The seeds have broad, fine, membranous wings. Some varieties which flower profusely are used chiefly for the young fruits, whereas others yield principally leaves.

Almost all parts of the plant are useful as food. Young plants from seeds are very tender and make an excellent cooked green vegetable. The shoot tips, leaves and flowers make an excellent spinach, high in vitamins, minerals, and protein. Young

pods have a flavor reminiscent of asparagus. The thick, soft roots have a strong flavor of horseradish due to an alkaloid, and they substitute for this condiment when peeled, dried, ground, and blended with vinegar. Seeds yield a fine edible oil, and they are used in water treatment: crushed seeds coagulate suspended particles in the water, helping to remove disease organisms present in turbid water.

Moringa is especially adapted to low elevations and to dry areas, and may resist several months of drought. It needs a well-drained soil. Propagation is usually by seeds, but cuttings may also be used. Plants are best started in areas where they will be used, and can be seeded heavily (every few inches) and thinned later to suitable distance. The trees are especially susceptible to termites, and in some areas their culture may be limited. The wood is soft, but useful for paper. The tree is weak, and limbs are easily broken. Medicinally the pulp of the root (or other parts) is used as a counter-irritant similar to "mustard plaster." Many more folk uses have been recorded, such as an ingredient in skin ointments and an antibiotic. This multipurpose tree is very productive in marginal growing conditions and is a reliable source of green leaves in areas where few other vegetables can be grown.

To residents of both temperate and tropical regions, palm trees (Palmae) are considered precious. They are usually attractive, often beautiful, and sometimes romantic. Thus it seems a travesty to destroy them, particularly in order to eat only a small portion. Nevertheless, the young growing terminal bud of many species is often used as a vegetable. This vital plant part is frequently served under the names "palm cabbage" or "millionaire's salad."

The number of palm species from which a suitable cabbage is taken is probably large. No one has systematically collected all the names of the edible species. Nevertheless, not all palms bear suitable cabbages. In some, removal of the cabbage is too difficult to justify the labor. In other species the flavor is not satisfactory. The cabbage is removed by cutting the palm if necessary, removing the fronds, and then opening the trunk with axe or machete. The edible part consists of the bases of the young developing fronds tightly enfolded one in another. The color is usually white. In Brazil, where the destruction of palms is often practiced to open new lands for agricultural purposes, the canning of the terminal bud is practiced on a commercial scale. Coconut palm plantations have been planted just for "cabbage."

Palm cabbage resembles true cabbage (*Brassica oleracea* L. var. *capitata*) only in having numerous thin layers of tissue. These are easily sliced finely to form a typical "slaw," which is flavored with oil, vinegar, etc., as it has little flavor of its own. The cabbage may also be cut into thick slices and cooked as a vegetable.

The chief palms used for cabbages are those palmitos of the genera *Irearta* and *Geonoma* of South America, the palmitos of North America, in Brazil the species *Euterpe oleracea* C. Martius and *Acrocomia sclerocarpa* Mart., in the Caribbean species of *Roystonea* and *Oreodoxa*, in Africa *Borassus*, and at the time of elimination of old trees, the oil palm *Elaeis guineensis* Jacq. In Southeast Asia many species are used. The most ubiquitous species is of course the coconut (*Cocos nucifera* L.), well known as one of the better sources of cabbage in all the regions in which it is grown.

The young, unfolding leaves of a few species of palm are also used as green vegetables. In Southeast Asia, for example, the fronds of *Arenga* (sugar palms) are so used. This method, which might be applicable to other species, avoids the

destruction of the tree for its cabbage.

A full review of edibility of palm leaves would be desirable. In the appendix a list of species reported to have edible cabbages is given.

CHAPTER VI

Tropical Leaves as Spices and Teas

In addition to their uses in salads, stews, and side dishes, leaves have a wide variety of uses that can classify them as spices. Since leaves are being considered here chiefly for their edible value, no great attention will be placed on the fact that spices, including leaves, were used for many centuries for other purposes: incenses, medicines, cosmetics, antidotes to poison, perfumes, aphrodisiacs, and preservatives for embalming. However, since not all substances used for such purposes are spices, it follows that "spice" should be used for still a smaller group of substances. Perhaps the word "spicy" is the clue, for it suggests aroma, or pungency, a sharp but pleasant taste. But some leaves used as spices do not add exactly that to the food with which they are used. Let us define a spice as a plant substance that is not eaten primarily as a food itself, but that is used to change the taste of food.

It follows that spices come from many parts of the plant, from leaves, stems, roots, bark, flower buds, seeds, etc. Distinctions between spices, herbs, and condiments can be forgotten here, for they are somewhat artificial. What is of interest is that many leaves of the tropics are used to flavor food. Nevertheless, the chief spices of the tropics are not from leaves, but from other plant parts, as with pepper, cloves, ginger, cinnamon, allspice, vanilla, chili peppers, cardamom, nutmeg, and mace. It is from the temperate zones that the principal leaves used for flavoring have come: basil, bay leaf, chervil, chives, savory, marjoram, oregano, mint, parsley, rosemary, tarragon, sage, and thyme.

For every well-known spice in the Western kitchen, there must be dozens of spices that are not common but that are used somewhere throughout the tropics. In the appendix of edible leaves, no attempt has been made to gather together the names of all the spices of tropical plants which have leaves used to flavor foods. For the most part, these native spices are not recorded in the botanical literature. From Burkill's treatment of the useful plants of the Malay Peninsula (1935), a partial list of the many species has been assembled (Table 2). This list does not include other species mentioned in this chapter.

Perhaps it is the ease with which the human palate is bored that has led to the use of spices. The staple but bland dish, rice, is frequently made more savory by the inclusion of a few leaves. Each area of the tropics is characterized by special leaves used for seasoning. Another use for spices in the past has been to mask the flavor of spoiled food. Stomachs and consequently tastes had to be stronger in those days. As the need for hiding spoilage has lessened, so has the need for spices.

Many of the plants used as a source of edible leaves belong either to the Umbelliferae (the family of the carrot) or the Labiatae (the mint family). These two families merit special mention. The Compositae family is of less importance.

Umbelliferae

This family, widespread throughout the temperate zone and not uncommon in the tropics, is characterized by flower clusters in the forms of an umbel. In

addition to species used as a source of edible leaves (see appendix), the family is also the source of a number of spices so common that they are known in almost every household. However, many species bear poisonous leaves. The spices of this family are not tropical in nature. Nevertheless, they are frequently grown in the tropics where they sometimes prove sufficiently adapted to yield a worthwhile crop.

Coriander or cilantro, *Coriandrum sativum* L., is grown chiefly for its edible seeds, the spice of commerce. It is a very old spice, recorded from the time before Christ and used in perfume, liquor, medicine, and aphrodisiacs. It is widely grown throughout the tropical highlands, where in some cases it has become commercial. The fresh leaf of coriander has a disagreeable odor related to the origin of the name coriandes, from bedbug. If the leaf is dried, the odor matures to resemble that of the seed. In both forms it finds a wide usage in the tropics, in flavoring rice, stews, soups, and with cooked meat. Although not often marketed as a leaf, the plant is common in dooryards where it can be readily used. It is normally grown as an annual. If some flowering and seeding occurs, it reproduces itself normally and is not consciously planted from year to year. The false coriander or culantro of Puerto Rico, *Eryngium foetidum* L., is used similarly for its spicy leaves (Fig. 31).

Parsley or perejil, *Petroselinum crispum* (Miller) A. W. Hill, is not as well adapted to the tropics as is coriander. It can best be grown as a potted plant in areas protected from excess heat. It does not necessarily flower, nor does it thrive in the tropics, but plants often survive several years, yielding a continuous quantity of ferny leaf used chiefly as a garnish, but to a minor extent to flavor food.

Fennel or hinojo, *Foeniculum vulgare* Miller, is an aromatic perennial of the Mediterranean that is now widely distributed and frequently weedy. A rather versatile species, some varieties are used as the source of the seed, the spice of commerce, whereas others are used for the edible qualities of their leaves or fleshy leaf bases. In the tropics fennel is now quite common. It succeeds best at altitudes of 500 meters or more. At lower altitudes the seeds are seldom produced, but this does not prevent the use of the leaves as flavoring both raw in salads or cooked. The leaves may also be dried and ground to be used as needed for flavoring.

Dill or eneldo, *Anethum graveolens* L., is not commonly seen in the tropics, but it has been introduced widely and is known to be well adapted. In Indonesia, time has brought about changes in this spice so that fully adapted forms are now available. It is grown commercially on a small scale, but probably more often for its spicy foliage than for its seeds, the usual spice. The leaves are used chiefly in soups and stews, but also have uses in folk medicine.

Chervil or cerafolio, *Anthriscus cereifolium* (L.) Hoffm., is a European annual with lacy foliage reminiscent of parsley, and is used in much the same way. It is more sensitive to the heat and is seldom seen in the tropics. The leaves are often used cooked in soups and stews.

Labiatae

The mint family is so widely distributed that it hardly needs introduction. There must be few people who have not found it volunteering in their own backyards, or who cannot recognize a member of the family by the squareness of the stems, the

diminutive irregular flowers frequently in whorls in the axils of the leaves, or by the scent of the leaves themselves. Many of the members of this large family are spicy (see appendix) and are utilized cultivated or wild to give food a special touch. In contrast to members of the Umbelliferae, the spice plants of the Labiatae are used chiefly for their aromatic leaves.

Perhaps the mints are known best, as every child remembers minty chewing gums. The principal mint species, *Mentha piperita* L. (peppermint) and *M. spicata* L. (spearmint), are native to the Mediterranean region, but now widespread; the latter is better adapted to the tropics. The Japanese peppermint *M. arvensis* L. is now the most widely distributed and important; while not the best in quality, it is the easiest to grow. The species hybridize easily and give the taxonomists trouble. All three species are perennial herbs, grown in certain temperate areas as commercial crops, but only more recently in the tropics. Mints are common enough in the tropics, often grown in pots for small-scale uses in the home. Most of the growth is vegetative. Flowers are seldom produced, an advantage which prolongs the life of the plant.

Mints have a variety of uses, as flavoring herbs and in cooking, desserts and appetizers, and scents and perfumes. Their history in the Mediterranean is long and well recorded, for their medicinal uses have also been important. Mint leaves are also served in teas, as a garnish, and as a flavoring for candies. The commercial preparation of mint is seldom the fresh or even the dry leaf, but the oils, removed from the leaf by steam distillation. For this purpose it is harvested in the tropics on a grand scale from commercial farms and dried before distillation.

The most important spices of the Labiatae are rather strong and are used principally with meat. Oregano is a good example. The name is used for the several fragrant-leaved species of the genus *Origanum*, and some confusion exists, especially when a distinction is attempted from marjoram. All are perennial plants of the Mediterranean region, but some are grown as annuals. "Oregano" is frequently applied in the tropics to other savory-leaved plants used as spices, but more properly its use should be restricted. The true oregano, *Origanum vulgare* L., and the Mexican "oregano," *Lippia graveolens* Kunth, are grown on only a limited scale in the tropics. A native *Lippia* of Puerto Rico is also called oregano (Fig. 32). They are chiefly confined to pots or produced on only a small scale. Marjoram (*Origanum majorana* L.) is a smaller plant more suitable for home usage in the tropics. It should not be confused with *O. onites* L., pot marjoram, a more common but less desirable species. "Oregano" in the Caribbean often is used for the species *Coleus amboinicus* Lour.

Thyme (*Thymus vulgaris* L.) is a small Mediterranean plant with quite small, very pleasantly aromatic leaves. Normally harvested and dried when the plants are beginning to flower, thyme is well adjusted to northern climes but is rare in the tropics. With care it can be grown in pots or the garden for use on a limited scale.

Basil or albahaca (*Ocimum basilicum* L.) is a spice of the Labiatae from the tropics which has been accepted in the temperate zone as sweet basil. It is an old species, cultivated in India for centuries, and probably better known there than anywhere else. The genus itself is widely distributed in the tropics where related species are used for religious, medicinal, and insecticidal purposes. Basil is a small plant, rather bushy, and somewhat woody at the base (Fig. 33). It is grown from seed as an annual, although in fact it is a perennial species. The foliage is normally

removed and dried in order to prepare the condiment. An essential oil is removed by steam distillation. Basil is already a tropical herb, perhaps the most important spice from leaves that has come from the tropics. It is well adapted everywhere and needs no special precautions. The leaves can be used fresh or sun dried in stews, with meats, or with vegetables. By custom it is often used with dishes that contain tomatoes. The liqueur chartreuse includes basil leaves in its recipe.

Three other spices seldom seen in the tropics are sage or salvia, (*Salvia officinalis* L.), savory or aphedrea, (*Satureja hortensis* L.) and rosemary or romero (*Rosmarinus officinalis* L.). On the small scale for which they are needed in the home, they can be grown in the tropical garden. A few sages have done very well in the tropics, and are used as spices, including *S. hispanica* L., in Indonesia.

Compositae

Among the plants of the Compositae useful as condiments, none is more important than the true tarragon, *Artemisia dracunculus* L. It is a bushy perennial from Southern Russia and western Asia that has now been widely grown throughout the temperate zone, but is almost unknown in the tropics. It is widely used in sauces, with meat and vegetables, and in vinegar where its licorice or anise-like aroma adds a distinctive touch. *Artemisia* has numerous wild, aromatic species of which a few have been introduced to the tropics and can be used as tarragon substitutes. Of these, wormwood (*A. vulgaris* L.) seems to be the most promising, and it has grown and produced well in Indonesia.

Other Families

Several species related to the onion (genus *Allium*, Liliaceae) find their place in the tropics. The most useful of these is *A. schoenoprasum* L., known as chives, cebolleta, or cebollino, grown not for its bulbs, which are insignificant, but for its leaves which are used more as a condiment than as a vegetable. Two other species, *A. fistulosum* L., the Welsh onion, and *A. tuberosum* Rottler ex Sprengel, Chinese chives, are used in a similar fashion. These plants are not at home in the tropics except at higher elevations. Where grown, they are popular, and are often marketed. Under the special conditions of the home garden all three can be grown; pot culture is recommended. A small number of plants, protected from an excess of heat and sun, can provide large quantities of leaves throughout the year for use in home cookery.

In Table 2 a list of species, the leaves of which are sometimes used for flavoring, is given. In most cases very little information is available on the plants, and readers who can obtain some of the species are warned that caution is appropriate. The list is not complete, for it emphasizes species native or introduced to Southeast Asia. Data on African and South American species are much more difficult to obtain.

Table 2. A list of plants of Southeast Asia with leaves used as condiments*

Scientific name	Common name	Family
Acacia farnesiana (L.) Willd.	Cassie flower	Leguminosae
Acronychia laurifolia Blume	Ketiak	Rutaceae
Aegle marmelos (L.) Corr. Serr.	Baelfruit	Rutaceae
Allium odorum L.	Chinese chives	Liliaceae
Ancistrocladus extensus Wallich	Ox-tongue	Ancistrocladaceae
Antidesma ghaesembilla Gaert.	Sekinchak	Euphorbiaceae
Begonia tuberosa Lam.	Tuberous begonia	Begoniaceae
Claoxylon polot Mer.	Rock blumea	Euphorbiaceae
Coleus tuberosus Benth.	African potato	Labiatae
Crypteronia paniculata Blume	Sempoh	Crypteroniaceae
Curcuma longa L.	Turmeric	Zingiberaceae
Cymbopogon citratus (Nees) Stapf	Lemon Grass	Graminae
Cyrtandra decurrens de Vriese	Sorrel flavor	Gesneriaceae
C. pendula Blume	Rock sorrel	Gesneriaceae
Dendrobium salaccense Lindl.	Cooking orchid	Orchidaceae
Derris heptaphylla Merr.	Seven finger	Leguminosae
Eugenia polyantha Wight	White kelat	Myrtaceae
Evodia roxburghiana Benth.	Sour-relish wood	Rutaceae
Gynura procumbens M.	Akar	Compositae
Homalomena griffithii Hook f.	Itch grass	Araceae
Hornstedtia spp.	Tepus	Zingiberaceae
Horsfieldia sylvestris Warb.	Pendarahan	Myristicaceae
Kaempferia galanga L.	Chekur	Zingiberaceae
K. rotunda L.	Kenchur	Zingiberaceae
Leucas lavandulifolia Smith	Ketumbak	Labiatae
L. zeylanica R. Br.	Ketumbak	Labiatae
Limnophila aromatica Merr.	Swamp leaf	Scrophulariaceae
L. villosa Blume	Swamp leaf	Scrophulariaceae
L. conferta Benth.	Swamp leaf	Scrophulariaceae
L. pulcherrima Hook. F.	Swamp leaf	Scrophulariaceae
L. rugosa Merr.	Swamp leaf	Scrophulariaceae
Lycium chinense Miller	Kichi, matrimony vine	Solanaceae
Lycopersicon esculentum Miller	Tomato	Solanaceae
Medinilla crispata Blume	Medinilla	Melastomataceae
M. hasseltii Blume	Medinilla	Melastomataceae
M. radicans Blume	Medinilla	Melastomataceae
Mentha longifolia (L.) Hudson	Longleaf mint	Labiatae
Murraya koenigii (L.) Sprengel	Curry-leaf tree	Rutaceae
Nauclea esculenta Afzel.	Pincushion	Rubiacea
Ocimum canum Sims	Hoary basil	Labiatae
Oenanthe javanica DC	Shelum	Umbelliferae
Ottelia alismoides (L.) Pers.	Pond lettuce	Hydrocharitaceae

Oxalis corniculata L.	Sorrel	Oxalidaceae
Pilea melastomoides	Sweet nettle	Urticaceae
Piper lolot C. DC	Pepper leaf	Piperaceae
P. caducibracteum C.D.	Pepper leaf	Piperaceae
P. umbellatum L.	Pepper leaf	Piperaceae
Pistacia lentiscus L.	Pistachio resin tree	Anacardiaceae
Pluchea indica (L.) Less.	Indian sage	Compositae
Polygonum hydropiper L.	Water pepper	Polygonaceae
Staurogyne elongata Kuntze	Cross flower	Acanthaceae
Trachyspermum involucratum Walff.	Wild celery	Umbelliferae

*This list does not include species mentioned in the text. From Burkill (1935).

Leaves Used as Tea

A wide variety of leaves are used throughout the world as teas. Many of the teas are really folk medicines that have seldom been investigated for their reputed values. Another class of teas are those that stimulate, usually because of the presence of the alkaloid caffeine. There may be teas also that are consumed only for the flavors, but this reason for drinking them is only a minor one.

The tea of commerce comes from the leaves of *Camellia sinensis* L. Kuntze (Theaceae), a native species of Assam or India. Tea is a subtropical bushy plant cultivated from seeds or cuttings. It is very well known in the tropics, and much of the world's production has come from India, Sri Lanka, and Indonesia. It is found at the equator in Africa, especially at high elevations. The true tea has not thrived in most places in the New World but is sometimes found on a small scale (as in Brazil).

Tea bushes require several years to mature, are harvested regularly for five or six years thereafter, and then are cut back in order to permit new growth. Only the youngest leaves of the plants are harvested, and this stimulates new growth. Thus, harvesting every two weeks is necessary. The leaves are dried immediately to produce green tea, or fermented after withering and crushing. Caffeine occurs in the leaf as 2 to 5 percent of the dry matter. Tannin content is high, and gives the body desired to the tea. Tea has very little value other than as a stimulant.

Another tea, this one of American origin, is that made from the leaves of maté, *Ilex paraguariensis* A. St-Hil. (Aquifoliaceae). This subtropical plant occurs wild and is extensively cultivated in Paraguay, Northern Argentina, and Southern Brazil. The use of maté is of ancient origin but the habit is now extensive and spreading. Maté is less astringent than "true" tea. It is somewhat bitter, aromatic, and very stimulating. The beverage is prepared by pouring hot or cold water over the crushed leaves. When ready, the infusion is drunk with a perforated tube, or one might say, a filtered straw.

Maté is at home in the subtropics but can be grown with some care in the hotter regions. In the temperate zone other species of *Ilex* such as *I. cassine* L. and *I. vomitoria* Aiton have been used for tea.

A tea little known to the Western world is khat, made from the leaves of *Catha edulis* (Vahl) Endl. (Celastraceae), an evergreen shrub of Arabia and Africa. The leaves are eaten uncooked, chewed, or brewed fresh or dry into a tea. As with other teas, its stimulating principle is an alkaloid much like caffeine. The cultivation of khat is very old, probably predating that of coffee.

The use of tropical leaves in other beverages should be mentioned. The leaves of coca, *Erythroxylum coca* Lam. (Erythroxylaceae) can be used, after removal of the cocaine, to make the popular cola drinks. Several leaves used in liqueurs have already been mentioned. To them should be added those of anise and peppermint used in creme de menthe.

A full list of tropical tea plants would be very difficult to develop. A short list of additional species, many of which are common, is given in Table 3.

Table 3. Other tropical plants, the leaves of which are used in teas

Scientific name	Common name
Acalypha siamensis Oliver	Hermit's tea
Baeckea frutescens L.	Childbirth tea
Bidens pilosa L.	Spanish needles
Camellia japonica L.	Garden camellia
Cassia mimosoides L.	Japanese tea
Sarcandra glabra Gardner	Tea scent
Citrus aurantium L.	Seville orange
Cratoxylum nerifolium Blume	Bebya tea
Cymbopogon citratus (Nees) Stapf.	Lemon grass
Diplospora kunstleri Kong	Wild coffee
D. macaccenense Hook f.	Wild coffee
Ehretia microphylla Lam.	Himalayan tea
Gaultheria fragrantissima Wall.	Wintergreen tea
Centella asiatica (L.) Urban	Long life tea
Ilex latifolia Thunb.	Holly tea
Lycium chinense L.	Matrimony vine
Melaleuca quinquenervia (Cav.) S.T. Blake	Paper bark tree
Peperomia pellucida (L.) Kunth	Greenhouse tea plant
Talauma ovata St-Hil.	Talauma tea
Vitis diffusa Miq.	Charek

CHAPTER VII

Temperate Zone Green Leaves in the Tropics

Was it chance, climate, or luck that the principal agricultural-based civilizations of the past developed in the temperate zone? Perhaps the cold weather made advanced planning and organization necessary. Food and fuel had to be obtained in times of plenty and stored for the lean months. Those who could not plan moved towards the equator or perished. Eventually the strong civilizations of the north, particularly of Europe, began to move south, where they profoundly influenced the history of the tropics. With the explorers went their foodstuffs, their edible plants developed in their own countries. Among these were edible green leaves.

Thus, it should come as no surprise that edible green leaves from northern climates are frequently seen in the tropics. They are often better known than the cultivated and wild greens found locally. But they are not necessarily happy in their new environments. The reasons are simple. Each species exists in a harmonious balance with its ambient. When the environment is changed, the species often does not respond favorably.

Elements of the environment that limit green-leaved plants from the temperate zone are temperature and length of day. The normal life cycles of such plants are regulated to coincide with cold temperatures, when growth is slow, and warm spring and summer temperatures when flowering and seeding occur. Although both temperature and daylength can be controlled on a small scale, control on the scale of commercial production is much more difficult to achieve. Temperate zone green-leaved plants are thus seldom at home in the tropics. But if their special requirements are met, they can be made to produce.

The Genus *Brassica*

Although about 100 species of *Brassica* (Cruciferae) have been described in Europe, Asia, and Africa, this genus is a particularly confusing one because of its many forms, its adaptation to many climates and ecological niches, its cultivated varieties and its noxious weeds. The species are mostly annual or biennial herbs. The biennials usually form a rosette of leaves during the winter season, often storing nutrients in thickened or tuberous roots. The mature plants are erect, sometimes branched, free of hair (usually), with pinnated lower leaves, and with white or yellow flowers. The flowers have 4 petals, 4 sepals, but 6 stamens.

The tendency to thicken, seen in the roots, is true also of leaves, stems, axillary buds, and flower clusters. It is probably this characteristic, and the edibility of most *Brassica* species, that led to cultivation of a few species and the eventual development, through breeding, of many botanical forms and thousands of varieties. Most of the edible types are considered cool season crops. The principal species and varieties of *Brassica* that bear edible green leaves are listed below. Others are included in the appendix. The truth is that the relationship of the species and botanical varieties is not well known, and therefore other classifications are equally feasible.

Brassica carinata	Ethiopian kale
B. hirta Moench	White or yellow mustard
B. integrifolia Schultz	Chevalieri, tropical African cabbage
B. juncea (L.) Czerniak	Indian mustard
B. napus L.	Rape, colza
Napobrassica group	Rutabaga
Pabularia group	Siberian kale
B. nigra (L.) Koch	Black mustard
B. oleracea L.	Wild cabbage
Acephala group	Kale, collards
Alboglabra group	Chinese broccoli
Botrytis group	Cauliflower, broccoli
Capitata group	Head and Savoy cabbage
Gemmifera group	Brussels sprouts
Gongylodes group	Kohlrabi
Italica group	Sprouting broccoli
B. rapa L. (*B. campestris*)	Field mustard
Chinensis group	Chinese mustard or cabbage, pak choi
Pekinensis group	Chinese cabbage
Perviridis group	Spinach mustard
Rapifera group	Turnip
B. tournefortii Gouan.	Wild turnip-rape

Cabbage

Cabbage is a generic term applied not only to a type of plant in which the leaves are closely packed, such as palm cabbage, but also to what is often called the "true" cabbage, *Brassica oleracea* L., Capitata group. In contrast to plants of the type that fit the generic name, the "true" cabbage includes forms that produce loose leaves as well as the heading varieties. Collards or colewort are leafy varieties of cabbage grown, harvested, and eaten in much the same way as for spinach. The name cabbage, however, has its origin in words that mean heads.

The original cabbage was of the non-heading type and grew wild in the eastern Mediterranean. It is believed to have been extended throughout Europe by the Celts years before the time of Christ. The existence of wild cabbage in England, France, and Denmark has encouraged the impression, however, that cabbage originated in western Europe. The wild forms differ tremendously in morphology and eating qualities.

Experimental work in England has shown that the wild, headless cabbage can be bred within a few generations to form a loose head. Or if the stems have a tendency to swell, the plants can be bred to form the turnip-rooted cabbages. The first cabbage varieties were therefore probably of the loose leaf type. The Savoy type cabbages of Southern Europe, which form rather loose heads, are representative of the primitive type of varieties, but differ in their rugose or blistered leaves. Some are attractively colored by anthocyanins of the epidermis.

The headed cabbage, on the other hand, also appears to be ancient in origin.

There is some suggestion that hard-headed cabbages came from northern Europe, but it is uncertain whether the historical distinctions found in the literature were only the result of growing similar varieties in different places. The heading tendency, for example, is much less evident in warm than in cold climates. Modern varieties can be conveniently divided into 5 varieties, depending on shape of the head (flat headed, spherical, egg-shaped, elliptical, and conical). All these various types are still represented by at least a few existing varieties.

Cabbages are slow-growing biennials which have three distinct periods. In the first period, the rosette of vegetation is formed. This is a relatively rapid phase, during the latter part of which the head forms. Cabbages then pass through a period of rest when the rudiments of the bloom are formed. Finally, the inflorescence develops rapidly, forming of the plant an upright, branched, prolifically flowering structure. However, seed production dictates some modification of the growth pattern. The plants are removed about the time of frost, stored until spring, then replanted. The heads are partially cut to permit the growing point to emerge with little obstacle.

Cabbage is definitely a cool season crop and reaches its perfection in cold climes. Cold temperatures of winter are necessary to stimulate flower production. Frosts are well tolerated; the collards, in fact, are much improved in flavor by frosts. The bulk of the world's cabbages are grown in the cold climates of the northern hemisphere. Nevertheless, cabbage, perhaps better than any other temperate zone green, can be grown successfully in the tropics (Fig. 34).

Perhaps the tropical area where cabbage and related crops have been most thoroughly studied is the Philippine Islands. Here a wide variety of geographical conditions, altitudes, shores, etc., blend to form a mosaic of climates. Cabbages are grown throughout the year in high, cool, moist regions (Fig. 35). Nevertheless, during the cool months of the short-day season, cabbages are also successful in the lowlands. In the latter case the plants may be established during warm weather, but plantings should be timed so that heading of cabbage corresponds to the cool weather.

Cabbages are not particular about their soil preferences. Earliness is associated with sandy soils, and high, late yields with clays. Soil pH of 6-6.8 is optimum. An important feature of the soil is its available moisture. An abundant supply of moisture is necessary for this crop. The soil is usually worked thoroughly and then formed into shallow beds of one or two rows. It is beneficial to incorporate an organic material or complete mineral fertilizer in the soil before planting.

Cabbage may be planted in special seedling beds and then transplanted, or it may be seeded directly in the garden. The former method makes possible careful soil sterilization as well as special attention to nutrient status. However, transplanting always delays the crop to some extent. The seeds are planted not more than 1.5 cm deep and germinate in a few days. Plants must be maintained in excellent condition, for those stunted by competition, drought, or poor nutrition do not yield satisfactory heads later. If plants grow too rapidly, they may be held back by withholding water. Generally about 4 weeks are needed to produce suitable plants. Plants should be exposed to harsh conditions for about a week to harden them before transplanting. Plants that are too large at transplanting (stem diameter of 6 mm or more) might have passed the juvenile stage. Exposure to cold temperatures can thus induce flowering instead of head formation. Transplanting in the garden is most convenient at about 0.5

meters, in rows one meter apart. However, optimum spacing depends on the variety. Plants should be removed from seed beds with some soil to avoid too much damage to the root system. Adequate irrigation is needed from the very beginning.

After the plants are well established, they benefit from extra nitrogen fertilizer. Because cabbages are shallow rooted, they must be irrigated frequently. For such fast-growing plants, weed competition is particularly deleterious. Commercial herbicides are often used after planting. Hand cultivation should be as shallow as possible to avoid damage to the root system. Cabbages are susceptible to attack by many insects, especially caterpillars, but control measures cannot be given here. It is interesting that in some areas dead insects collected on the plants are mixed in a spray to spread the diseases that killed them, a simple but effective biological control. Nematodes may cause severe stunting.

Cabbage is ready for harvest 3-5 months after planting (Fig. 36). Although the leaves are edible at any time, the plants are generally left until a hard head is formed. The time required is chiefly a function of variety. Most cabbage harvesting is still done by hand. The stalk is cut with a sharp knife. For marketing, heads are trimmed of most of the outer leaves. Once harvested, storage characteristics are usually pretty good. Fresh heads can be stored at cool temperatures up to 6 weeks without serious loss. Much longer storage is feasible if quality loss is tolerated. When stored cabbage is removed from the cold, it deteriorates rapidly. Early Jersey, Wakefield, Copenhagen Market, Brunswick, Golden Acre and many more varieties have been suitable in the tropics; hybrids are often widely adapted and quite vigorous.

Cabbage is one of the best sources of edible green leaves, not only because its yields are very good, but because of its nutritive value. Water content is very high, about 92%. It is a very good source of calcium and vitamin C, a fair source of energy and A and B vitamins, and it is a good source of protein. Because of its high production, it is usually an inexpensive food. Cabbage is also versatile in its uses. It is an excellent salad plant, but some people object to its strong odor caused by a sulfur compound. As a cooked vegetable it is used in a variety of forms, including stews with other vegetables. It can be preserved by pickling to give sauerkraut.

Other Cole Crops

The leaves of practically all *Brassica* species are edible, but the strong flavors of some species are disagreeable or too strong for most people's taste. Most of the important species have been mentioned earlier. The edible leaves are usually not eaten, however, in special forms such as broccoli and cauliflower. Of the various species, Chinese cabbage, *Brassica rapa* L., is surely the most important except for cabbage itself.

As its name implies, Chinese cabbage is a native of eastern Asia. Its history is long; it is believed to have been cultivated before the time of Christ. From there it was introduced to adjacent islands in pre-Columbian times. Therefore, Chinese cabbage is well known and distributed in the Asian tropics, but little known elsewhere. It resembles lettuce in many ways. The leaves are usually rugose and are formed into heads which are less compact than the heads of typical cabbage. While heads form rapidly, sometimes in as little as two months after planting, they vary in

shape. The Pekinensis forms are narrow and upright and resemble romaine lettuce. The Chinensis forms do not form solid heads but are more open and resemble Swiss chard, especially because of their prominent white petioles.

The species is a short-lived annual which usually is planted either during the winter or spring. It is highly responsive to differences in both temperature and daylength. High temperatures, while useful in reducing flowering tendency, lead to bitter flavors and soft heads. High-quality Chinese cabbage can only be produced at cool temperatures, such as 15-20°C. Daylength also influences plant growth. The long days of summer are conducive to flowering, but so are cool days. Areas of the tropics where Chinese cabbage has been very successful include Southeast Asia, the Philippine Islands, Puerto Rico, Central America, Sierra Leone, Nigeria, and Hawaii.

Chinese cabbage is usually produced as a late fall or early summer crop. Unless special precautions are taken to protect it from long days, it is not grown for heads during long, hot summers. Nevertheless, something edible can be had from Chinese cabbage at all seasons and climates of the tropics. Plants for transplanting are usually produced in carefully tended beds where frequent watering is necessary and mulch can be used to maintain the humidity. The plants grow rapidly and are ready for transplanting 3-3 1/2 weeks after seeding. They require a rich, well-fertilized soil. After transplanting they are maintained in lush condition by applications of nitrogen fertilizer and by frequent irrigations. The mature plants may be ready for harvesting in as little as 20 days after transplanting. More frequently the total cycle from seeding to maturity is 2 or 3 months.

Chinese cabbage has many uses. It is commonly used raw as a salad or is cooked as a green. It may also be fermented and stored in salt to give a unique dish. It is sometimes dried for later use. In addition, it can be stored under cool conditions for up to 3 months. Chinese cabbage is a good source of calcium and vitamins A and C. Because of its rapid growth, it is a food produced very efficiently.

The leafy species of *Brassica*, collards, kale, and mustard, while less popular and more strongly flavored than the cabbages, merit more attention in the tropics for several reasons. They are more amenable to the continuous cropping desirable in the home garden. Because of their open structure, they are greener. They are more nutritious than the cabbages for their weight. Whereas the former require a cool temperature, tropical mustards can be grown in the tropics almost year-round.

Brassica carinata A. Braun (Ethiopian kale, Abyssinian mustard), unlike many other species, sets seed readily in the tropics. It is rich in protein. Tender leaves and stems are eaten raw or cooked, and the inflorescence is used like broccoli. Older leaves may be boiled as a vegetable; they are satisfactorily used as small animal feed as well. With its prolific seed set, it may reseed an area, creating in the garden an area for constant production of this low-maintenance vegetable. Ethiopian kale has proven highly successful from tropical lowlands to equatorial elevations of 2600 m. It merits trial in a wide variety of locations.

As a summary, the *Brassica* species are very useful in the tropics when care is taken to give them appropriate environmental conditions and treatments. They merit more extensive trial in the home garden and more extensive breeding work to eliminate hot weather sensitivity. In contrast to most green leaves of the tropics, *Brassica*s are easily available from seeds stores and thus available almost anywhere.

Other Leafy Crops

Endive and chicory. Two closely related leafy crops of the family Compositae sometimes grown in the tropics are endive (*Cichorium endivia* L.) and chicory (*C. intybus* L.). The former species is believed to have originated in eastern India, probably from high elevations or cool climates. However, it is best known and has been developed as a vegetable chiefly in Europe. In the tropics, on the other hand, endive has been grown frequently in tropical highlands where its cool requirements are met. Chicory originated in Europe where it has been used for a number of distinct purposes. It is seldom seen in the tropics, and indeed requires somewhat more stringent conditions than endive. Whereas endive is grown as an annual or biennial, chicory is known as a perennial.

Endive is a good substitute for lettuce in the tropics. Although a cool season crop, endive withstands heat better than lettuce. It is normally sown either in the fall or very early spring so that its growth cycle is finished before the coming of very hot weather. The leaves of endive can be used as a fresh green in salads or as a cooked green. Their flavor is strong and bitter, however. In order to avoid this taste and to produce a more succulent product, the leaves are blanched before harvest. This is done by gathering up the large outer leaves into a loose bundle and tying them with a string. Blanching requires 10 days to 3 weeks in the tropics. When the plant is harvested by cutting it away from the roots, the large, outer leaves are discarded. Blanching must be avoided in wet weather because the inner head rots easily. Some varieties, such as Broad-leaved Batavian, form loose, natural heads, which are self-blanching and less susceptible to rot. Other varieties are sometimes blanched by crowding plants in the row.

In common with most greens, endive requires rich cultural conditions, high fertility, and lots of water. Seeds should be started in the area where the mature plants are desired, as they do not transplant well. Plants are spaced 25-30 cm apart. The plants should be forced along to maturity as rapidly as possible. In the tropics endive has been reported successful, chiefly at high altitudes, in Puerto Rico, the Philippine Islands, West Africa, Madagascar, and Hong Kong.

In contrast to endive, chicory is seldom seen in the tropics and merits further trial, especially at high altitudes. It is somewhat more fussy than endive in its requirements, which probably accounts for its neglect. Chicory is best known as an adulterant for coffee. The perennial tap roots are washed, sliced, dried, and ground to make a coffee-like product. Chicory is also used as a pot herb, but the coarse leaves are so bitter that two changes of cooking water are recommended. Such leaves are seldom marketed. However, although seldom practiced, the leaves of chicory can be blanched in much the same way as those of endive. Another practice is to bank soil around the plants to blanch the leaves.

Chicory is at its best when blanched in the dark. The roots are removed at maturity and stored in a cool place until desired. Then, when placed in a warm place, they begin to sprout. Although this can be done in light, in the darkness the new leaves are blanched and tender. If soil is heaped over the roots, or if straw or another substitute is used, the germinating shoot forms a soft, delicate head commonly known as whitloof. This vegetable is highly esteemed.

Chicory appears to be widely adapted, for weedy forms have been introduced throughout the temperate zone and in some parts of the tropics. Because of its excellent quality as a specialty leaf vegetable, it merits attention to see if its culture can be adapted to the tropics.

Spinach. The word "spinach" is often used for many kinds of edible green leaves. Nevertheless, its most widely understood usage is as a common name for the species *Spinacia oleracea* L. (Chenopodiaceae), the spinach of the temperate zone. It was introduced into Europe from southwestern Asia, where it has continued to evolve as a cool season crop. Spinach may be eaten either raw in salad or cooked as a pot herb.

The habit of spinach is to develop a seed stalk rapidly in the tropics. This characteristic is related primarily to daylength but also is influenced by temperature. Therefore, spinach is not successful in most areas of the tropics. It is rarely grown, and then only at altitudes of 1000 meters or more.

Spinach grows rapidly, especially when well fertilized with nitrogen, and thus needs a rich soil and much attention. A rosette of leaves forms first, from which the flower stalk originates. Normally the plants are harvested just once from 6 weeks to 3 months after planting. For all its vaunted food value, its high vitamin, mineral and protein content, spinach has one defect: a high content of oxalic acid. Because oxalic acid combines with calcium to make it unavailable to the body, too much spinach in the diet can be detrimental. In contrast to most plants, spinach is relatively rich in the essential amino acid methionine. Species of plants, like people, differ in their ability to adjust away from home. The true spinach has not found a home in the tropics.

Swiss chard and beet greens. One of the most ancient of European vegetables is *Beta vulgaris* L. (Chenopodiaceae), a very diversified species with many cultivars including the well-known sugar beet, the table beet (red and yellow forms), and Swiss chard. Lesser-known forms include other chards (red, "black"), the sea-beet, the silver-leaf beet, and the mangold. The species also has wild forms that extend from the Canary Islands through the Mediterranean to western India. They are eaten as pot herbs. The origins of the numerous varieties of *B. vulgaris* are not well known, but many forms were described before the time of Christ.

Although the leaves of all *B. vulgaris* varieties are edible, including table beets and sugar beets (Fig. 37), only Swiss chard (subsp. *cicla* (L.) Koch) merits attention here. The other chards are too difficult to obtain and are seldom seen on the market. Chard is simple to grow and very tolerant of differences in soils. Although a cool season crop, chard is quite adapted to cool regions of the tropics, can tolerate some heat, and produces reasonably well in the lowlands. The seeds are large and encased in a corky coat. They germinate rapidly and furnish edible greens within a few weeks. Leaves may be cut at any time for use as a spinach (never as a salad green). With care the entire loose head may be taken, leaving the base of the leaves and part of the stem for regrowth. A better practice is to cut only the large outer leaves. This continuous cropping feature of chard recommends it for the home garden. Furthermore, chard is biennial and may be cropped a second year unless seed stalk formation occurs. Leaf stalks are sometimes prominent and may be cooked separately from the leaf in the form of celery or asparagus.

Yields of chard are spectacular. Careful culture, based on small-scale

experiments, has yielded up to 400 metric tons of edible greens per hectare in the tropics. Varieties include both smooth-leaved and savoyed (rugose) types. No special varieties have been developed for the tropics, but those from temperate zones such as Fordhook Giant, Dark Green White Ribbed, and Lucullus serve well in the tropics. Red-stalked varieties include Rhubarb and Vulcan. Swiss chard has been successfully grown in Tanzania, West Africa, the Philippine Islands, Puerto Rico, Curacao, and without doubt in many other areas of the tropics. As an old standby, a prolific and dependable source of greens, it merits much more extensive use.

Celery. *Apium graveolens* L. (Umbelliferae), is not usually grown for its green leaves, but its fleshy petioles. As a popular salad vegetable as well as pot herb it merits consideration here. It is a wild plant of marshy places, found native from as far north as Sweden to as far south as Algeria. However, by now it is widespread as an occasional weed throughout the temperate zones. It is apparently a Johnny-come-lately among cultivated vegetables, although it was used earlier as a wild plant for medicinal purposes. It is interesting to note that a tuberous form of celery exists in the temperate zone, celeriac. The thickened crown is used as a vegetable. Leaves and petioles of celery may be dried for later use.

The culture of celery is rather specialized, especially when blanched petioles are desired. Its requirement for cool weather is met only at higher altitudes of the tropics. At higher temperatures (lower altitudes), the petioles of celery tend to be tough and stringy. A variety grown in the Philippines with short, compact stems is heat resistant. Rich soils are required, and this generally involves the use of manure. The small seeds are normally germinated in a separate bed, where they are seeded very near the surface. Seedlings are transplanted when five or more centimeters high, and must be protected from the sun for a few days. High nitrogen fertilizer and frequent irrigation is essential for best growth. The growing season is rather long, about five months. During the last few weeks, green varieties are sometimes tied up with paper to blanch the petioles.

For its long season and special requirements, celery is not recommended as an important source of edible leaves. It has been grown successfully, however, in Tanzania, the Philippines, Puerto Rico, Hong Kong, and other parts of the tropics.

Miscellaneous Species

A few green-leaved crops from the temperate zone are seldom seen in the tropics but for completeness should be mentioned here. From Europe: *Atriplex hortensis* L. (mountain spinach), *Taraxacum officinale* Wigg. (dandelion), *Lepidium sativum* L. (garden cress), *Valerianella locusta* (L.) Betcke (corn salad), *Angelica archangelica* L. (ground ash), and *Anthriscus cereifolium* (L.) Hoffm. (chervil). *Eruca vesicaria* (L.) Cav. subsp. *sativa* (Miller) Thell. (rocket salad) is native to the Mediterranean region, and *Rheum rhaponticum* L. (rhubarb) is from southern Siberia.

Thus, it can be seen that while temperate zone green leaves are not exactly strangers to the tropics, neither are they perfectly at home. Most species can be grown successfully at high altitudes or during the cool season. On the other hand, a few are of much value in the hot, moist tropical lowlands.

CHAPTER VIII

Lettuce in the Tropics

The queen of the salad plants, the leaf that is synonymous with salad in most of the temperate zone, that exquisite, crisp foundation for the salad dish that also shreds into a fine and almost neutral medium for a variety of tasty sauces, is, of course, lettuce, *Lactuca sativa* L. (Compositae). Lettuce is not only salad, but it is money, a vegetable crop of sizeable importance to temperate zone economies. It is a modern crop that has emerged from primitive agriculture to be one of the most tenderly handled farm products, yet it is produced in a mechanized manner surpassed in few instances. Fortunes are made and occasionally lost in lettuce as growers scramble to anticipate and to dominate the vagaries of the lettuce market. With respect to lettuce, society has reached new heights of agricultural perfection and marketing integration. It is just a leaf, but there is no other leaf like lettuce.

Lactuca, the genus to which lettuce belongs, comes from the Latin word *lac* which refers to the milky juice found in all species. The plants are annual or perennial, mostly herbaceous, and mostly distributed throughout the tropics. No systematic attempts have been made to resolve the taxonomy.

The genus *Lactuca* has its origin in the basin of the Mediterranean, where four closely related species occur. These, like so many weeds of the area, are now widely distributed. One, *L. serriola* L., inhabits the south shore. In many ways, though wild, it resembles cultivated lettuce. Furthermore, it can be hybridized with lettuce, and apparently such hybridization occurs in nature. The rather similar morphologies, the fact of hybridization, and the similarity of chromosome number suggest that cultivated lettuce originated from something like this wild species. On the other hand, the wild *L. serriola*, as we know it, has also undoubtedly been influenced by its proximity to the cultivated forms. The interchange of germplasm has probably been continuous. The result has been the production of a cultivated species with a high degree of genetic plasticity and a wild species that has spread throughout the tropical world.

Paintings in Egyptian tombs dating from about 4500 B.C. reveal a type of lettuce with long pointed leaves, not much different from romaine lettuce. Lettuce was eaten by the Persian kings as early as 550 B.C. It was cultivated at a very early date in Greece, and later in Rome. The varieties of lettuce were leaf types. In a "herbal" or plant notebook of 1543, a lettuce in bloom is depicted, but with the name *Lactuca capitata*, the first historical record of head lettuce. Lettuce introduced to China in A.D. 600-900 developed along different lines, and in fact the fleshy stem became the principal part eaten. Lettuce was introduced into the New World with almost the first of the explorers, but the records show that it was first cultivated in the Caribbean.

Modern varieties of lettuce may be divided into four groups. The cos lettuce varieties are those such as romaine with long, upright, blunt-tipped leaves and a marked midrib almost to the tip. The leaves are somewhat folded and grouped into loose heads. Leaf lettuces (Fig. 38), on the other hand, are almost orbicular and rather prostrate. The midrib is much branched into smaller veins. Cabbage lettuce has much the same type of leaf but the leaves are gathered into a tight and succulent head.

Asparagus lettuce varieties are seldom seen. The young stems are tender and edible whereas the light grey leaves are unpalatable. In addition to these, many primitive forms have been found that do not fit well into any classification.

The life cycle of lettuce is closely related to its cultural requirements. The general tendency of lettuce is to form a rosette of leaves near ground level during the cool months of winter or spring. As temperature increases, flowering is stimulated. From the rosette develops an upright stem, characterized by few leaves, that rapidly comes to flower. Thus, lettuce is an annual plant, or when planted very late in the year it can be said to be a biennial. The annual habit and the tendency to flower when temperatures are too high are characteristics which influence the success of different classes of lettuce in the tropics, but within each class, varietal differences with respect to heat tolerances are well known. In contrast to its heat sensitivity, lettuce is not responsive to photoperiod changes.

The cos varieties are the most heat-tolerant lettuces. Most such varieties were developed in the warm southern regions of Europe, but cool-requiring varieties are also known in England. The head type lettuces are the most demanding in their environmental requirements, while the leaf varieties are variable and intermediate.

Lettuce has little value as a food. Its water content is 94-95 percent. Protein and vitamin B and C contents are much lower than those of almost all other green-leaved vegetables. Lettuce contains worthwhile amounts of calcium and vitamin A, however. The chief value of lettuce in the diet appears to be that it adds bulk and serves as a medium for other items.

Many varieties of lettuce have been tested and reported as successful in the tropics. Some varieties of head lettuce include Great Lakes (especially 118, 456, 659), Iceberg, New York, Webb's Wonderful, and Trocadero, all suitable for high altitudes; Oswego, Calmar (mildew resistant), Imperial (44, 847), Sutton's, Yatesdale, Winterlake, Pennlake, Laepili, and Kulanui, for medium elevations; and the heat-resistant Minetto, Montello, Kauwela, and Anuenue. Of the leaf and cos lettuces, the following have been reported as successful and mostly heat resistant: Queensland (extremely heat-resistant, even difficult to bolt for seed production), Mignonette (soft head, good for home gardens), White Boston, Black Seeded Simpson, Early Curled Simpson, Slobolt (common), Ruby, Salad Bowl, Paris White Cos, and Parris Island Cos (mosaic tolerant). More varieties should be tested for their suitability in specific sites. The tropical gardener interested in lettuce should consult Facciola (1990) for information and seed sources for over 140 varieties of heading and leaf lettuces.

Soil Requirements

Lettuce is grown throughout the world on many different types of soils. The commercial production in New York is chiefly on muck soil rich in organic matter. In California the soils are much lighter and loamier, or even somewhat sandy. A heavier soil is desirable when the crop matures in hot weather. The root system of lettuce is not extensive, and thus the soil must be capable of holding sufficient water. Nevertheless, poor drainage is not tolerated. Lettuce does not thrive on soils too acid in reaction, but it can tolerate some alkaline soils. The optimum soil pH is 6-6.8. Liming an acid soil in excess of needs can cause chlorosis of lettuce.

Modification of the Climate

In the tropics (Fig. 39), lettuce is generally grown at high elevations of 1,000 meters or more. When grown in coastal lowlands, it is usually successful only during the cooler months of the year. Nevertheless, on the scale of the home garden, some modification of the microclimate is possible to extend the season when lettuce can be successfully produced. The most important climatic modification is the reduction of temperature. High temperatures not only lead to bolting, but are also responsible for the bitterness of lettuce. Any of the following methods are useful: partial shading with plastic screens, slow-maturing plants of other crops or *Lactuca indica* L.; maintaining cool conditions near the soil by appropriate watering; or mist spray during the hottest hours of the day. Structures built to give shade have the further advantage of protection of the plants from torrential rains. Screens break large drops into small particles, which usually do not harm the delicate new leaves.

Culture

Lettuce seeds are small, and the plants established from them are weak and slow to establish themselves. Special care in starting and tending plantings is desirable, and pays dividends in terms of future yields. Shallow wooden boxes or flats are convenient for sorting the plants. The soil should be loamy, finely sifted, fertile, and sterilized (small quantities of soil can be sterilized in the oven of the kitchen). The seeds planted in furrows can be covered with about 0.5 cm of fine soil. Protection from ants, which carry off the seed, may be necessary. Germination requires cool temperatures and these may be hard to obtain in the tropics. Watering should be managed with extreme caution. When plants have grown to the 4 or 5 leaf stage, they should be transplanted without pruning to the garden beds of carefully prepared, fertilized soil. The beds should be watered in advance and then allowed to drain so as to avoid mud on transplanting. If the seed flat is also watered shortly before planting, the seedlings can be removed easily with minimum damage to the roots. The plants are transplanted at distances of 15 to 20 cm.

As an alternative, the lettuce seeds may be scattered over the very carefully prepared bed, covered with a light cap of soil, and watered with care. The extra plants can be thinned out after germination, leaving the largest to grow.

The newly planted beds need some protection from hot tropical sun and from torrential rains. Temporary shelters may be useful, or if shade is not too intense, may be used throughout the growing season. Plantings must be irrigated with care. Subsoil irrigation is a common practice. Because of its shallow root system, lettuce needs frequent watering. Several weeks after transplanting, a fertilizer high in nitrogen (such as ammonium sulfate) is required to keep plants in a vigorous, succulent condition. The beds should be weeded periodically, and plants that begin to bolt (develop flowering spikes) should be removed. If such plants are caught early enough, they are still useful as salad.

Still another convenient way to grow lettuce, especially the leafy varieties, is to sow or transplant among growing corn, tomato, pepper, or eggplants. The shade is beneficial for the lettuce and the plants usually complete their development before

the shade-giving crop begins to mature.

A variety of insect pests attack lettuce, but these are seldom a serious problem. Because the life cycle of lettuce is short, diseases are not usually severe. It is beyond the scope of this book to consider pest control problems.

One advantage of leaf lettuce plantings is that some leaves may be harvested at practically all seasons. Even the small plants are edible. The larger leaves of developing plants can be removed at any time. An alternative means of harvest is to cut all of the leaves of the plant without damaging the growing point. A new set of leaves will rapidly develop. Or, the entire plant can be removed from the soil, and the root cut away. The more tender portions of the plant receive some protection from the coarser outermost leaves. The bulk of the leaf lettuce harvest can be expected 35-40 days after sowing. Transplanting delays maturation. Head lettuce varieties are normally not harvested until a firm head is produced (Fig. 40). Two or three months of growth are usually required. The hardness of the head is determined by feeling, for appearances are not reliable. The interval when head lettuce is best for harvest may be very short during warm weather. The outermost leaves are seldom suitable and are cut away.

The growing of lettuce seed is a special and interesting operation quite unlike the production of the green leaf. The heat of summer weather is necessary to stimulate flower stalk formation (Fig. 41). In the case of head lettuce, the heads are often forced open to permit the stalk to emerge.

Distribution and Experimental Studies in the Tropics

Lettuce is not grown throughout the tropics, although it can probably be grown almost anywhere. It is produced commercially in Queensland and in small quantities in Hong Kong, the Philippines, West Africa, and the Caribbean. Expatriate markets have encouraged the establishment of lettuce production near urban centers.

Although not of major importance anywhere in the tropics, lettuce has been investigated in many agricultural research institutes. Variety trials have been reported in Tanzania, Trinidad, Curacao, New Britain, and the Philippines. Breeding of heat-resistant varieties has been done in Hawaii. Growth rate and fertilization was studied in Ghana. In the Philippine Islands, lettuce has been well studied from the agronomic standpoint. Disease control with sprays and drenches was reported from Trinidad. In Queensland the disease known as tipburn has been investigated with respect to mineral nutrition. Seasonal effects on vitamin content were found in Puerto Rico.

Because lettuce is a green-leaved vegetable of choice, good, dependable varieties are needed for the tropics. Further searches for heat resistance in the species of *Lactuca* are desirable, and more breeding is necessary in order to develop truly heat-resistant varieties. Until extensive efforts are made, the queen of the salad plants will have only a modest place in the hot tropics.

Other Species

In addition to *Lactuca sativa*, other species of lettuce are sometimes used as food. *L. alpina* (*Cicerbita alpina* (L.) Wallroth, mountain sow-thistle) is a weed of

76

Europe, the milky stem of which is peeled and eaten by the Laplanders. The species *L. plumieri* grows wild in Southern France where it is used for its edible leaves. In the tropics of the Orient, the species *L. indica* L. (tropical or Indian lettuce) is commonly grown for cooked greens, but can also be eaten as a salad (Fig. 42), sometimes with vinegar to cover any bitterness. It is a tall, erect, annual herb with bright yellow flowers. This species of lettuce may be used as a light shade for *L. sativa*, or for other vegetables. An African edible species is *L. taracifolea*, and in the near east is found *L. tuberosa*. *L. intybacea*, a tall, branching herb of which entire young leaves are taken for cooking, is widespread through the tropics. The appendix can be consulted for names of other edible species.

The European species *L. virosa* produces a sedative or narcotic, lactucarium, sometimes known as lettuce opium. It is found to some extent in all of the cultivated species. Few of those who enthusiastically eat their salads daily suspect that they are being dosed in small quantities with such a drug.

CHAPTER IX

Tropical Leaves That Are Poisonous

The function of the leaf of the plant is to intercept the energy of the sun and to use it in the synthesis of carbohydrates from carbon dioxide and water. Thus, leaves are factories, very important to the survival of the plant. It is not surprising that leaves are desirable food for animals and that plants have defenses in order to protect themselves from animal predators. The chief of these is to synthesize poisonous compounds.

Although the leaves of the vast majority of tropical species are harmless if eaten, many poisonous species also occur and some are common. Because in this book over 400 species with edible leaves are mentioned, it would be a tragic error to believe that all leaves are edible, or that by simple trial and error the edible can be distinguished from the inedible leaves. Persons with a strong interest in edible wild plants are cautioned to identify plants carefully before testing their edible properties, and then to proceed with extreme caution.

The subject of plant poisoning is a very complex area treated in detail by numerous texts. As a general rule, the plants of no one family can be singled out as particularly dangerous, but some families have more poisonous species than others. Many edible plants have near relatives with poisonous parts or are themselves poisonous at times. Not every individual of a poisonous species is necessarily poisonous. Of a poisonous plant, some parts may be poisonous while other parts are not. These parts may be poisonous at one time, and not poisonous at another. Leaves, for example, are most often poisonous when they are mature, but exceptions occur. Fruits, on the other hand, are most often poisonous just before maturity, but on maturity the poisonous substances are remetabolized. Seeds are particularly likely to be poisonous. Furthermore, plants that are very common and are not thought of as poisonous may be poisonous under certain circumstances, for example, when they accumulate toxic substances from the soil. Species of plants that are toxic to one species of animals are not necessarily toxic to other species. Thus, the entire subject of toxicity is complicated by special considerations. When plants are known to be poisonous, very special knowledge of the conditions under which they are not toxic or can be detoxified is necessary. Even the experts do not have all of the facts. Thus, with leaves a good rule is, "If in doubt, don't eat it."

The poisonous substances in plants can be classified in many ways. For example, they can be considered primary and secondary substances. The primary substances, those which are common to all or almost all plants, play an important role in the growth and metabolism of the plant, and are necessary for the continuance of plant life. Such primary substances are seldom poisonous. However, under unusual conditions and occasionally even in normal circumstances, such substances accumulate to the point that they are toxic. Secondary substances are not found in all plants, but occur especially in certain species that we identify as poisonous. They are not necessary to the normal metabolism of the plant but fill special roles. It is generally believed that poisonous substances give the plant some protection from animal pests, and that they have thus evolved as mechanisms of protection. In the majority of the

poisonous species, the function of the poisonous substance in the plant is unknown. In addition to these classes of poisonous substances, poisons can exist in the leaves that were taken from the soil and then retained or partially metabolized by the plant.

Poisonous plants can be classified by their physiological actions which differ considerably, but three classes can be distinguished. Some poisonous plants are toxic on contact. Their effects may be immediate, resulting in itching or pain, or may be delayed, with itching, dermatitis, or blistering occurring several days after contact. The resulting condition can last for a few hours or for days and weeks. The poisonous substance from such plants is often found in the milky juice or resinous secretion. Such poisoning by contact must be distinguished from mechanical irritation (Fig. 43). For the sake of completeness a few leaves that mechanically irritate are considered here, but such irritation may not be associated with poisonous substances. In a few cases mechanical irritation and contact poisoning go hand in hand.

A second class of substances includes those that interfere with normal bodily functions and thus are usually not harmful unless ingested. Such substances may be immediately toxic in small quantities, chronically toxic over long periods of time with cumulative effects, or toxic only when taken in such quantities that the body cannot throw off the effects rapidly enough. The principal compounds are classified as alkaloids, glycosides, resinoids, and organic acids. Inorganic compounds, such as selenium, also can be classified here.

A final important class, more important for animals than for people, is of those plant poisons that sensitize the skin to light. After ingesting sufficient quantities of the foliage, and only after exposure to sunlight, characteristic diseases develop which can result in death. Skin color apparently can provide some protection against photodynamic plant poisoning, perhaps by impeding the deep penetration of light rays.

A classification of poisonous principles of plants principally by J. M. Kingsbury (1964) is useful to point out the diversity of plant poisons:

Alkaloids	Phenolics and tannins
Polypeptides	Resins and resinoids
Amines	Toxalbumins
Glycosides	Minerals
Cyanogenic	Copper, lead, fluorine, manganese
Goitrogenic	Nitrogen (as nitrates, nitrites,
Irritating oils	nitroses, and gaseous oxides)
Coumarin derivatives	Selenium
Steroid and triterpenoid derivatives	Molybdenum
Cardiac glycosides	Photosensitization compounds
Saponins	Primary photosensitization
Oxalates	Heptagenic photosensitization

Approximately 6000 plant species with toxic compounds and over 10,000 chemical compunds are listed by Watt and Breyer-Brandwijk (1962). Duke (1985) offers an exceptionally complete listing of chemicals' toxicity and their distribution in plant genera; this resource is recommended to those with specific interest.

From the standpoint of chemical constitution, the most important group of

poisonous substances found in leaves are alkaloids. These are secondary plant substances, always organic (carbon-containing) in nature and always containing nitrogen. In addition, they are normally physiologically active in animals; that is, they profoundly influence normal physiological processes, and because these effects are disruptive, the substances are poisonous. Alkaloids are potent compounds often active in very small quantities. Much of the value of folk medicine lies in the utilization of naturally occurring alkaloids. Alkaloids have a long history of use in legitimate medicine and of abuse as poisons for human beings.

Alkaloids are most common in seed-bearing plants, especially the Dicotyledons. They are uncommon but not unknown in fungi and simple plants (cryptograms). They are not very common in Monocotyledons. More than 2000 alkaloids have been described, and new compounds are constantly being discovered. Extensive searches are being made of the flowering plants in search of new alkaloids of possible medicinal value. One report by J. J. Willaman (1961) lists 3671 species known to contain alkaloids. This is only a very small portion of the number of species of plants in existence. In about half of these species the leaves themselves contain alkaloids. Since some alkaloids are the most deadly of poisons, experimentation with new species should begin by checking the species name against the body of information already available, such as the above references.

Certain plant families have more alkaloid-bearing species than others. Some with many poisonous alkaloid-bearing species include Apocynaceae (at least 220 species), Compositae (200), Euphorbiaceae (75), Labiatae (50), Lauraceae (65), Leguminosae (500), Liliaceae (120), Loganiaceae (70), Menispermaceae (70), Papaveraceae (100), Ranunculaceae (125), Rubiaceae (175), Rutaceae (180), Sapindaceae (45), and Solanaceae (260). However, the distribution of particular alkaloids and classes of alkaloids throughout the plant kingdom is so irregular that no generalization or safe rules are possible. It must be remembered that many edible plants, especially potatoes, contain alkaloids, and that in small or normal quantities these plants are not considered poisonous.

Many plant poisons belong to a class of substances called glycosides. These are usually bitter, white, and crystalline. Compounds of many types are held together in this group solely by the fact that their molecules include sugar side chains which increase their solubility in water. These sugars may be broken from the main molecule (hydrolyzed), an action which often increases the effects of the poisonous substances. Many alkaloids are also glycosides, and thus the classes overlap.

The cyanogenic glycosides are substances which yield the extremely poisonous gas hydrogen cyanide (HCN, prussic acid) on hydrolysis. These are very common throughout the flowering plants; Duke (1985) lists over 200 genera with hydrocyanic acid, including some of the most familiar. Leaves of the following plants contain cyanogenic glycosides: loquat (*Eriobotrya japonica* (Thunb.) Lindley), rose apple (*Syzygium jambos* (L.) Alston), macadamia nut (*Macadamia* spp.), grenadilla (*Passiflora quadrangularis* L.), sorghum (*S. bicolor* (L.) Moench), and hydrangea (*H. macrophylla* (Thunb.) Ser.).

The physiological action of HCN is to inhibit respiration at the cellular level, thus causing a type of asphixiation. Hydrolysis occurs readily, and can be used to rid the tissues of the poison, which escapes as gas. The hydrocyanic acid present in many

leaves is volatilized through the process of heating; in these cases, cooking allows the HCN to be released into the air, thus reducing or eliminating the leaves' toxicity. Raw or insufficiently cooked leaves (and other parts) containing hydrocyanic acid can be very dangerous and must be avoided. Because this type of compound is so important in cassava (*Manihot esculenta*), it is discussed more fully in Chapter II.

Goitrogenic glycosides are those that prevent the body from accumulating iodine, and thus stimulate the formation of goiters. Species of several families, including Cruciferae, Rosaceae, and Umbelliferaceae, are especially prone to this type of poison. Effects may be cumulative; acute poisoning is unusual.

Irritating oils which are glycosides occur in the Cruciferae as isothyocyanates, and as other substances in Ranunculaceae. While usually recognized as skin irritants, they can be toxic if ingested in excessive amounts.

Under appropriate circumstances of fermentation or ensilage, coumarin can be converted into a poisonous glycoside which acts as a hemorrhagic agent. The compound, and poisoning resulting from it, are chiefly associated with the clovers (*Melilotus*) and also present in *Gliricidia sepium*, although it is widely distributed.

Steroidal and triterpenoid substances can be divided into cardiac glycosides, such as digitalis, and saponins. Cardiac glycosides are particularly potent substances found principally in the Scrophulariaceae, the Liliaceae, and the Apocynaceae. Saponins are very widely scattered throughout the plant kingdom; Duke (1985) lists over 160 genera. Their action is chiefly to cause gastrointestinal irritations.

Oxalic acid and oxalates are normal, widespread substances that can be metabolized by the body in small quantities, but which are poisonous if taken in excess. The soluble oxalates reduce the level of available calcium in the blood. They are widespread and often reduce the value of otherwise very nutritious leaves. Some leaves with high oxalic acid content are rhubarb, spinach, beet green, *Talinum*, *Portulaca*, amaranth, and many leaves with a sour flavor. The insoluble forms occur as crystal raphides that irritate the mouth and throat on ingesting them. Most species of aroids (Araceae) contain insoluble oxalates. Oxalates can often be reduced by boiling leaves in ample water and discarding the cooking water before eating.

Phenolics and their complex conjugation products, tannins, are very common in leaves and other plant tissues. While often not considered poisonous, they react with other substances and produce off colors and off odors. Tannins combine with proteins during food preparation, making the protein difficult or impossible to digest. Cassava leaves have a high protein content, but because of their tannins, that protein may not be digested when eaten.

Resins or resinoids are a variety of compounds found in sap that harden into vitrious substances and are inflammable. The poisons of the milkweed family (Asclepiadaceae) are of this type.

Occasional specialized proteins, toxalbumins, are found, which have unexpected physiological effects, such as the agglutination of erythrocites and often powerful enzymatic action. The leaves from castor bean (Fig. 44) and tung contain such proteins.

Inorganic or mineral substances often are associated with poisoning. This may be due to an excess of these substances in the soil, the selective absorption and accumulation of such substances by certain plants that have an affinity for them, or

the residues left by pesticides sprayed on the plants. Selenium is actually required by some species, such as *Astragalus*, and such plants reveal the presence of selenium by their own abundant growth on selenium-containing soils. Molybdenum may poison by itself, or by its low concentration may stimulate copper poisoning. Lead is a common contaminant in soils, with disastrous effects in people, particularly in children.

Nonorganic compounds produced by the plants, including nitrates, nitrites, nitroses, and even gases of oxidized nitrogen, released by fermentation processes, can be quite toxic. Unfortunately these compounds are very widespread including among species generally thought to be edible (lettuce and sweet potato leaves, for example). Sometimes external agents, such as herbicides and fertilizers, stimulate excessive production of these compounds, so that normally safe leaves become poisonous. Nevertheless, poisoning is usually confined to animals.

Photosensitization compounds are called primary if, as in the case of pigments from buckwheat, the substances themselves cause the poisoning when the skin is exposed to the sun. If the compounds are metabolized into poisonous pigments after ingestion, the effect is called heptagenic photosensitization. Such compounds occur in the leaves of *Lantana* species, *Tribulus terrestris,* and *Brassica napus*.

Thus, the poisonous substances from leaves are extremely varied in nature, physiological action, and distribution. It is frightening to know that so many leaves are poisonous. At least 10 percent of the species of plants in every environment bear poisonous leaves. Nevertheless the probability of poisoning from most plants is very small. The reason is that in most cases during the normal course of events, the contact between plant and human is too inconsequential to permit poisoning. Eating the leaves provides a very intimate contact, but even so, depending on the kind of poison, small quantities of some poisonous leaves can be eaten without causing harm.

In considering the plants with poisonous leaves, it is not necessary, desirable, nor possible to list all of the poisonous species here, since this book is a treatise concerning edible leaves, not poisonous ones. The leaves that are treated are only those of common plants widespread throughout the tropics, common to the garden (including as weeds), and thus most likely to be a source of poisoning. For convenience the poisonous plants are listed by families. However, many families that include poisonous species are not mentioned here.

Acanthaceae. Relatively few plants yield leaves which are poisonous, generally due to alkaloids. These include *Justicia* spp. and *Thunbergia alata* Bojer ex Sims (clock vine). Nevertheless, leaves of the latter are reported to be edible.

Aizoaceae. This family includes New Zealand spinach, which contains small amounts of an alkaloid and a saponin. Members of the family tend to be high in oxalic acid and often in alkaloids as well.

Amaranthaceae. A few common herbs, including species of *Amaranthus, Celosia,* and *Gomphrena* have been reported to contain small, probably insignificant quantities of alkaloids. However, the poisonous substance in livestock loss has been excessive quantities of nitrate. Overfertilized amaranths are a risk for babies.

Anacardiaceae. The cashew family is noted for its poisonous substance which stimulates strong rashes in some people and not in others. In the American tropics, an insidious group of plants of the genus *Comocladia* (*C. dodonaea* (L.) Urban, *C. glabra* (Schultes) Spreng) irritate the skin in much the same manner as do

poison oak and poison ivy of the temperate zone. Unfortunately, the irritation appears several days after touching the plant, and therefore a person walking through dense brush can accumulate in a short time what will explode into a violent irritation later. The irritating principal can be carried through the body and can result in eruptions far from the area of contact.

The common mango, *Mangifera indica* L., is both a contact and stomach poison for many people. Although eating the fruit is generally considered the source of inflammation, contact with the leaves and especially the sap of the tree or unripe fruit can be equally harmful. In spite of this, the young leaves are sometimes eaten.

Annonaceae. Leaves of several common species of *Annona,* including *A. squamosa* L. (sugar apple) and *A. reticulata* L. (custard apple), contain alkaloids and are potentially poisonous. The leaves of some *Polyalthias*, ornamentals grown for their attractive foliage, are also poisonous.

Apocynaceae. This widespread family is well known throughout the tropics for its poisonous plants. The sap of the lovely ornamental shrub *Allamanda cathartica* L. is dangerously purgative if taken in quantity. Leaves of the fruit-bearing *Carissa* species contain alkaloids. The garden oleander, *Nerium oleander* L. (Fig. 45) and some of its tropical relatives (*Thevetia* spp.) contain dangerous amounts of toxic glycosides. It is said that a single leaf of oleander is sufficient to kill a person. Poisoning may result from the routine handling and pruning of these widespread plants, or from inhalation of the smoke when the vegetative parts are burned. It is a dangerous plant for children, and has only a doubtful place in the home garden. The leaves of the frangipanis (*Plumeria* spp.) contain unknown alkaloids.

As reported earlier, the young leaves of *Catharanthus roseus* (L.) G. Don f. (Madagascar periwinkle) are sometimes edible. The older leaves of this and related species contain alkaloids. Leaves and roots are used in folk medicine to induce vomiting, for their purging effects, or for the treatment of worms. *Strophanthus* spp. leaves contain a poisonous alkaloid.

Araceae. This family includes many species with edible leaves. The aroids are obnoxious chiefly for the crystals of calcium oxalate which sting the skin or the roof of the mouth when ingested. Practically all species contain some such crystals under some circumstances, and appropriate cooking methods are therefore required. Other species contain alkaloids in their leaves.

The common *Dieffenbachia*, used as an attractive broad-leaved ornamental plant, has an interesting poisoning effect thought to be due to toxin as well as calcium oxalate crystals. After ingestion of juice or vegetative plant parts, the throat swells, preventing speech. The poisoning is usually temporary, but fatalities have been reported in Brazil.

Asclepiadaceae. The milkweeds, *Asclepias* spp., of the temperate zones and the tropics are usually recognized as hazards to grazing animals. All parts of mature plants contain a poisonous resinoid, and glycosides and alkaloids are sometimes found. Symptoms include apathy, loss of muscular control, rapid pulse, and labored respiration. Young leaves of broad-leaved but not narrow-leaved species are sometimes cooked and eaten.

The giant milkweed, *Calotropis procera* (Aiton) Aiton f., very common in the tropics is also toxic, such that the juice from the plant was used in arrow poisons

and acts as a depilatory. A glycoside of the alkaloid calotropin and a cardiac glycoside have been reported to be the poisons. They stimulate the heart excessively and can kill rapidly in small doses. An extract of this species is used in the poison curare.

Cryptostegia grandiflora R. Br., the rubber vine (Fig. 46), is a very attractive shrub widely planted for its large lovely flowers, and for its adaptability to dry areas. The milky sap of the leaf or stem contains a toxic glycoside that produces an irritation of the skin, or if taken internally, a severe diarrhea and heart failure. Teas prepared from the leaves have proved fatal. Poisoning often occurs when the plants are routinely pruned. This species thus hardly merits a place in the home garden.

Compositae. Among the composites there are many species with alkaloids or many other poisonous principles in the leaves, including species from genera of which the leaves are eaten, such as *Artemisia, Senecio, Vernonia,* and *Xanthium.* Frequently unknown, the alkaloids are often not present in harmful concentrations.

Euphorbiaceae. This is a family usually recognized for its irritating and poisonous plants. The substances, usually alkaloids of the milky sap, are often poisonous on contact, and may be harmless after cooking. Individuals vary in sensitivity to poisoning by Euphorbiaceous species.

Aleurites species, especially *A. fordii* Hemsley (Fig. 47), the source of tung oil, are highly toxic due to the presence of a saponin and an unidentified poisonous substance. These trees are grown as ornamentals for their large, attractive leaves. Poisoning symptoms include loss of appetite, depression, and hemorrhagic diarrhea.

The leaves of most species of *Croton*, which are common, somewhat woody weeds of the tropics, contain a purgative oil of formidable strength. Especially well known in dry places, *Crotons* are seldom taken as food or feed, but because of their ubiquitous nature, constitute a constant hazard.

In another portion of this text the young leaves of *Euphorbia pulcherrima* Willd. ex Klotzsch (poinsettia) are described as edible. Nevertheless, many persons are susceptible to the milky sap of the leaves or stem, which causes a wicked irritation of the skin. This may crack open and become infected. Pruning the plants in the garden is a frequent cause of poisoning. Poisoning of children from eating the leaves has been reported. Strong stomach pains are a symptom. A dilemma thus exists, for young leaves are edible cooked.

Most species of *Jatropha* are poisonous due to purgative oil and a still unidentified substance. Boiling is said to render the poisonous seeds harmless.

The very succulent species of *Euphorbia*, often leafless or with leaves during only part of their life cycle, also contain a toxic milky sap that is very irritating to some humans. Among the common plants causing poisoning is *E. tirucalli* L., the pencil tree. This plant also poisons the soil by release of a carcinogenic substance taken up by edible plants.

The famous machineel tree, *Hippomane mancinella* L., of the Caribbean is well appreciated in literature or by those who have come in contact with it. An attractive tree of the beaches and of dry areas, an apple-like fruit is produced, which has often been consumed with fatal results. The sap of the tree is a very strong irritant of the skin, and poisoning has been reported from resting under the boughs. Some persons are more susceptible than others. One of the poisons is an alkaloid

thought to be physostigmine, but other substances are not yet identified.

The sandbox tree, *Hura crepitans* L., is planted throughout the tropics for its attractive form, or used as a living fencepost. It is the sap of the species, which can be obtained from the stems or leaves, which contains an unidentified emetic and cathartic substance, and another poison. The seeds are particularly poisonous.

The castor bean, *Ricinus communis* L., is often seen in gardens grown as an ornamental. In spite of the fact that the young leaves are cooked and eaten, mature leaves as well as seeds contain alkaloids associated with the protein. Symptoms of poisoning include nausea, vomiting, pains of the abdomen, feverish skin, accelerated pulse, and blurred vision. Most poisoning occurs from eating the seed, but all parts contain some poison.

Illiciaceae. *Illicium anisatum* L., the Shikimi tree, has leaves which are toxic due to an alkaloid. The seeds are also toxic.

Labiatae. The mint family includes many species that contain poisonous volatile oils. An attractive mint-like weed characterized by whorls of small flowers at the nodes, *Leonotis nepetifolia* (L.) R. Br., is often a source of irritation to persons allergic to it. The burning irritation is associated either with the fine hairs of the leaf or with the pollen. Nevertheless, the leaves are often fed to rabbits and may not be toxic to humans.

Leguminosae. Perhaps no family contains as many poisonous species as the legume family. On the other hand, few families have given to humanity so many edible species. Poisonous principles of the legumes are principally the alkaloids (of which a wide variety occur), toxalbumins, and toxic metals. Genera with poisonous leaves include *Acacia, Albizia, Cassia, Crotalaria, Erythrina, Genista, Lupinus, Pachyrhizus, Pithecellobium, Sesbania, Sophora,* and *Tephrosia.*

Wild coffee, *Cassia occidentalis* L., is one of those ubiquitous small trees that are useful and poisonous at the same time. The seeds are weakly poisonous until roasted, when they are used as a coffee substitute. The leaves, used in folk medicine, contain lesser quantities of the substance chrysarobin. *Cassia siamea* Lam., very common in the tropics, has foliage especially attractive to pigs, and fatal. The poisonous substance is an alkaloid. *Cassia* species in general tend to contain alkaloids and can be considered a dangerous group.

Species of *Crotalaria* (Fig. 48), attractive legumes of the tropics, contain the alkaloid crotaline, or related substances. Sometimes grown in the garden for their attractive yellow flowers or inflated pods, *Crotalaria*s should be considered a risk wherever children are near. Poisoning can be rapid or very slow. Symptoms include bleeding of the stomach. Leaves are less toxic than the deadly seeds.

Because of the large variety of toxic substances, all fruits, seeds, and leaves of the Leguminosae are suspect. Even the edible species should be eaten in small amounts as a precaution.

Liliaceae. Tropical lilies, as in the case of temperate zone species, frequently are poisonous. The alkaloids or other substances are usually present chiefly in the bulb, as in the case of *Crinum* and *Hymenocallis*, but the leaves may contain small quantities. *Gloriosa superba* L. (climbing lily) leaves are poisonous due to alkaloids. All lily leaves should be thought of as potentially poisonous.

Meliaceae. The chinaberry, *Melia azedarach* L., a beautiful ornamental tree

now distributed through the tropics, is generally recognized as poisonous. The fruits are well liked by pigs and have caused serious poisoning. Other domestic animals are less susceptible. Human poisoning from eating the leaves is not common. The leaves contain an alkaloid, paraisine, distinct from that of the fruits, azaridine.

Solanaceae. This extremely common family contains a number of strongly poisonous species, and the leaves of almost all species can be considered dangerous. Particularly dangerous genera in the tropics are *Datura, Nicotiana, Physalis,* and especially *Solanum.* The poisonous substances are alkaloids of several classes, including glycoalkaloids with a steroid nucleus, a useful raw material for the synthesis of steroidal drugs and birth-control pills. These substances are common in the edible species and their leaves, making them potentially dangerous. Some forms of arthritis appear to be caused by even small amounts of these edible vegetables.

Leaves of the genus *Datura,* including jimson weed, are extremely poisonous, and these plants should be kept out of the garden. A series of alkaloids increase the pulse and rate of respiration. Diarrhea, dilation of the pupils of the eyes, and rigidity of the body are common symptoms. Children have been killed by chewing or sucking the attractive flowers.

Verbenaceae. The *Lantana*s of the tropics, familiar weeds of neglected areas, are often taken into cultivation for their attractive umbels of bicolored flowers (Fig. 49). The leaves are poisonous due to the presence of alkaloids, in some cases lantanine. However, amounts of leaves insufficient to kill may have a photosensitizing effect. Light skin exposed to the sun becomes yellow, swollen, hard, and painful. The fruits may also be poisonous.

For more information. Morton (1995) gives descriptions with color plates and accounts of many poisonings from over 110 of the most common tropical ornamental and wild species. Some tropical species are reviewed by Oakes (1962). The species covered by Watt and Breyer-Brandwijk (1962) include many common throughout the tropics and subtropics. Full coverage of poisonous plants of the United States is given in Kingsbury's book (1968). Duke (1985, 1992) discusses the toxic properties of a tremendous number of edible and medicinal plants.

Experimenting with the edible properties of leaves

Knowledge of the edible and poisonous properties of leaves must have developed slowly over a long period of time. Since cases of fatal poisoning from eating leaves continues, it is obvious that experimentation has not ceased and that eating leaves can be dangerous. Therefore, any person interested in trying new leaves as food should be fully aware of the dangers, and should practice extreme caution. Some very important points include:

1. Know the species before attempting to eat the leaves. Consult authorities if possible and become a reasonable expert on the plant involved before trying it out.
2. Avoid leaves of plants with milky sap, unless absolutely identified as safe.
3. Do not eat new leaves raw. Cook them, and throw away the cooking water.
4. If cooked leaves are bitter, avoid them.

5. If leaves are very sour they may contain excessive amounts of oxalic acid. Avoid eating too much of them.
6. Try out new but identified leaves in very small amounts and progress gradually with time towards the use of larger amounts.
7. Leave experimentation with unknown leaves to the laboratory of experts.

The problem of identifying new edible leaves in the laboratory is a difficult one that will not be solved easily. Species that bear leaves that are sufficiently succulent can be tested for the presence of alkaloids and the more obvious classes of poisonous substances. After that small animal trials can be used to establish edibility. These are not simple. The long-term effects of an item of the diet can only be solved by laborious experimentation. On the other hand, if deleterious effects are found, isolation and identification of the poisonous substance may need years of study.

Thus, we suggest to the lover of green leaves: "Caution is always appropriate; experimentation is dangerous."

CHAPTER X

Culture and Care of Green-Leaved Vegetables

All green-leaved vegetables bear both edible and non-edible leaves. The edible leaves are invariably the young and succulent leaves near the tip of the shoot. Older leaves tend to be tough and fibrous or may accumulate bitter substances. Therefore, the appropriate cultural conditions are those that stimulate succulent growth or maximize the production of succulent leaves. These conditions will not be the same for all species that bear edible green leaves. Local experimentation in production methods will always be necessary.

Climate

Climate is the average condition prevailing in an area, as affected by rainfall, winds, light intensity, atmospheric pressure, and annual changes. Weather is the daily variation in the climate. The climate and weather influence the success of green-leaved vegetables, most importantly through temperature, light, and water.

In discussing climate one must always distinguish between macro- and micro-climate. Whereas any area can be characterized by its climate in general, local influences, many under the gardener's control, can effectively modify the climate in a given area. Small pockets where local influences prevail are said to have particular microclimates. Gardeners, once aware of the climatic needs of their plants, can modify their treatments to approximate optimum conditions.

Tropical climates are varied. Within the tropics and subtropics, rainfall varies from 200 to 10,000 mm per year. Rainfall is seldom uniformly distributed, however, so wet and dry seasons can be distinguished. Temperature varies from the hottest measured to near the lowest (in tropical alpine areas). Light intensity varies among macro- as well as microclimates due to local conditions including latitude and atmospheric conditions. Only daylength, directly related to latitude, cannot reach extremes. Because of the wide range of geographic situations in the tropics, suitable climates occur for almost all green-leaved vegetables, although the growth patterns of typical summer vegetables of the temperate zone may be adversely affected by the relatively short summer days of the tropics.

Tropical temperatures vary with latitude, altitude, atmospheric conditions, and proximity of large bodies of water. Low temperatures limit the growth of green-leaved vegetables in very few locations. Indeed, some of the cooler tropical climates are optimal for temperate zone leafy greens, especially spinach, brussels sprouts, broccoli, cabbage, and lettuce. High temperatures, however, frequently inhibit plant growth, especially when associated with winds and inadequate moisture. High daytime temperatures can be modified with light shading. Although this can be accomplished with relatively open-canopied trees, such as *Inga vera* Willd. (guaba) and *Gliricidia sepium* (Jacq.) Walp., these may compete with garden plants because of their ramified root systems. Shelters of palm leaves, branches, ferns, or saran cloth (Fig. 50) can be constructed cheaply and in the case of the latter, are durable. The modified climate below such shelters can be further changed by irrigation during the hottest weather.

The effects of wind on local temperature conditions can be modified by windbreaks. These need to be set to the windward side of the garden area and should be of tall, relatively narrow materials. Some plants (*Panax* species, Fig. 51) provide attractive windbreaks and ornamental hedges. The effective distance of a windbreak is usually calculated at only 2 1/2 times its height. This distance is multiplied when the windbreak is used in conjunction with a shade-producing shelter.

Light intensity is seldom a limiting factor in the tropics. This may not be the case in very cloudy climates or during intense rainy seasons. The modification of the climate to increase light intensity is seldom necessary. On the other hand, light intensity may be reduced, as needed, by appropriate shading.

Effects of daylength are particularly marked in the tropics. Contrary to popular belief, tropical plants are more, not less sensitive to daylengths; in fact, their vegetative versus flowering phases may be controlled by daylength differences of a half hour or less. Most of the green amaranth varieties do not produce well during short days, as they begin to flower when the plants are too small for good leaf production. This response to short days can often be corrected by additional illumination (Fig. 52). Such light need not be intense nor of long duration, but its effects on plant growth may be striking.

Moisture

Water is necessary, of course, for plant growth. Two classes of problems can be distinguished associated with water: scarcity of water and excess water. For gardening of green-leaved vegetables, adequate water is a necessity. Without water the desired succulence of the foliage cannot be obtained or maintained. Growth rates, furthermore, are reduced. The amount of water needed by the plant cannot be judged only by the wetness of the surface of the ground. A dry surface can occur naturally, while large quantities of water still remain available to the plant. On the other hand, wilting suggests a condition of dryness that has already gone too far. Established plantings should not be permitted to dry to the point of wilting, for even if the plants recover after irrigation, their growth has been impeded.

Excess moisture is the cause of many problems. Moisture on the leaves promotes fungal growth. Excess water in the soil promotes disease. Waterlogging impedes the respiration of roots and can even lead to wilting. In addition, heavy rains can injure plants, even destroying young seedlings. Excess rainfall and dew are difficult to control. Nevertheless, if such conditions are expected, the gardener can partially modify conditions in order to minimize deleterious effects. Shelters constructed for shading also reduce the force of heavy rains. Planting on ridges with adequate drainage ditches to carry off excess water reduces waterlogging and disease. If night dews are a problem, orienting the garden with respect to night breezes may help maintain drier conditions.

The wise gardener studies local climatic conditions and modifies them to achieve desired effects. Since green-leaved vegetables also differ, some understanding of the specific needs of the various species is also desirable so that cultural practices can be controlled.

Soils

Tropical soils vary tremendously. Although exact recommendations cannot be given in advance of the study of particular soils and their characteristics, the choice of soil for the garden is extremely important in determining its success. However, a variety of soils can be made productive with proper management.

Clay soils (those containing principally very fine particles) are sometimes quite fertile, but their heavy textures impede drainage and proper aeration. Furthermore, such soils are often hard to manage. Plowing or soil preparation when the soil is too wet may lead to the formation of durable clods. When finely broken up, however, such soils can be productive. Structure of the soil can be improved by the addition of organic material. Ridging the soil improves drainage and aeration.

Sandy soils, on the other hand, are often lacking in sufficient nutrients. In addition, although aeration can be excellent, drainage is often excessive. Such soils need organic materials to improve the retention of water and nutrients. Nematodes, which injure the roots and reduce vigor and yield, are often a problem on sandy soils.

The ideal soil, a loam, consists of mixtures of particles of different sizes: large (sand), small (clay), and intermediate (silt). Such a soil will have good drainage and yet retain sufficient air, water, and nutrients for good plant growth.

The hydrogen ion content (pH) of the soil exerts a great influence on the growth of plants. If the soil is too acid (low pH) or too alkaline (high pH), the retrieval by the plant of essential minerals will be impeded. A pH of 6.0-7.0 is most desirable for most green-leaved vegetables, but tolerance to both high and low pH varies. Low pHs can be corrected by adding lime (calcium carbonate) to the soil in fairly large quantities (5 tons/hectare). This may be supplied in many fashions, including burned lime, hydrated lime, crushed limestone, shell, etc. Once applied, the lime is not immediately effective. Benefits increase with time. High pH is corrected by the addition of sulfur, usually in the form of powder, at average rates of 1000 kg/hectare or more. Tables have been published for calculating the appropriate quantity of lime or sulfur for different soils, depending on the pH found and the correction desired (Knott, 1957). Without adequate tests of pH and study of the soil type, additives will not usually be used in correct proportions.

Organic materials improve the soil structure, leading to good drainage, aeration, and nutrient availability. However, the material should be well-rotted or it will tend to tie up the nitrogen available in the soil and thus deprive the growing plants of this essential element. In contrast to mineral fertilizer, organic materials release nutrients for a relatively long, continuous period. Such amendments are often preferred over mineral fertilizers, but the latter may also be necessary.

Fertilization

Tropical soils are often badly leached by heavy rainfalls, and are not productive unless appropriately treated. Although the addition of organic material is one of the surest ways to improve soil fertility, especially on the scale of the home garden, such materials are often not available. Mineral fertilizers are desirable in such cases, but may also supplement the addition of organic materials to the soil.

For most crop plants, and especially for green-leaved vegetables, nitrogen is the most important element in a mineral fertilizer. Nitrogen is an important building block of amino acids, proteins, and other plant constituents. It promotes vegetative growth in contrast to root growth. For green-leaved vegetables, nitrogen darkens the green color and improves succulence. Nitrogen, supplied to the soil chiefly by decay of organic materials and by bacterial fixation, is easily leached from the soil by rains. It is the element most likely to be lacking sometime during the course of the growth of the plant, and the single element most likely to stimulate growth of green-leaved vegetables. Lack of nitrogen leads to general yellowing of the foliage (Fig. 53). Organic sources include manure, leaves of green manure legumes or grass clippings, fish meal, blood meal, and many other products found on the farm. Mineral fertilizer for green-leaved vegetables should be fairly high in nitrogen.

Phosphorous is also a very important element in nutrition of green-leaved plants. It is a component of the natural buffer system of plants, and is extremely important in energy transfer. Phosphorous in the soil is formed by the breakdown of normal minerals and is often relatively plentiful. Nevertheless, it often occurs in insoluble forms that are of no benefit to the plant. It may not be lacking except when intense cultivation is practiced. Phosphorous is not leached rapidly from the soil, and the effect of application may last for several seasons. Phosphorous deficiency is difficult to diagnose; symptoms include unnaturally dark green leaves and reddish tinges of leaves and stems. It can be added through bone meal and rock phosphate. Mineral fertilizer for leafy vegetables needs only moderate amounts of phosphorous.

Potassium is another element of much importance to growing plants. It is associated with carbohydrate and protein synthesis and with many growth processes. Potassium in the soil comes from the weathering of common minerals. Nevertheless, in highly leached soils potassium is frequently limiting. Potassium deficiency is usually seen in terms of local symptoms, including mottling, chlorosis, and necrosis, especially near the margins and tips of the leaf. The amount of potassium suitable for green-leaved vegetables can hardly be predicted in advance. Ashes and animal and plant (especially banana and cacao) residues are sources of potassium. Without specific knowledge of needs, a fertilizer for green-leaved vegetables should contain moderate to high amounts of potassium.

Nitrogen (N), phosphorous (P), and potassium (K) are the most necessary elements of a mineral fertilizer. When all three are present, the fertilizer mixture is said to be balanced. The percentage of these elements in the fertilizer mixture is indicated on the bag by numbers such as 12-5-10 (12% N, 5% P, 10% K). However, other elements are frequently lacking and may limit production in specific soils. These include calcium, magnesium, sulfur, iron, manganese, and others. When it is possible to buy fertilizer mixtures with added "minor elements," these generally provide an insurance against shortages. For the home gardener it is usually impractical to determine the special needs for these minerals in small garden plots.

Balanced mineral fertilizer can be applied before seeding at the rate of a handful per meter of row, buried under the planting ridge. Additional nitrogen can be applied after seedlings are established, dissolved in water or applied along the ridge but not in direct contact with the plant. The entire subject of fertilization is beyond the scope of this book. The serious student must look elsewhere.

Preparation of Soil and Planting

Soil preparation for green-leaved vegetables is no different from that for tropical vegetables in general. Excess vegetation must be cleared from the area. Discarded plant remains can be composted for later use in the garden. The soil can be loosened or turned over with fork, shovel, or plow. At this stage lime may be added to improve the texture and fertility of the soil. If the land can be left alone for several weeks and then turned again, many of the weed seeds will have germinated and will be eliminated. Large lumps of soil should be broken up to prevent the formation of hard troublesome clods.

The soil should then be formed into ridges or beds to permit drainage (Fig. 54). Mineral fertilizers can be added at this time, buried below the furrow if desired. The beds should be raked smooth leaving finely divided soil near the surface.

Tropical greens are often planted from cuttings. Although some, such as cassava and sweet potato, are planted directly in the field, it is usually more satisfactory to root cuttings first in moist sand before field planting. Large seeds can be planted directly in the garden but small seeds will germinate better in boxes or pots of finely sieved soil (Fig. 55). This suggests the desirability of a nursery area in the garden where small plants can be produced under suitable conditions.

A useful technique in establishing the garden is to cover the prepared area with a thin black plastic sheet (Fig. 56). The cloth can be weighted in the furrows or drainage ditches. To permit the penetration of water, holes or slits can be cut rapidly with hoe or machete. Seeds or seedlings are then planted directly through holes cut in the plastic. This technique results in very satisfactory weed control.

Care and Harvest

Once planted, all tropical greens are subject to pests and disease. It is often difficult to control these conditions in a small garden, and methodology is also well beyond the scope of this presentation. Particular problems encountered with some of these species are mentioned in the descriptions of the species. It must be emphasized that cultural details have not been worked out for many of the leaf crops mentioned herein. A certain amount of experimentation is always necessary and desirable. Alert gardeners rapidly learn the requirements of their particular crops.

Many green vegetables can be harvested many times during their life cycle. Although the youngest leaves are usually the most tender, and in some cases, the most free of obnoxious or irritating principles, the older leaves sometimes have stronger flavors which appeal to the more initiated tastes. With any species, the first few harvests will rapidly demonstrate the qualities of the younger versus older leaves. When older leaves can be eaten, it is preferable to do so, for the younger leaves are necessary for the continued growth of the plant. A system of harvesting older but not overmature leaves will generally permit the most rapid recovery of the plant, and the rapid production of a new crop. Treating the garden with ammonium sulfate, about 1 kg per 35 meters of row, helps maintain the plants in succulent condition. Each species differs and must be treated separately. As with all crops, leafy vegetables require care for the best production. Quality treatment gives rewarding results.

1. The 'Tigerleaf' variety of edible amaranth

2. Quail grass, *Celosia argentea*, a dependable and attractive plant

3. Leaves of *Xanthosoma* (left) and *Colocasia* (right)

4. *Basella alba*, Malabar spinach, a succulent and productive perennial vine

5. *Telfairia occidentalis* leaves at the stage they are marketed in West Africa

6. *Manihot esculenta*, cassava, a common green already growing in the field

7. The nutritious and tasty shrub, katuk, *Sauropus androgynus*

8. The delicate edible inner leaves of corn

9. 'Green Jade' edible hibiscus, *Abelmoschus manihot*, more productive than most greens

10. *Cassia alata*, ringworm senna, a medicinal and edible leaf

11. Leaves of *Euphorbia pulcherrima*, the poinsettia, a debatable species

12. Chaya, *Cnidoscolus chayamansa*, a tolerant and productive ornamental shrub

13. Leaves of *Anacardium occidentale*, the cashew

14. The edible leaves of the durian, *Durio zibethinus*

15. A branch of tamarind, *Tamarindus indica*, with edible tips and young fruits

16. Young leaves of mulberry, *Morus alba*

17. A clump of the edible weed, *Justicia insularis*

18. Leaves and flowers of *Thunbergia alata*, susana

19. *Bidens pilosa*, Spanish needles, a widely distributed edible weed

20. Foliage and flower of the beach morning glory, *Ipomoea pes-caprae*

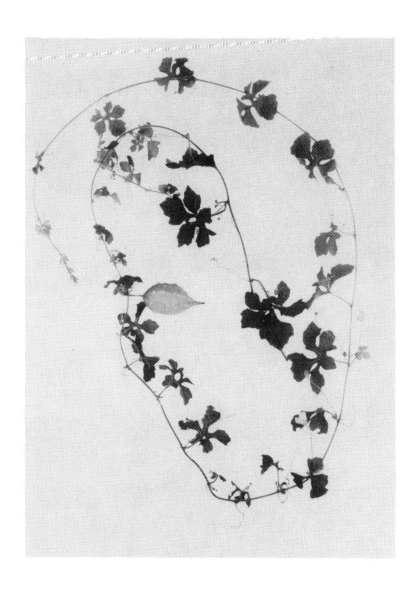

21. Leaves and mature fruit of the wild balsam pear, *Momordica charantia*

22. *Peperomia pellucida*, a common edible weed of greenhouses

23. An edible *Portulaca* from the fields of Puerto Rico

24. Mature plant of *Talinum triangulare*

25. Edible leaves and ripe pods of *Erythrina berteroana*, dwarf bucare

26. Leaves of mother-of-cacao, *Gliricidia sepium*

27. The pinnate leaves of the weedy tree *Leucaena leucocephala*

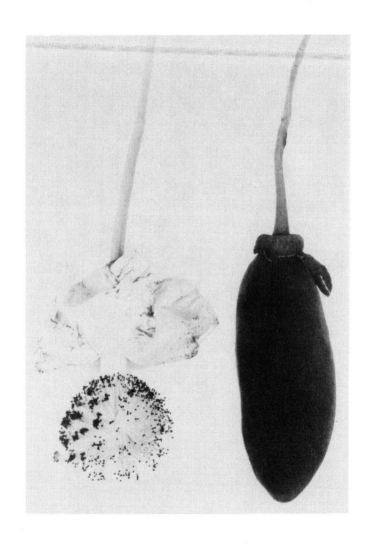

28. The flower and fruit of *Adansonia digitata*, baobab

29. Leaves and fruit of *Morinda citrifolia*

30. Leaves and pods of *Moringa oleifera*, the horseradish tree

31. Culantro, the false coriander of Puerto Rico with spicy leaves

32. The oregano of Puerto Rico, *Lippia helleri*

33. Basil or albahaca, as grown for its leaves in Puerto Rico

34. Cabbage in a garden clearing in the Caribbean

35. A hillside planting of cabbage, established and cultivated by hand, in the mountains of Puerto Rico

36. Harvesttime, and the most reliable way to get cabbages out of the field

37. A sugar beet field in Puerto Rico, with large edible leaves

38. A leaf lettuce, Black-leaved Simpson, which does well in the tropics

39. Gardening for lettuce on a small commercial farm of Puerto Rico

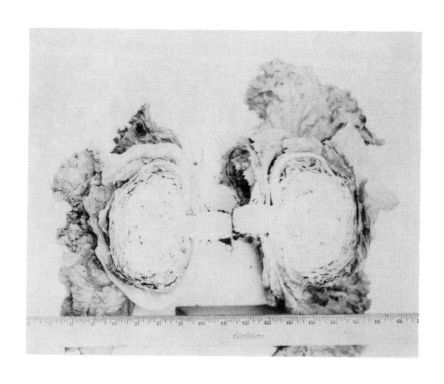

40. Head lettuce grown at a medium elevation, showing a semi-solid head

41. Lettuce flowering

42. Tropical lettuce, *Lactuca indica*, edible and used for shade

43. Ortiga, *Urera baccifera*, a stinging nettle of the Caribbean

44. Castor bean, poisonous plant, the leaves of which are processed for eating

45. *Nerium oleander*, one of the most dangerous of garden shrubs

46. Leaf and flower of *Cryptostegia grandiflora*, erroneously called
the purple allamandra

47. *Aleurites fordii*, tung, the source of oil and poisonous leaves

48. *Crotalaria retusa*, its colorful flowers and poisonous leaves

49. *Lantana camara* with its colorful flowers and fruits

50. A saran cloth shelter used to reduce light intensity and temperature

51. A *Panax* hedge which reduces wind under the glass roof

52. A field illuminated with light at night to avoid short day effects

53. Plants showing symptoms of nitrogen deficiency (right) compared to healthy plants of the same age (left)

54. Garden beds planted with many green-leaved vegetables

55. Seedling flats of green-leaved vegetables

56. Tahitian taro growing in a bed covered with plastic mulch

Seed Sources and Resources

For those seeking to test commercial varieties or find seed or cuttings of rare plants, the value of *Cornucopia: A Source Book of Edible Plants* (Facciola 1990) cannot be overemphasized. A short description, further reading, and seed sources are listed for each plant or variety. It is available from Kampong Publications, 1870 Sunrise Drive, Vista, CA 92084, USA (book or software), and from ECHO's bookstore (book only).

The following are some sources of commercial, specialty, or specially-adapted varieties of edible-leaved vegetables:

J.L. Hudson, Seedsman (Star Route 2, Box 337, La Honda, CA 94020, USA) offers a tremendous variety of seeds in the "Ethnobotanical Catalog of Seeds," including agroforestry species, unusual vegetables, flowers and ornamentals, plants used medicinally, and many wild plants difficult to find elsewhere, in small packets and at reasonable prices.

Seed Savers Exchange (3076 North Winn Rd., Decorah, IA 52101, USA) members maintain a tremendous variety of rare heirloom vegetable, herb, fruit, and other seeds. They may be able to help you locate rare seeds as well.

Native Seeds/SEARCH (2509 N. Campbell Ave. #325, Tucson, AZ 85719, USA; phone 520/327-9123; fax 520/327-5821; http://desert.net/seeds/home.htm) offers a 50% discount to native peoples on their tremendous selection of amaranth (13 varieties), beans, chili peppers, corn, cucurbits, okra, tomatoes, flowers, and more, suitable for very hot and dry conditions; some are adapted to higher altitudes as well.

B&T World Seeds (Route des Marchandes, Paguignan, 34210 Olonzac, FRANCE; phone 04 6891 2963; http://compuserve.com/homepages/b_and_t_world_seeds) is one of the largest seed distributors in the world, with an unbelievably comprehensive listing of many kinds of seeds.

Known-You Seed Co., Ltd. (26, Chung Cheng 2nd Road, Kaohsiung, Taiwan, R.O.C.; phone 886-7-224-1106; fax 886-7-222-7299) has many Oriental leaf vegetables, many hybrids, in their catalog.

Nichols Garden Nursery (1190 North Pacific Highway NE, Albany, OR 97321, USA; phone 541/928-9280; fax 541/967-8406) offers many Oriental leaf vegetables and several wild or weedy greens.

Richters Herb Specialists (Goodwood, Ontario LOC 1AO, CANADA; phone 905/640-6677; fax 905/640-6641; e-mail orderdesk@richters.com; www.richters.com) has an exceptionally complete herb listing with descriptions of the plant uses.

Hawaii Fruit and Forest Nursery (Box 333, Hakalau, HI 96710, USA) offers a variety of tropical perennial vegetables and more.

The University of Hawaii (Seed Program, Department of Horticulture, 3190 Maile Way, Room 112, Honolulu, HI 96822, USA; they only ship to US addresses; phone 808/956-7890) offers high-quality seed of select varieties of solo papaya, pole bean, heat-resistant lettuce, sweet corn, eggplant, tomato, and other vegetables.

Bountiful Gardens Seeds (18001 Shafer Ranch Road, Willits, CA 95490, USA; phone 707/459-6410) lists a good selection of leafy vegetables, including weedy salad greens. Enthusiasts may ask for their rare seeds catalog.

Twilley Seed Co. (P.O. Box 65, Trevose, PA 19053, USA; phone 215/639-8800) has common temperate vegetable and flower seeds, including commercial varieties of leafy greens.

Indiana Seed Company (P.O. Box 1745, Noblesville, IN 46060, USA; phone 800/562-2459 or 317/773-5813; fax 317/773-9290) offers bulk quantities of the most popular temperate vegetables at very reasonable prices.

ECHO (17430 Durrance Road, North Fort Myers, FL 33917, USA; phone 941/543-3246; fax 941/543-5317; e-mail ECHO@xc.org; http://www.xc.org/echo) maintains a seedbank of species with potential to produce well under marginal growing conditions. ECHO's concentration is in the area of underexploited plants, assisting people working in marginal conditions to perform trials with these plants to identify those with promise for their region. Seeds or cuttings for small-scale experiments are supplied to people working in tropical agricultural development programs. Among the most valuable annual and perennial leafy vegetables normally available from ECHO are the following (* indicates cutting): amaranth, bush okra, chaya*, Ethiopian kale, false roselle, katuk, lettuce (Anuenue, Maioba, Montello, Queensland), Malabar spinach, moringa, Okinawan spinach*, quail grass, roselle, sissoo spinach*, and tropical lettuce. Many more species have edible leaves as a secondary use. Write or see the web site for the full seed catalog.

Those interested in leaves in nutrition may want to contact the following:

Leaf for Life (US)/Find Your Feet (UK) is an organization which teaches people to make best use of green leaf crops to improve their nutrition and encourage the development of sustainable food systems. They publish and distribute extensive, practical information for making leaf concentrate, dried leaves, and other food uses for a wide range of tropical plants. Information guides field workers through technical, agricultural, and economic decision-making about using leaf crops. They are involved in small projects in several countries. Contact David Kennedy, Leaf for Life, 260 Radford Hollow Road, Big Hill, KY 40405, USA; phone/fax 606/986-5418; e-mail dlkennedy@skn.net.

The Xerophthalmia Club Bulletin is supported by Sight Savers and the International Vitamin A Consultative Group. This valuable resource summarizes and discusses

recent findings on vitamin A deficiency and directs readers to a great number of contacts who work in this area. An issue can be used as a reference and a source for ideas in health promotion. Subscription is free; write to the Editor, International Centre for Eye Health; Institute of Ophthalmology, Bath Street, London, EC1V 9EL, UK; fax 44 1903 206770.

A directory of food composition tables from various regions of the world can be found at http://www.crop.cri.nz/foodinfo/infoods/infoods.htm.

Cookbooks:

Development projects interested in promoting leafy vegetables should first try to incorporate greens into existing local recipes. But for the gourmet, some recent cookbooks may be of interest. Although few local markets in the tropics could supply all of the ingredients in these books, substitutions can be tried and the recipes may inspire you to prepare and serve leaves in new ways:

Greens Glorious Greens!: More Than 140 Ways to Prepare All Those Great-Tasting, Super-Healthy, Beautiful Leafy Greens. By Johnna Albi and Catherine Walthers. New York: St. Martin's Press, 1996. ISBN 0-312-14108-4.

Leafy Greens. By Mark Bittman. New York: Macmillan, 1995. ISBN 0-02-860355-9.

The Greens Book. By Susan Belsinger and Carolyn Dille. Loveland, Colorado: Interweave Press, 1995. ISBN 1-883010-05-5.

Salad Gardens: Gourmet Greens and Beyond. By Karan Davis Cutler (ed.). New York: Brooklyn Botanic Garden, 1995. ISBN 0-945352-89-1.

Selected Bibliography for Edible and Poisonous Leaves

Abbiw, D.K. 1990. Useful plants of Ghana: West African uses of wild and cultivated plants. Intermediate Technology, London, and Royal Botanic Gardens, Kew. 337 pp.

Aglibut, A.P., L.G. Gonzalez, and A.C. Garcia. 1951. The influence of varying amounts of water on surface-irrigated lettuce fertilized with ammonium sulphate. Phil. Agric. 35:304-318.

Akoroda, M.O. 1988. Cultivation of jute (*Corchorus olitorius* L.) for edible leaf in Nigeria. Trop. Agric. (Trinidad) 65(4):297-299.

Al Azharia Jahn, S. 1995. Traditional Indonesian and Ethiopian recipes for tree vegetables. Agriculture and Rural Development, January 1995:64-66.

Almazan, A.M., and R.L. Theberge. 1989. Influence of cassava mosaic virus on cassava leaf-vegetable quality. Tropical Agriculture 66:305-308.

Anonymous. 1970. Cabbage, cauliflowers, and related crops. Queensland Agric. Jour. 96:588-597, 697-703.

Arnold, H.L. 1968. Poisonous plants in Hawaii. Charles E. Tuttle Co., Rutland, Vermont. 71 pp.

Bailey, J.M. 1992. The leaves we eat. South Pacific Commission, Noumea, New Caledonia. 97 pp.

Bawa, S.F., and S.P. Yadav. 1986. Protein and mineral contents of green leafy vegetables consumed by Sokoto population. J. Sci. Food Agric. 37:504-506.

Bhaskarachary, K., D.S. Sankar Rao, Y.G. Deosthale, and V. Reddy. 1995. Carotene content of some common and less familiar foods of plant origin. Food Chemistry 54:189-193.

Bittenbender, H.C. 1992. Handling and storage of cowpea *Vigna unguiculata* (L.) Walp. as a leaf vegetable. Trop. Agric. (Trinidad) 69:197-199.

Booth, S., R. Bressani, and T. Johns. 1992. Nutrient content of selected indigenous leafy vegetables consumed by the K'ekchi people of Alta Verapaz, Guatemala. Journal of Food Composition and Analysis 5:25-34.

Booth, S., T. Johns, and C.Y. Lopez-Palacios. 1993. Factors influencing the dietary intake of indigenous leafy greens by the K'ekchi peope of Alta Verapaz, Guatemala. Ecol. Food Nutr. 31:127-145.

Brown, W.H. 1951. Useful plants of the Philippines. Tech. Bull. 10(1-9), Phil. Dept. Agric. and Natural Resources, Manila. 1610 pp.

Burkill, H.L. 1935. A dictionary of the economic products of the Malay Peninsula. Crown Agents for the Colonies, London. 2402 pp.

Burns, B. 1988. Wild edible plants in the Greater Noakhali District of Bangladesh. Mennonite Central Committee, Dhaka. 93 pp.

Bye, R.A. 1981. Quelites: ethnoecology of edible greens--past, present, and future. J. Ethnobiol. 1(1):109-123.

Chadwick, C.I., T.A. Lumpkin, and L.R. Elberson. 1993. The botany, uses and production of *Wasabia japonica* (Miq.) (Cruciferae) Matsum. Econ. Bot. 47(2):113-135.

Chatfield, C., and S. Adams. 1937. Proximate composition of fresh vegetables. U.S. Department of Agriculture Circular 146.

Chopra, R.N., R.L. Badluvar, and S. Ghosh. 1965. Poisonous plants of India. 2nd ed. Indian Council of Agricultural Research, New Delhi. 972 pp.

Coursey, D.G. 1968. The edible aroids. World Crops, September 1968:3-8.

De Pee, S. 1996. Food-based approaches for controlling vitamin A deficiency: studies in breastfeeding women in Indonesia. Netherlands Foundation for Scientific Research, Wageningen. 192 pp.

Deutsch, J.A. 1977. Genetic variation of yield and nutritional value in several *Amaranthus* species used as a leafy vegetable. Ph.D. Dissertation. Cornell University, Ithaca, New York. 193 pp.

Diaz-Bolio, J. 1974. La chaya: planta maravillosa, alimenticia y medicinal. Area Maya, Merida, México. 48 pp.

Duke, J.A. 1985. Handbook of medicinal herbs. CRC Press, Boca Raton, Florida. 677 pp.

_____. 1992. Handbook of edible weeds. CRC Press, Boca Raton, Florida.

Edie, H.H., and B.W.C. Ho. 1969. *Ipomoea aquatica* as a vegetable crop in Hong Kong. Econ. Bot. 23(1):32-36.

Enyi, B.A.C. 1965. Effect of age of seedling, height and frequency of cutting on growth and yield of African spinach (*Amaranthus oleraceus*). Nigerian Agr. Jour.

155

2(1):35-38.

Facciola, S. 1990. Cornucopia: a source book of edible plants. Kampong Publications, Vista, California. 678 pp.

Fajardo, P.S. 1952. Pechay growing. Phil. Agric. 36:218-224.

FAO. 1994. Food composition data. Food, Nutrition and Agriculture 12:1-41.

Food Policy and Food Science Service, Nutrition Division, FAO. 1970. Amino acid content of foods and biological data on proteins. FAO Nutritional Studies No. 24. FAO, Rome. 285 pp.

Gilbert, J.C., D.C. McGuire, J.E. Tanaka, and C.F. Poole. 1961. Vegetable breeding in Hawaii. Proc. Trop. Reg. Amer. Soc. Hort. Sci. 5:21-25.

Godfrey-Sam-Aggrey, W., and B.V. Williams. 1972. Upland soils of Sierra Leone for selected vegetable crops. World Crops 24:30-34.

Goode, P.M. 1989. Edible plants of Uganda: the value of wild and cultivated plants as food. FAO, Rome. 146 pp.

Gooding, E.G.B., and A.G. Garcia. 1963. Growing vegetables in Colombia. Proc. Trop. Reg. Amer. Soc. Hort. Sci. 7:37-40.

Greensill, T.M. 1956. The application of commercial methods of vegetable growing in the eastern region of Nigeria. Trop. Agr. 33:18-34.

Grubben, G.J.H. 1976. The cultivation of amaranth as a tropical leaf vegetable. Comm. 67. Royal Tropical Institute, Amsterdam. 207 pp.

_____. 1977. Tropical vegetables and their genetic resources. International Board for Plant Genetic Resources, Rome. 197 pp.

Gupta, K., and D.S. Wagle. 1988. Nutritional and antinutritional factors of green leafy vegetables. J. Agric. Food. Chem. 36:472-474.

Harlan, J.R., and J.M.J. de Wet. 1965. Some thoughts about weeds. Econ. Bot. 19(1):16-24.

Henderson, C.P., and I.R. Hancock. 1988. A guide to the useful plants of Solomon Islands. Ministry of Agriculture and Lands, Honiara. 481 pp. (Includes a unique discussion of nine edible fern species.)

Herklots, G.A.C. 1947. Vegetable cultivation in Hong Kong. The South China Morning Post, Ltd., Hong Kong. 208 pp.

_____. 1972. Vegetables in South-east Asia. Hafner Press, New York. 525 pp.

Hodnett, G.E., and J.S. Campbell. 1963. Effect of spacing on yield of cabbage and lettuce in Trinidad. Trop. Agr. 40:103-108.

Hurtado Fuertes, C., and B. Balbin Ordaya. 1986. Domesticación de nuevas plantas herbáceas para integrarlas a la alimentación latinoamericana. Universidad San Martín de Porres, Lima. 93 pp. (A unique commentary on traditional uses of leaves and recipes of South America.)

Igile, G.O., W. Oleszek, S. Burda, and M. Jurzysta. 1995. Nutritional assessment of *Vernonia amygdalina* leaves in growing mice. J. Agric. Food Chem. 43:2162-2166.

Jacquat, C. 1990. Plants from the markets of Thailand. Duang Kamol, Bangkok. 251 pp. (Exceptionally artistic photographs.)

Jardin, C. 1967. List of foods used in Africa. FAO, Rome. 320 pp.

Joseph, S., and K.V. Peter. 1985. Curry leaf (*Murraya koenigii*), perennial, nutritious, leafy vegetable. Econ. Bot. 39(1):68-73.

Kailasapathy, K., and T. Koneshan. 1986. Effect of wilting on the ascorbate content of selected fresh green leafy vegetables consumed in Sri Lanka. J. Agric. Food Chem. 34:259-261.

Kennedy, D. 1993. Field manual for small-scale leaf concentrate programs. Leaf for Life, Big Hill, Kentucky. 192 pp.

Kingsbury, J.M. 1964. Poisonous plants of the United States and Canada. Prentice-Hall, Inc., Englewood Cliffs, New Jersey. 626 pp.

Knott, J.E. 1962. Handbook for vegetable growers. John Wiley & Sons, New York.

_____, and J.R. Deanon, Jr., eds. 1967. Vegetable production in Southeast Asia. Univ. of Philippines Press, Laguna, Philippines. 406 pp.

Kuhnlein, H.V., and O. Receveur. 1996. Dietary change and traditional food systems of indigenous peoples. Annual Review of Nutrition 16:417-442.

Kunkel, G. 1984. Plants for human consumption: an annotated checklist of the edible phanerogams and ferns. Koeltz, Koenigstein. 393 pp. (The serious student with positive botanical identification may check if edibility has been reported.)

Lancaster, P.A., and J.E. Brooks. 1983. Cassava leaves as human food. Econ. Bot. 37(3):331-348.

Laungaroon, S., and P.A. Abella. 1966. Effects of distance of planting on growth and yield of cabbage at the Central Luzon State University. Scient. Jour. 1(1):15-19.

Lazan, H., Z.M. Ali, A. Mohd., and F. Nahar. 1987. Water stress and quality decline during storage of tropical leafy vegetables. Journal of Food Science 52(5):1286-1288.

Leon, J. 1968. Fundamentos botánicos de los cultivos tropicales. Instituto Interamericano de Ciencias Agrícolas de la OEA, San José, Costa Rica. 487 pp.

Levi-Strauus, C. 1952. The use of wild plants in tropical South America. Econ. Bot. 6:252-270.

Lindquist, K. 1960. On the origin of cultivated lettuce. Hereditas 46:319-350.

Lorenz, O.A., and D.N. Maynard. 1980. Knott's handbook for vegetable growers. 2d ed. John Wiley & Sons, New York. 390 pp.

Lugod, G.C. 1970. Wild plants used as vegetables. In Knott, J.E., and J.R. Deanon, Jr., eds. Vegetable production in Southeast Asia. Univ. of Philippines Press, Laguna, Philippines, pp. 342-347.

Mabberley, D.J. 1987. The plant-book: a portable dictionary of the higher plants. Cambridge University Press, Cambridge. 707 pp.

Mapes, C., F. Basurto, and R. Bye. 1997. Ethnobotany of quintonil: knowledge, use and management of edible greens *Amaranthus* spp. (Amaranthaceae) in the Sierra Norte de Puebla, México. Econ. Bot. 51(3):293-306.

Meitzner, L.S., and M.L. Price. 1996. Amaranth to zai holes: ideas for growing food under difficult conditions. ECHO, North Fort Myers, Florida. 404 pp.

Mercadante, A.Z., and D.B. Rodriquez-Amaya. 1991. Carotenoid composition of a leafy vegetable in relation to some agricultural variables. J. Agric. Food Chem. 39:1094-1097.

Mondonedo, J.R. 1969. Some sources of unusual vegetable foods. Proc. Trop. Reg. Amer. Soc. Hort. Sci. 13:88-90.

Moreno-Payuno, E. 1959. The oxalic acid content of some Philippine food plants. Philippine J. Sci. 88(2):221-224.

Morgan, C.N. 1962. Summer lettuce growing is highly specialized. Queensland Agric. J. 88:554-556.

Mortensen, E., and E.T. Bullard. 1964. Handbook of tropical and subtropical horticulture. U.S. Department of State, Washington, D.C. 260 pp.

Morton, J.F. 1962. Spanish needles (*Bidens pilosa* L.) as a wild food resource. Econ. Bot. 16(3):173-179.

_____. 1967. The balsam pear, an edible, medicinal, and toxic plant. Econ. Bot. 21(1):57-68.

_____. 1968. Tropical fruit tree and other exotic foliage as human food. Proc. Florida State Hort. Soc. 81:318-329.

_____. 1972. Cocoyams (*Xanthosoma caracus, X. nigrum*), ancient root- and leaf-vegetables growing in economic importance. Proc. Fla. Sta. Hort. Soc. 85:85-94.

_____. 1975. Cattails (*Typha* spp.)--weed problem or potential crop? Econ. Bot. 29(1):7-29.

_____. 1987. Fruits of warm climates. Morton, Miami. 505 pp.

_____. 1991. The horseradish tree, *Moringa pterygosperma* (Moringaceae)--a boon to arid lands? Econ. Bot. 45(3):318-333.

_____. 1994. Pito (*Erythrina berteroana*) and chipilin (*Crotalaria longirostrata*), (Fabaceae), two soporific vegetables of Central America. Econ. Bot. 48(2):130-138.

_____. 1994. Lantana, or red sage (*Lantana camara* L. [Verbenaceae]), notorious weed and popular garden flower; some cases of poisoning in Florida. Econ. Bot. 48(3):259-270.

_____. 1995. Plants poisonous to people in Florida and other warm areas. Hallmark Press, Miami. 176 pp.

Mpuchane, S., and B.A. Gashe. 1995. Prevalence of coliforms in traditionally dried leafy vegetables sold in open markets and food stores in Gaborone, Botswana. Journal of Food Protection 59(1):28-30.

Mullison, E.G., and W.R. Mullison. 1949. Vegetable varieties for the tropics. Proc. Amer. Soc. Hort. Sci. 54:452-458.

Munier, P. 1967. Le chou-palmita (palm cabbage). Fruits 22(1):42-43.

Nakagawa, Y., and R.R. Romanowski. 1967. A guide to chemical weed control in vegetable crops in Hawaii. Circ. Cooper. Ext. Serv., Univ. of Hawaii. 17 pp.

Nicklow, C.W., P.H. Comas-Haezebrouck, and W.A. Feder. 1983. Influence of varying soil lead levels on lead uptake of leafy and root vegetables. J. Amer. Soc. Hort. Sci. 108(2):193-195.

Nwufo, M.I. 1994. Effects of water stress on the post-harvest quality of two leafy vegetables, *Telfairia occidentalis* and *Pterocarpus soyauxii*, during storage. J. Sci. Food Agric. 64:265-269.

Oakes, A.J., and J.O. Butcher. 1962. Poisonous and injurious plants of the U.S. Virgin Islands. Misc. Publ. No. 882. Agricultural Research Service, U.S. Department of Agriculture.

Ochse, J.J., and R.C. Bakhuizen van den Brink. 1931. Vegetables of the Dutch East Indies. Dept. of Agriculture, Industry and Commerce of the Netherlands. East Indies, Buitenzorg. 1004 pp.

Oke, O.L. 1965. Chemical studies of some Nigerian vegetables. Exp. Agr. 10(1-2):125-129.

_____. 1966. Chemical studies on the more commonly used leaf vegetables in Nigeria. Jour. W. Afr. Sc. Assoc. 11(1-2):42-48.

Okeibuno Badifu, G.I. 1991. Effect of long-term storage of processed Nigeria-grown edible leafy green vegetables on vitamin C content. J. Agric. Food Chem. 39:538-541.

Okigbo, B. 1986. Broadening the food base in Africa: traditional food plants. Food Nutr. 1(12):4-17.

Okoli, B.E., and C.M. Mgbeogu. 1983. Fluted pumpkin, *Telfairia occidentalis*: West African vegetable crop. Econ. Bot. 37(2):145-149.

Oomen, H.A.P.C. 1964. Vegetable greens, a tropical undevelopment. Chron. Horticult. 4(1):3-5.

_____, and G.J.H. Grubben. 1977. Tropical leaf vegetables in human nutrition. Comm. 69. Royal Tropical Institute, Amsterdam. 136 pp.

Pace, R.D., T.E. Sibiya, B.R. Phills, and G.G. Dull. 1985. Ca, Fe and Zn content of 'Jewel' sweet potato greens as affected by harvesting practices. Journal of Food Science 50:940-941.

Pal, M., and T.N. Khoshoo. 1971. Evolution and improvement of cultivated

amaranths. Jour. Heredity 63:78-82.

Paterson, A.S. 1967. Lettuce observations at Vudal Agricultural College, New Britain, Papua and New Guinea. Agr. Jour. 19(3):138-139.

Peters, C.R., E.M. O'Brian, and R.B. Drummond. 1992. Edible wild plants of Sub-Saharan Africa: an annotated checklist, emphasizing the woodland and savanna floras of Eastern and Southern Africa, including the plants utilized for food by chimpanzees and baboons. Royal Botanic Gardens, Kew. 239 pp.

Poole, C.F. 1959. New sweet potato and lettuce varieties developed by HAES. Hawaii Farm Sc. 8:1-2.

Porter, R.H. 1961. Maté--South American or Paraguay tea. Econ Bot. 4(1):37-51.

Prakash, D., P. Nath, and M. Pal. 1995. Composition and variation in vitamin C, carotenoids, protein, nitrate and oxalate contents in *Celosia* leaves. Plant Foods for Human Nutrition 47:221-226.

Prakash, V. 1990. Leafy spices. CRC Press, Boca Raton, Florida. 114 pp.

Purseglove, J.W. 1968. Tropical crops. Dicotyledons, Vols. I and II. Longman Group, London. 719 pp.

_____. 1972. Tropical crops. Monocotyledons, Vols. I and II. Longman Group, London. 607 pp.

Ram, J., and N. Glover. 1994. Pacific Islands Farm Manual: Tropical Perennial Vegetable Leaflets #1-11. ADAP Project, Honolulu. (Available from ECHO.)

Ramachandran, C., K.V. Peter, and P.K. Gopalakrishnan. 1980. Drumstick (*Moringa oleifera*): a multipurpose Indian vegetable. Econ. Bot. 34(3):276-283.

Rangarajan, A. 1997. Personal communication on summary of forthcoming Ph.D. dissertation, Michigan State University.

Rogers, D.J., and M. Milner. 1963. Amino acid profile of manioc leaf protein in relation to nutritive value. Econ. Bot. 17(3):211-216.

Ryder, E.J. 1979. Leafy salad vegetables. AVI, Westport, Connecticut. 266 pp.

Samaka Service Center. 1962. The Samaka guide. Manila, Philippines. 64 pp.

Samson, J.A. 1972. Tropical spinach from *Amaranthus*, *Ipomoea*, and *Xanthosoma*. Surinaamse Landbouw 20(1):15-21.

Schippers, R. and L. Budd, eds. 1997. Workshop on African indigenous vegetables held in Limbe, Cameroon, January 13-18, 1997. IPGRI, Nairobi and NRI, Kent, UK. 154 pp.

Schmidt, D.R. 1971. Yield and chemical components of tropical leafy vegetable species as influenced by environmental variables and plant nutrition. Ph.D. Dissertation. Cornell University, Ithaca, New York. 223 pp.

Simwambanu, M.S.C., T.U. Ferguson, and D.S.O. Osiru. 1992. The effects of time to first shoot removal on leaf vegetable quality in cassava (*Manihot esculenta* Crantz). J. Sci. Food Agric. 60:319-325.

Singh, H.B., and R.K. Arora. 1978. Wild edible plants of India. Indian Council of Agricultural Research, New Delhi. 89 pp.

Terra, G.J.A. 1964. The significance of leaf vegetables, especially of cassava, in tropical nutrition. Trop. Geogr. Medicine 16(2):97-108.

_____. 1966. Tropical vegetables: vegetable growing in the tropics and subtropics, especially of indigenous vegetables. Comm. 54e. Dept. Agric. Research Royal Tropical Institute, Amsterdam, Holland.

Tindall, H.D. 1965. Fruits and vegetables in West Africa. FAO, Rome. 259 pp.

Van Epenhuijsen, C.W. 1974. Growing native vegetables in Nigeria. FAO, Rome. 113 pp.

Van Eynatlen, C.L.M. 1969. Observations on protein of tropical leafy vegetables and some other food stuffs from West Africa. Nederf, Amsterdam. 11 pp.

Watt, J.M., and M.G. Breyer-Brandwijk. 1962. The medicinal and poisonous plants of southern and eastern Africa. E & S Livingstone, Edinburgh. 1457 pp.

Wesche-Ebeling, P., R. Maiti, G. García-Díaz, D.I. González, and F. Sosa-Alvarado. 1995. Contributions to the botany and nutritional value of some wild *Amaranthus* species (Amaranthaceae) of Nuevo León, México. Econ. Bot. 49(4):423-430.

West, C.E., and E.J. Poortvliet. 1993. The carotenoid content of foods with special reference to developing countries. VITAL, Arlington, Virginia. 210 pp.

Wester, P.J. 1921. The food plants of the Philippines. Philippine Agricultural Review 14(3):384 ff.

Whitaker, T.W. 1969. Salads for everyone--a look at the lettuce plant. Econ. Bot. 23(3):261-264.

Whitner, L.D., F.A.I. Bowers, and M. Takahashi. 1939. Taro varieties in Hawaii. Bull. 84, Hawaii Agr. Exp. Sta. 86 pp.

Willaman, J.J. 1961. Alkaloid-bearing plants and their contained alkaloids. Agric. Res. Service, U.S. Dept. Agric. Technical Bulletin No. 1234 287 pp.

Wilson, F.D., and M.Y. Menzel. 1964. Kenaf (*Hibiscus cannabinus*), roselle (*Hibiscus sabdariffa*). Econ. Bot. 18(1):80-91.

Winters, H.F. 1963. Ceylon spinach (*Basella rubra*). Econ. Bot. 17(3):195-199.

Wolff, X.Y., and R.R. Coltman. 1990. Productivity of eight leafy vegetable crops grown under shade in Hawaii. J. Amer. Soc. Hort. Sci. 115:182-188.

Yadav, S.K., and S. Sehgal. 1995. Effect of home processing on ascorbic acid and beta-carotene content of spinach (*Spinacia oleracea*) and amaranth (*Amaranthus tricolor*) leaves. Plant Foods for Human Nutrition 47:125-131.

Yamaguchi, M. 1983. World Vegetables. AVI, Westport, Connecticut. 415 pp.

Appendix: Tropical Plants Reported to Have Edible Leaves

Warning: Being listed in this table does not indicate that all leaves of these species are safe to eat. Some must be detoxified with special treatments, while others may be unappetizing regardless of preparation. Refer to Chapter 9 for further precautions when investigating the edible properties of unfamiliar species.

Species	Source	Type
ACANTHACEAE		
Acanthus montanus T. And.	Congo	Shrub
Afromendoncie gilgiana Lind.	Congo	Herb
Asystasia gangetica T. And.	Tropical Africa	Herb
A. schimperi T. And.	Tropical Africa	Herb
A. vogeliana Benth.	Tropical Africa	Herb
Barleria opaca Nees.	Tropical Africa	Shrub
B. talbotii S. Moore	Africa	Shrub
Brillantaisia alata Anders.	Congo	Herb
Climacanthus nutans	Vietnam	Shrub
Dicliptera chinensis Juss.	Southeast Asia	Herb
D. papuana Warb.	New Guinea	Herb
D. umbellata Juss.	Africa	Herb
Dipteracanthus longifolia Hochs.	Pantropical	Herb
Eremomastax polysperma (Benth.) Dandy	Central Africa	Shrub
Hygrophila auriculata Heyne	Africa	Herb
H. quadrivalvis Nees.	Tropical Asia	Herb
H. salicifolia Nees.	India	Herb
H. serpyllum T. And.	India	Herb
H. thonneri de Wild	Congo	Herb
R. Br.	Africa	Herb
Justicia flava Vahl.	Indian coast	Herb
J. galeopsis T. And.	Southeast Asia	Herb
J. gendarussa L.	Tropical Asia	Herb
J. glabra Koen. ex Roxb.	Africa	Herb
J. insularis T. And.	West Africa	Herb
J. japonica	India, Japan	Herb
J. melampyrum S. Moore	West Africa	Herb
J. metammensis Oliv.	South Africa	Herb
J. pectoralis Jacq.	Mexico	Herb
J. procumbens L,	India	Herb
J. quinqueangularis Koen. ex Roxb.	India	Herb
J. rostellaria Lindau	Mexico	Herb
J. schimperi Hochst.	West Africa	Herb
J. striata Klotzsch	Africa	Shrub
Lankesteria barteri Hook. f.	Congo	Herb
Nelsonia brunelloides O.K.	Congo	Herb
Pseuderanthemum bicolor Radlk.	Philippines	Shrub
P. racemosum Radlk.	Southeast Asia	Shrub
P. reticulatum Radlk.	Philippines	Shrub
P. tunicatum Milne-Redh.	Gabon	Shrub
Rhinacanthus calcaratus Nees.	Burma	Herb
R. nasutus Kurz.	Southeast Asia	Herb
Rungia grandis T. And.	Tropical Africa	Herb
R. klossii S. Moore	Pantropical	Herb
Ktze.	Southeast Asia	Herb
Thunbergia alata L.	Caribbean	Vine
T. bogoriensis de Wilc.	Congo	Vine
T. grandiflora Roxb.	Burmea, India	Vine
T. lancifolia T. And.	Africa	Vine
T. oblongifolia Olr.	Africa	Vine
AIZOACEAE		
Aizoon canariense L.	Africa	Herb
Anicosa pugionformis N.E. Br.	South Africa	Herb
Aptenia cordifolia (L.) Schwantes	South Africa	Herb
Camellia sinensis L. (Kuntze)	Southeast Asia	Shrub
Cryophytumaitonis (Jacq.) N.E. Br.	South Africa	Herb
C. crystallinum (L.) N.E. Br.	Pansubtropical	Herb
Ginus lotoides Loefl.	Africa	Herb
Gisekia pharnaceoides L.	India, Africa	Herb
Glinus lotoides Loefl.	India	Herb
G. oppositifolius	Pantropical	Herb
Lithops hookeri (A. Berger) Schwantes	South Africa	Herb
Mesembryanthemum angulatum Thunb.	Africa	Herb
M. aequilaterale Haw.	Southwest Africa, Australia	Herb

M. crystallinum L.	Pansubtropical	Herb
Mollugo nudicaulis Lam.	Congo	Herb
M. oppositifolia L.	Southeast Asia	Herb
M. pentaphylla L.	Tropical Asia	Herb
Opophytum forskallii	Egypt, Sudan	Herb
Sesuvium portulacastrum L.	Pantropical	Herb
S. Repens	Tropical Asia	Herb
Tetragonia decumbens Mill.	Southern Africa	Herb
T. tetragonoides (Pall.) O. Kuntze Z.	New Zealand	Herb
T. fruticosa L.	Southern Africa	Herb
T. portulacastrum L.	Tropical Asia, Africa	Herb
Zaleya pentandra	Tropical Asia, Africa	Herb

ALISMATACEAE

Sagittaria sagittifolia L.	Eastern Asia	Herb
S. sinensis Sims.	China	Herb

AMARANTHACEAE

Achyranthes aspera L.	Pantropical	Herb
A. bidentata Blume	Tropical Asia	Herb
A. rubrofusca Wight	Tropical Asia	Herb
Acnida cuspidata Bert.	America	Herb
Aerva javanica (Burm. f.) Juss. ex Schult.	Subtropical Africa, India	Herb
A. lanata (L.) Juss. ex Schult.	Pantropical	Herb
A. tomentosa Forsk.	Africa	Herb
Allmania albida R. Br.	Southeast Asia	Herb
A. nodiflora R. Br.	Sri Lanka, Philippines	Herb
Alternanthera amoena (Lem.) Voss.	Pantropical	Herb
A. maritima St. Hill	Tropical America, West Africa	Herb
A. nodiflora R. Br.		Herb
A. triandra Lam.	Tropical America, West Africa	Herb
A. versicolor L.	Tropical America, West Africa	Herb
Amaranthus blitum L.	Worldwide	Herb
A. caudatus L.	South America	Herb
A. chlorostachys Miq.	Worldwide	Herb
A. cruentus L.	Pantropical	Herb
A. dubius Mart. et Thell	South America	Herb
A. frumentaceus Buch.	India, Sri Lanka	Herb
A. gracilis Desf.	Worldwide	Herb
A. hybridus L. sp. cruentus (L.) Thell.	Congo	Herb
A. hybridus L. sp. hybridus	East Africa, Tropical America	Herb
A. hypochondriacus	Mexico	Herb
A. lividus L.	Mediterranean	Herb
A. mangostanus Justen	China	Herb
A. mantegazzianus Passer	Argentina	Herb
A. nodiflora	West Africa	Herb
A. oleraceus L.		Herb
A. paniculatus L.	Pantropical	Herb
A. patulus Bertol.		Herb
A. philoxeroides Griesb.	Indonesia	Herb
A. polygamus L.	India	Herb
A. polygonoides L	India, Sri Lanka	Herb
A. sessilia R. Br.	Pantropical	Herb
A. spinosus L.	Pantropical	Herb
A. thunbergii Miq.	Tropical Africa	Herb
A. triandra Lam.	Pantropical	Herb
A. tricolor L.	China	Herb
A. versicolor L.	Pantropical	Herb
A. viridis L.	Southeast Asia, Africa	Herb
Celosia argentea L.	India	Herb
C. bonnivairii Schinz.	Tropical Africa	Herb
C. cristata L.	Worldwide	Herb
C. laxa Schum. et Thonn.	West Africa	Herb
C. Leptostachye Benth	Tropical Africa	Herb
C. trigyna L.	Tropical Africa	Herb
Cyathula prostrata Bl.	Congo	Herb
Deeringia amaranthoides Bantji (Lam.) Merr.	Southeast Asia	Shrub
Digera arvensis Forsk.	India, Africa	Herb
Gomphrena globosa L.	Pantropical	Herb
Mengea tenuifolia Miq.	India	Herb
Pandiaka heudelotii (Moq.) Hook. f.	Cameroon	Herb
Philoxarus vermicularis R. Br.	Pantropical	Herb
Sericostachys scandens Gilq. et Lepr.	Congo	Herb
Telanthera polygonoides Miq.	South Pacific	Herb

AMARYLLIDACEAE

Agave cantata Roxb.	Indonesia	Herb
A. sisalana Perr.	Pantropical	Herb
Cyrtanthus bicolor R. A. Dyer	Africa	Herb
Pancratium trianthum Herb.	West Africa	Herb

AMPELIDACEAE

Vitis quadrangularis Wall	India	Vine

ANACARDIACEAE

Anacardium occidentale L.	Pantropical	Tree
Bouea macrophylla Griff.	Southeast Asia	Tree
B. oppositifolia Misn.	Thailand	Tree
Dracontomelon dao (Blanco) Merr.	Malaysia to Fiji	Tree
D. manqiferum	Tropical Asia	Tree

Species	Distribution	Habit
Gluta velutina Blume	Malaysia	Tree
Lannea acida A. Rich	West Africa	Shrub
L. grandis Engl.	Tropical Asia	Tree
L. microcarpa Engl. et K. Krause	West Africa	Tree
L. oieosa A. Chev.	Tropical Africa	Tree
Mangifera caesia Jack.	Indonesia	Tree
M. indica L.	Pantropical	Tree
Pseudospondias mierocarpum Engl.	Congo	Tree
Rhus javanica Thunb.	Subtropical Asia	Shrub
Rhus taitensis Guill.	Pacific islands	Shrub
Semecarpus cassuvium Roxb.	Indonesia	Tree
Spondias cytherea Sonn.	India	Tree
Spondias dulcis Forst.	Pantropical	Tree
S. mombin L.	Pantropical	Tree
S. pinnata Kurz.	Philippines	Tree
S. purpurea L.	Pantropical	Tree
ANNONACEAE		
Annona muricata L.	Tropical America	Tree
Cleistopholis patens Engl. et Pzantl.	Africa	Tree
Enneastemon foliosus (Engl. et Diels) Robyns et Chesq.	Tropical Africa	Tree
APOCYNACEAE		
Agonosma marginata G. Don.	Thailand	Vine
Alafia lucida Stapf.	Congo	Vine
Catharanthus roseus (L.) G. Don.	Congo	Herb
Cerbera manghas L.	Pantropical,	Tree
Chilocarpus eantleyi King.	Southeast Asia	Vine
C. denudatus Bl.	Indonesia	Herb
Fernaldia pandurata R. E. Woodson	America	Herb
Isonema smeathmannii Roem et Schult.	West Africa	Shrub
Lochnera pusilla K. Shum.	India	Herb
L. rosea L. f.	India	Herb
Pyenobotrya nitida Benth.	Congo	Herb
Vallaris heynii Spreng.	Thailand	Shrub
Wrightia tinctoria	India	Shrub
AQUIFOLIACEAE		
Ilex integra Thunb.	Taiwan	Shrub
Ilex paraguayensis St Hil.	South America	Shrub
I. vomitoria Ait.	South America	Shrub
ARACEAE		
Aglaonema pictum Kunth	Malaysia, Southeast Asia	Herb
Alocasia indica Schott	East Asia	Herb
A. campanulatus (Roxb.) ex Decne.	Indonesia, India	Herb
A. macrorrhiza Schott	Sri Lanka	Herb
Amorphophalluscampanulatus (Roxb.) Blume ex Decne.	Philippines, Indonesia	Herb
A. rivieri var. konjac Engl.	China	Herb
A. schweinfurthii N. E. Br.	Sudan	Herb
A. variabilis Blume	Indonesia, Philippines	Herb
Anadendrum montanum Schott	Southwest Asia	Herb
Arisaema speciosum Mart.	Pantropical	Herb
Caladium bicolor Vent.	Pantropical	Herb
Colocasia esculenta (L.)	Southeast Asia	Herb
C. gigantea Hook. f.	India	Herb
Cyrtosperma chamissonis	Southeast Asia	Herb
C. sp.	South Pacific	Herb
Lasia spinosa Thw.	Southeast Asia	Aquat.
Pistia stratiotes L.	Pantropical, Sudan, China	Aquat.
Remusatis moluccana Blume	Malaysia, Indonesia	Herb
R. vivipara Schott	Burma, India	Herb
Rhaphidophora lobbii Hassk	Malaysia	Vine
Schismatoglottis calyptrata Zoll. et Mor.	Southeast Asia	Herb
Spathiphyllum communatum Schott	Southeast Asia	Herb
S. phrynifolium Schott	Central America	Herb
Stylochiton hypogeum Lepr.	Africa	Herb
S. warneckii Engl.	Tropical Africa	Herb
Typhonium bulbiferum Dalz.	India	Herb
T. divaricatum Decne.	Tropical Asia, Pacific islands	Herb
T. trilobatum Schott	India, Sri Lanka	Herb
Xanthosoma albertii	Pantropical	Herb
X. brasiliense Engl.	Brazil	Herb
X. caraca Koch. et Bouche	Venezuela	Herb
X. jacquini Schott	South, Central America	Herb
X. mafaffa Schott	South, Central America	Herb
X. violaceum Schott	Tropical America	Herb
Zantedeschia aethiopica Spreng.	Africa	Herb
ARALIACEAE		
Aralia cordata Thumb.	Japan	Herb
Boerlagiodendron palmatum Harms.	Indonesia	Shrub
Nothopanax	Indonesia	Shrub

Species	Location	Growth form
fruticosum Miq.		
N. pinnatum Miq.	Indonesia	Shrub
N. scutellarium Merr.	Indonesia	Shrub
Schefflera aromatica Harms.	Southeast Asia	Shrub
Trevesia cheirantha Ridl.	Malay Peninsula	Shrub
T. sundaica Miq.	Dutch Indies	Shrub
ASCLEPIADACEAE		
Asclepias affinis de Wild.	Africa	Herb
Boucerosia aucheriana Decne	India	Vine
Caralluma dalsiclii N.E. Brown	West Africa	Herb
C. europea N.E. Brown	North Africa	Herb
C. knobelii Phill.	South Africa	Herb
C. moureti A. Chev.	Africa	Herb
Ceropegia papillata N.E. Brown	Africa	Vine
C. stenantha K. Schum	Africa	Vine
Chlorocoda whitei Hook	Congo	Vine
Cynanchum ovalifolium Wight.	Indonesia	Herb
C. pauciflorum R. Br.	Sri Lanka	Vine
C. schistoglossum Schlecht.	Madagascar	Vine
C. tetrapterum (lurcz.)	East Africa	Vine
C. virens Steud	South Africa	Vine
Desdichium spp.	Polynesia	Vine
Dregia volubilis Benth	Sri Lanka	Herb
Duvalia polita N. E. Brown	South Africa	Herb
Ectadiopsis oblongifolia Schlecht.	Africa	Shrub
Finlaysonia maritima Backer	Indonesia	Vine
F. obovata Wall.	Southeast Asia	Vine
Grossonema ooveanum Decne.	Africa	Herb
G. varians Benth.	India	Herb
Gomphocarpus albens Decne	Africa	Herb
Gymnema lactiferum R. Br.	Sri Lanka	Herb
G. sylvestre R. Br	Congo	Vine
G. syringifolium Boerl.	Malaysia	Vine
Holostemma annularis K. Schum.	India	Vine
Leptadenia hastata Decne.	Africa	Vine
L. lancifolia Decne.	West Africa	Shrub
L. pyrotechnica Decne.	Africa, India	Vine
L. reticulata Wight et Arn.	India	Vine
Oxystelma esculentum R. Br.	India, Sri Lanka	Herb
Pentarrhinum insipidum E. Mey.	South Africa	Vine
Pergularia africana N. E. Br.	Congo	Herb
P. daemia Chiov.	India	Herb
P. extensa N.E. Br.	Tropical Africa	Herb
Periploca aphylla Decne	Africa	Vine
Rymnena sylvestre R. Br.	Tropical Africa	Vine
Sarcostemna viminale R. Br.	Africa	Shrub
Secamone sp.	Africa	Herb
Stapelia kwebensis N.E. Br.	South Africa	Herb
Telosma cordata Merr.	Southeast Asia	Vine
T. minor Craib.	Thailand	Vine
Trichocaulon pillansii N. E. Br.	South Africa	Herb
Tylophora silvatica Decne	Central Africa	Herb
Xysmolobium umbellatum Ait.	South Africa	Herb
X. undulatum (L.) Ait.	South Africa	Herb
BALSAMINACEAE		
Impatiens balsamina L.	Pantropical	Herb
I. flaccida Arn.	Sri Lanka	Herb
I. giorgii Wild.	Zaire	Herb
BARRINGTONIACEAE		
Barringtonia insignia Miq.	Indonesia	Tree
B. racemosa Roxb.	Pacific islands	Tree
B. spicata Blume	Malaysia, Indonesia	Tree
BASELLACEAE		
Anredera scandens	Central America	Vine
Basella alba L.	Southeast Asia	Herb
B. rubra L.	Southeast Asia	Herb
Ullcus tuberosus Caldas	South America	Herb
BATIDACEAE		
Batis maritima L.	Pantropical	Herb
BEGONIACEAE		
Begonia hirtella Link.	Gabon	Herb
B. kotoensis Hay.	Taiwan	Herb
B. malabarica Lam.	India	Herb
B. poggei Warb.	Congo	Herb
B. siriculata	Gabon	Herb
B. tuberosa Lan.	Southeas Asia	Herb
BIGNONIACEAE		
Adenocalymna alliaceum	South America	Herb
Antidesma bunius Spreng.	Southeast Asia	Tree
Dolichandrone stipulata Benth. et Hook. f.	Burma	Tree
Oroxylum indicum Vewt.	Southeast Asia	Tree
Radermachera fimbriata K.Sch. Thailand	Southeast Asia	Tree

BIXACEAE

Species	Origin	Form
Cochlospermum tinctorium A. Rich	Africa	Tree

BOMBACACEAE

Species	Origin	Form
Adansonia digitata L.	Tropical Africa	Tree
A. grandieri Baill.	Madagascar	Tree
A. madagascariensis Baill.	Madagascar	Tree
A. Za Baill.	Madagascar	Tree
Bombax buonopozense P. Beauv.	Tropical Africa	Tree
B. malabarica D.C.	Indonesia	Tree
B. unguicarpum Ulbr.	Tropical America	Tree
Ceiba caribaea D.C.	Caribbean	Tree
C. guineensis A. Chev.	Tropical Africa	Tree
C. pentandra Gaertn.	Pantropical	Tree
C. thonningii A. Chev.	Tropical Africa	Tree
Durio zibethinus Murr.	Southeast Asia	Tree
Pachira aquatica Aublet	Tropical America	Tree
Pochota glabra (Pasq.) Bullock	Equatorial Africa	Tree

BORAGINACEAE

Anchusa sp.	North Africa	Shrub
Ansinckia lycopsioides Lehm.	California	Herb
Borago officinalis L.	North Africa	Herb
Cordia dichotoma Forst. f.	Tropical East Hem.	Tree
C. francisci Ten.	Near East	Tree
C. myxa L.	Near East	Tree
C. obliqua Willd	Pantropical	Tree
C. olitoria Blanco	Near East	Tree
Echium sp.	North Africa	Tree
Ehretia microphylla Lam.	Philippines	Shrub
E. orbicularis Hutch et Bruce	Africa	Herb
Symphytum officinals L.	Tropical Asia	Tree
Tournefortia argentea L.	Africa	
Trichodesma ceylanicum R. Br.		

BROMELIACEAE

Bromelia karatas L.	Tropical America	Herb
B. pinguin L.	Caribbean	Herb

BURSERACEAE

Bursera javanica Baill.	Indonesia	Tree
B. simaruba Sarg.	West Indies	Tree
Commiphora sulcata Chiov.	Africa	Herb
Protium javanieum Burm. f.	Indonesia	Tree

BUTOMACEAE

Species	Origin	Form
Limnocharis flava (L) Buch.	Tropical America	Aquat.
L. loanigensis	Africa	Aquat.

CACABOMACEAE

Brasenia schreberi J.F. Gmel.	Africa	Herb

CACTACEAE

Species	Origin	Form
Myrtillocactus geometricans Cons.	America	Shrub
Nopalea coccinellifera Solms-Dyck	America	Shrub
Opuntia subulata Engelm.	America	Shrub
Pereskia aculeata Mill.	Tropical Americas	Vine
P. bleo D.C.	Brazil	Vine

CAMPANULACEAE

Centropogon surinamensis Presl.	South America, Africa	Shrub
Lobelia alsinoides Lam.	India	Herb
L. fervens Thumb.	Africa	Herb
L. filiformis Lam.	Africa	Herb
L. pusilla K. Schum.	India	Herb
L. succulenta Blume	Southeast Asia	Herb
L. trigona Roxb.	India, Africa	Herb
Pentaphragma begoniaefolium Wall.	Malaysia, Southeast Asia	Herb
P. ellipticum Poulsem.	Indomalaysia	Herb
P. horsefieldii Airy Shaw.	Indomalaysia	Herb
Spenoclea zeylanica Gaertn	Southeast Asia	Herb
Wahlenbergia androsacea A. D.C.	South Africa	Herb
W. undulata A. D. C.	South Africa	Herb

CAPPARIDACEAE

Boscia angustifolia A. Rich.	Africa	Herb
B. salicifolia Oliv.	Tropical Africa	Shrub
B. senegalensis Lam.	Africa	Tree
Cadaba farinosa	Tropical Africa	Shrub
Capparis corymbosa Lam.	West Africa	Shrub
C. decidua Edgew	Northern Africa	Shrub
C. horrida L.	Tropical Asia	Herb
C. rupestris Sibth.	India	Herb
Cleome ciliata Schum et Thonn.		
C. gynandra L.	Malaysia	Herb
C. hirta Oliver	Africa	Herb
C. icosandra L.	Pantropical	Herb
C. monophylla L.	Africa	Herb
C. rutidosperma AC.	Tropical Africa	Herb
C. speciosa AC.	Mexico	Herb

Species	Distribution	Habit
C. viscosa L.	El Salvador	Herb
Crateva adansonii DS.	Southeast Asia	Tree
C. macrocarpa Kurz	Indochina, Southeast Asia	Shrub
C. nurvala Buch. Ham.	India, Burma	Tree
Clitandra lacourtiana De Wild.	Central Africa	Herb
Euadenia trifoliata Benth. et Hook.	Africa	Shrub
Gynandropsis gynandra (L.) Briq.	Indonesia	Herb
Maerua anggiensis UC.	Tropical Africa	Tree
M. crassifolia Forsk.	Africa	Tree
M. oblongifolia (Forsk.) A. Rich.	North Cameroon	Tree
Polanisia hirta Pax	Congo	Herb
CAPRIFOLIACEAE		
Sambucus javanica Reinw.	Tropical Asia	Shrub
CARDIOPTERICACEAE		
Cardiopteris lobata Wall	India to Indonesia	Vine
C. moluccana Blume	Indonesia	Vine
CARICACEAE		
Carica papaya L.	South America	Tree
CARYOPHYLLACEAE		
Silene agyptiaca L.	Near East	Herb
S. vulgaris (Moench) Gareke	Algeria	Herb
Stellaria aquatica Cyr.	India	Herb
S. media Cyr.	Near East	Herb
Salacia pynaertii de Wild.	Africa	Shrub
Catha edulis Forsk.	Tropical Africa	Shrub
CHENOPODIACEAE		
Arthrocnemum indicum Miq. Del.	India	Herb
A. pachystachyum Bunge	India	Herb
Atriplex arenaria Nutt	Sandy beaches	Herb
A. crassifolia C. A. Mey.	India	Herb
A. halimus L.	Sahara	Herb
A. hortensis L.	Worldwide	Herb
A. repens Roth	India, Sri Lanka	Herb
Beta vulgaris L. var cicla	Temperate Europe	Beet
Boussaingaultia baselloides HBK	Sri Lanka	Herb
Chenopodium album L.	India	Herb
C. amaranticolor Coste et Beyn	Madagascar	Herb
C. ambrosioides L.	Philippines	Herb
C. berlandieri Miq.	Mexico	Herb
C. bonus-henricus L.	Pantemperate	Herb
C. foliosum Aschers.	Pantemperate	Herb
C. giganteum G. Don	Madagascar	Herb
C. glaucum L.	South Africa	Herb
C. murale L.	Subtropical Africa	Herb
C. nuttalliae Saff.	South America	Herb
C. quinoa Willd.	Tropical America	Herb
Dondia linearis Millsp.	Beaches and salt marshes	Herb
Salicornia ambigua Michx.	Beaches and salt marshes	Herb
S. arabica L.	North Africa	Herb
S. bigelonii Torr	Beaches and salt marshes	Herb
Spinacia oleracea L.	Pantropical	Herb
Suaeda maritima Dumont	Pantropical	Herb
S. nudiflora Miq.	India	Herb
Ullucus tuberosus Cald.	Andes	Herb
CLEOMACEAE		
Cleome ciliata Schum. et Thonn.	West Africa	Herb
C. heptaphylla Oliver	Tropical America	Herb
C. hirta Oliver		Herb
C. icosandra L.	Pantropical	Herb
C. monophylla	Tropical Africa	Herb
C. strigosa Oliver		Herb
Gynandropsis gynandra L. Briquet	Africa	Herb
G. speciosa D.C.	Pantropical	Herb
CHLORANTHACEAE		
Chloranthus officinalis	Southeast Asia	Shrub
COMBRETACEAE		
Combretum micranthum G. Don	Gabon	Shrub
C. mooreanum Exell.	West Africa	Vine
C. paniculatum Vent.	West Africa	Vine
C. platyphyllum Hutch. et Dalz.	Africa	Shrub
C. racemosum P. Beauv.	West Africa	Shrub
Guiera senegalensis J. F. Gmel.	Africa	Tree
Lumnitzera racemosa Willd.	Southeast Asia, Polynesia	Tree
Quisqualis indica L.	Southeast Asia	Vine

COMMELINACEAE

Species	Distribution	Habit
Aneilema dregeanum Kunth	Africa	Herb
A. malabaricum Merr.	Southeast Asia	Herb
A. nudiflorum R. Br.	Southeast Asia, Malaysia	Herb
A. spiratum R. Br.	Southeast Asia	Herb
Commelina benghalensis L.	Eastern Hemisphere	Herb
C. claessinsii de Wild.	Pantropical	Herb
C. clavata C. B. Clarke	Congo	Herb
C. collestis Willd.	Tropiocal Asia	Herb
C. diffusa Burm. f.	Mexico	Herb
C. farskalei Vahl	Old World Tropics	Herb
C. latifolia Hochst.	Africa	Herb
C. nudiflora L.	Ethiopia	Herb
C. obliqua Buch. - Ham.	Southeast Asia	Herb
C. paleata Hassk.	Tropical Asia	Herb
C. zambezica D. C.	Malaysia	Herb
Cyanotis cristata Roem. et Schultes	Africa	Herb
C. cristata G. Don	Southeast Asia	Herb
C. nodiflora Kunth	Southeast Asia	Herb
Floscopa schweinfurthii G. G. Cl.	Africa	Herb
Forrestia glabrata Hassk	Guinea Coast	Herb
F. marginata Hassk.	Southeast Asia	Herb
F. mollissima Kds.	Southeast Asia	Herb

COMPOSITAE

Species	Distribution	Habit
Ambrosia maritima L.	Congo	Herb
Artemisia dracunculus L.	Caspian Sea, Siberia	Herb
A. vulgaris L.	Europe, North America	Herb
Aster amellus L.	Near East	Herb
Atractylis gummifera L.	North Africa	Herb
Bidens bipinnata L.	Africa, Asia	Herb
B. chinensis Willd.	Africa, Asia	Herb
B. leucantlla Willd.	Africa, Asia	Herb
B. pilosa L.	Africa, Asia	Herb
Blumea balsamifera D.C.	SW China	Herb
B. chinensis A. D.C.	China	Herb
B. lacera A. D.C.	Old World Tropics	Herb
B. myriacephala D.C.	Indochina	Herb
Carthamus tinctorius L.	Pansubtropical	Herb
Castalis pubescens (Willd) Blume	Pantropical	Aquat.
Centaurea pallescens Del.	North America	Herb
Cichorium endivia L.	Near East	Herb
C. intybus L.	Mediterranean	Herb
Chrysanthemum coronarium L.	Near East, Malaysia	Herb
C. indicum L.	India	Herb
C. segetum L.	Indochina	Herb
Calinsoga parviflora Cav.	Philippines	Herb
Conyza aegyptiaca Ait.	Congo, Sudan	Herb
Cosmos caudatus H.B.K	Madagascar	Herb
C. sulphureus Cav.	Tropical Asia	Herb
Crassocephalum biafrae S. Moore	Pantropical	Herb
C. crepidioides S. Moore	West Africa	Herb
C. rubens S. Moore	West Africa	Herb
C. vitellinum S. Moore	West Africa	Herb
Crepis aspera L.	Near East	Herb
C. reuteriana Boiss, et Heldr.	Near East	Herb
Cymboseris palestinae Boiss.	Near East	Herb
Cynara cardunculus L	Worldwide	Herb
C. scolymus L.	Mediterranean	Herb
Cynara sp.	Mediterranean region, and Canary Islands	Herb
Eclipta alba Hassk.	Java	Herb
E. prostrata L.	Pantropical	Herb
Emilia coccinea G. Don	Pantropical	Herb
E. flammea Cass.	Pantropical	Herb
E. sagittata D.C.	New World Tropics	Herb
E. sonchifolia A. D.C.	Pantropical	Herb
Enhydra fluctuans Lour.	Tropical Asia	Herb
E. paludosa D.C.	Tropical Asia	Herb
Erechtites hieracifolia Rafin. ex. D.C.	East India	Herb
E. valerianaefolia D.C.	Subtropical America	Herb
Erigeron sumatrensis Retz	Southeast Asia	Herb
Ethulia conyroides L.	East Africa	Herb
Galinsoga parviflora Cav.	Java	Herb
Glossocardia bosvallia D.C.	India	Herb
Gnaphalium affine D. Don	Southeast Asia	Herb
G. hypoleucum D.C.	Southeast Asia	Herb
G. indicum L.	Southeast Asia	Herb
Gundelia tourneforteii L.	Asia Minor	Herb
Gynura bicolor D. C.	Tropical Asia	Herb
G. cernua Benth.	Tropical Africa	Herb
G. procumbens Backer	Indonesia	Herb
G. sarmentosa D.C.	Indonesia	Herb
Hedypnois polymorpha D.C.	Africa	Herb
Hyoseris radiata L.	Liberia	Herb
Inula crithmoides L.	Near East	Herb
Koelpinia linearis Pallas	Africa	Herb
Lactuca alpina Benth et Hook. f	Europe	Herb
L. capensis Thunb	South Africa	Herb
L. dracoglossa Mak.	Subtropical Asia	Herb
L. indica L.	Subtropical Asia	Herb
L. intybacea Jacq.	Madagascar	Herb
L. plumieri	France	Herb
L. sativa L.	Pantropical	Herb
L. scariola L.	Worldwide	Herb
L. taraxacifolia Sch. et Thon	Nigeria	Herb
L. tuberosa	Near East	Herb

Species	Distribution	Habit
Laggera alata Sch. Kip.	Congo, West Africa	Herb
Launaea glomerata Hook. f.	Sahara	Herb
L. nudicaulis Hook. f.	Near East	Herb
L. sarmentosa Aeston.	Tropical Asia	Herb
L. taraxifolia Amin.	Tropical Africa	Herb
Microglossa afzelii O. Hoffm.	Sierra Leone	Herb
Mikania cordata Blume	West Africa	Herb
M. scandens Willd.	Pantropical	Herb
Myriactis wallichii L.	India	Herb
Nidorella macrocephala Steetz.	Africa	Herb
Ornopodonsp.	Africa	Herb
Pacourina edulis Aubl.	Guiana, Brzil	Herb
Petasites Japonicus F. Schmidt.	Japan	Herb
P. palmatus Ase Gray	California	Herb
Petasites sp.	Pacific Islands	Herb
Pluchea indica Less.	Southeast Asia	Tree
Rhaponticumacaule D. C.	Libya	Herb
Scolymus grandiflorus Desf.	North Africa	Herb
Scolymus hispanicus L.	North Africa, Canaries	Herb
S. maculatus L.	North Africa	Herb
Scorzonera alexandrina Briss.	Libya	Herb
S. hispanica L.	Europe	Herb
S. congolensis de Wild	Congo	Herb
S. gabonensis	Gabon	Herb
S. undulata Vahl	Mediterranean	Herb
Senecio biafrae Oliv.	Tropical Africa	Herb
S. gabonensis Oliv.	West Africa	Herb
S. oleracea Crevost et Lemairee	Vietnam	Herb
S. triafrae Olw. et Hiern.	Africa	Herb
Silybum marianum Gaertn.	North Africa	Herb
Sonehus arvensis L.	Old World	Shrub
S. asper Hill	Old World	Shrub
S. bipontini Arch	Old World	Herb
S. exauriculatus 0. Hoffm.	Old World	Herb
S. oleraceus L.	Old World	Herb
Spilanthes acmella Merr.	Pantropical	Herb
S. jabadicensis H. H. Moore	Tropical America, Africa	Herb
S. ocymifolia A. H. Moore	Tropical America, Africa	Herb
S. oleracea Jacq.	Pantropical	Herb
S. paniculata Wall. ex D. C.	Pantropical	Herb
Stevia rebaudians	Tropical America	Herb
Struchium sparganophora 0. Ktz.	Africa	Herb
Synedrella nodiflora Gaertn.	Malaysia	Herb
Tagetes patula L.	Zaire	Herb
Taraxacum officinale Weber	Worldwide	Herb
Tragopogon porrifolius	Subtropics	Herb
T. pratensis L.	Near East	Herb
Urospermum picroides F. W. Schmidt.		Herb
Vernonia appendiculata	Madagascar	Herb
V. amygdalina Dal.	West Africa	Herb
V. appendiculata Less.	Madagascar	Herb
V. biafrae Oliv. et Hiern.	Zaire	Herb
V. calvoana Hook. f.	Cameroon	Herb
V. chinensis Less.	Worldwide	Herb
V. cinerea Less.	Southwest Africa	Herb
V. colorata Drake	Worldwide	Herb
V. fastigiata Oliv. et Hiern	South Africa	Herb
V. gastigiata Oliv. et Hiern.	Worldwide	Herb
V. perrotteti Sch. Bip.	Sierre Leone	Herb
V. senegalensis L.	West Africa	Herb
Wedelia biflora D.C.	Pantropical	Herb
Zinnia elegans Jacq.	Mexico	Herb

CONNARACEAE

Species	Distribution	Habit
Agelaea hirsuta de Wild.	Congo	Herb
Castanola paradoxa (Gilg.)	South Nigeria	Herb
Connarus semidecandrus	Indonesia	Tree

CONVOLVULACEAE

Species	Distribution	Habit
Aniseia martinicensis Choisy	Malaysia	Vine
Argyreia populifolia Choisy	Sri Lanka, India	Vine
Calligonum polygonoidesL.		Shrub
Calonyction aculeatum House	Pantropical	Vine
C. bona-nox Boj.	India	Vine
C. muricatum G. Don.	India	Vine
Calystegia sepium (L.) R. Br.	China	Vine
Dipteropeltis poranoides Hall. f.	Central Africa	Vine
Ipomoea aquatica Forsk.	China	Vine
I. batatas (L.) Poir	Tropical America	Vine
I. biloba Forsk.	Pantropical	Vine
I. cairica (L.) Sweet	Pantropical	Vine
I. cordofana Choisy	Pantropical	Vine
I. crassicaulis R. L. Rob.	Tropical America	Shrub
I. digitata L.	Pantropical	Vine
I. eriocarpa R. Br.	India, Tropical Africa	Vine
I. hochstetteri House	South Africa	Vine
I. illustris Prain.	India	Vine
I. involucrata P. Beauv.	Tropical Africa	Vine
I. lugardi N.E. Br.	India	Vine

Species	Habit	Distribution
I. pes-caprae (L.) R. Br.	Vine	Pantropical
I. sepiaria Koenig ex Rob.	Vine	India
I. triloba L.	Vine	Pantropical
I. uniflora Roem. et Schult.	Vine	Pantropical
Jacquemontia sandwicensis A. Gray	Vine	Hawaii
J. tamnifolia (L.) Griseb.	Herb	Pantropical
Lettsonia setosa Roxb.	Vine	India
Merremia emarginata Hall.	Vine	India
M. rhyncorhiza Hall. f.	Vine	India
M. umbellata Hall. f.	Vine	Pantropical
Neuropeltes acuminata Benth.	Vine	Equatorial Africa
Operculina turpethum (L.)S. Manso.	Vine	Pantropical
Porana volubiles Burm. f.	Vine	Tropical Asia
Quamoclit pinnata Boyer	Vine	Pantropical
Rivea hypocrateriformis Choisy	Vine	India
R. ornata Choisy	Vine	India, Sri Lanka / Asia

CRUCIFERAE

Species	Habit	Distribution
Barbarea verna Asch.	Shrub	Pantemperate.
Brassica alba Baiss	Herb	Europe
B. alboglabra L. H. Bail.	Herb	Asia
B. campestris L. a.o.		
var. sarson Prain		India
var. toria		Eastern Asia
B. chinensis L.	Herb	Eastern Asia
B. hirta Moench	Herb	Pantropical
B. integrifolia Schultz.	Herb	Tropical Africa
B. juncea Czern. et Coss.	Herb	Pantropical
B. napus	Herb	Pantropical
B. nigra (L.) Koch.	Herb	Eurasia
B pekinensis (Lour.) Rupr.	Herb	Tropical Africa, Madagascar
B. rapa L.	Herb	Africa
B. rugosa Prain	Herb	Africa, India
B. schimperi Boiss.	Herb	East Africa
B. tournefortii Gonan	Herb	Africa, India
B. sinensis Juslen.	Herb	Tropical Africa
Cakile fusiformis Greene	Herb	South Florida
Capsella bursa-pastoris (L.) Medik	Herb	Near East, North Africa
Cardamine hirsuta R.	Herb	India
Cochlearia armoracea L.	Herb	Southeast Asia
Coronopus squamatus Asch.	Herb	Near East
Crambe abyssinica Hochst. ex R.E. Fries	Herb	Ethiopia
C. cordifolia Steven	Herb	India, Ethiopia
C. maritima L.	Herb	Western Europe to Southwest Asia
Diplotaxis duveyrierana Coss.	Herb	Africa
D. pendula D.C.	Herb	Africa
Eruca sativa Mill	Herb	Mediterranean
Lepidium africanum D.C.	Herb	South Africa
L. chilense Kunze	Herb	Chile
L. draba L.	Herb	India
L. myriocarpum Lond.	Herb	South Africa
L. sativum L.	Herb	Europe
L. virginicum L.	Herb	North America
Nasturtium barbariaefolium Baker	Herb	Africa
N. fluviatilis R. A. Dyer	Herb	Africa
N. heterophyllum Bl.	Herb	Southeast Asia
N. mierophyllum	Herb	Worldwide
N. officinale R. Br.	Herb	Europe
N. sarmentosum Shulz	Herb	New Guinea
Pugionium cornutum Geertn.	Herb	Mongolia
Morel.	Herb	Asia
R. sativus L.	Herb	Eurasia
Raphia faranifera (Gaertn.) Hylander	Palm	Madagascar, Tropical Africa
Rapistrum rugosum All	Herb	Near East
Rorippa humifusa (Gull. et Perr.) Hiern.	Herb	Congo
Senebiera coronopus Poir	Herb	Pantropical
S. lepidioides Coss. et Dur.	Herb	North Africa
S. pinnatifida D.C.	Herb	California
Sinapis alba L.	Herb	Mediterranean

CRYPTERONIACEAE

Species	Habit	Distribution
Crypteronia paniculata Bl.	Tree	Malaysia

CUCURBITACEAE

Species	Habit	Distribution
Benincasa hispida (Thunb.) Cogn.	Vine	Southeast Asia
Bryonopsis laciniosa Naud.	Herb	India
Cephalandra quinqueloba Schrad	Herb	Africa
Citrullus lanatus (Thunb.) Mansf.	Vine	South Africa
Coccinia cordifolia Cogn.	Herb	Southeast Asia
C. rehmannii Don	Herb	Tropical Africa, Asia
C. sessilifolia Cogn.	Herb	South Africa
Cogniauxia podolaena Baill.	Herb	Africa
Corallocarpus sphaerocarpus Ait.	Herb	Africa
Cucumello robicchii Chior.	Herb	Africa
Cucumeropsia mannii Maud.	Vine	Tropical Africa
Cucumis africanus Lincl.	Vine	Africa
C. egrestis Creb.	Vine	Africa

Cucurbitaceae (continued)

Species	Distribution	Habit
Spach.	East Africa	Vine
C. ficifolius A. Rich	Tanzania	Vine
C. hirsutus Sond.	Southeast Africa	Vine
C. maderaspatanus L.	India	Vine
C. prophetarum L.	Africa	Vine
C. sativus L.	South Asia	Vine
C. zeyheri Sond.	South Africa	Vine
Cucurbita maxima Duch. ex Lam.	South America	Vine
C. moschata Duch. ex Poir.	Central America	Vine
C. pepo L.	Mexico	Herb
Cyclanthera pedata Schrad.	Tropical America	Vine
Kedrostis rostrata Cogn.	India	Vine
Lagenaria siceraria (Molina) Strand.	India	Vine
L. sphaeriea (E. Mey. ex Sond.) Naud.	Malawi	Vine
Luffa acutangula (L.) Roxb.	Tropical Asia	Vine
Melothria heterophylla Cogn.	India	Vine
Momordica charantia L.	Old World Tropics	Vine
M. cochiachinensis (Lour.) Spreng.	Southeast Asia	Vine
Polakowskia tacaco Pitt.	Central America	Herb
Rhynchocarpa foetida Schrad.	West Africa	Vine
Sechium edule Swartz.	Tropical America	Vine
Sphaerosicyos sphericus Hook. f.	Africa	Herb
Telfairea occidentalis Hook. f.	Africa	Vine
T. pedata Hook.	Africa	Vine
Trichosanthes anguina L.	Indonesia	Vine
T. celebica Congn.	Indonesia	Vine
T. cucumerina L.	India	Vine
T. dioica Roxb.	Tropical Asia, North Australia,	Vine

Species	Distribution	Habit
ERICACEAE		
Rhododendron arboreum Sm.	Sri Lanka	Shrub
Vaccinium varingiaefolium Miq.	Indonesia	Shrub
EUPHORBIACEAE		
Acalypha australis L.	Philippines	Shrub
Acalypha boehmeroides Miq.	Malaysia	Shrub
A. caturus Bl.	Indonesia	Shrub
A. indica L.	India	Shrub
A. paniculata Miq.	Malaysia	Herb
A. siamensis Oliv.	Thailand, Malaysia	Shrub
A. wilkesiana Muell. Arg.	South Sea Islands	Shrub
Anthriscus arefolium Hoffm.	Tropical Asia	Herb
Antidesma bunius Spreng.	India	Tree
A. diandra Spreng.	India	Tree
A. ghaesembila Gaertn.	Malaysia, India	Tree
Aporosa maingayi Hook. f.	Southeast Asia	Tree
Baccaurea sapida Muell. Arg.	Southeast Asia	Tree
Baliospermum micranthum Muell. Arg.	India	Herb
Breynia discigera Muell. Arg.	Malaysia	Tree
B. reclinata Hook. f.	Indomalaysia	Shrub
B. rhamnoides Muell. Arg.	Malaysia	Shrub
Bridelia scleroneura Muell. Arg.	Africa	Tree
Cicca acida Merr.	Pantropical	Tree
Claoxylon longifolium Muell. Arg.	Southeast Asia	Tree
C. oleraceum Prain	Zaire	Tree
C. polot (Burm. f.) Merr.	Southeast Asia	Tree

Species	Distribution	Habit
Cleistanthus heterophyllus Hook. f.	Southeast Asia, Malaysia	Shrub
Clusianthus heterophyllus Hook. f.		
Cnidoscolus chayamansa McVaugh	Malaysia	Shrub
Codiaeum variegatum Bl.	Mexico	Shrub
Croton mubange Muell. Arg.	Pantropical	Shrub
Crotonogyne poggei Pax	Congo	Shrub
Endospermum moluccanum Becc.	Tropical Africa	
Erythrococca columnaris Prain	Indomalaysia	Shrub
E. oleracea Prain	Tropical Africa	Shrub
Euphorbia antiquorum L.	Tropical Africa	
E. balsamifera Ait.	Java	Herb
E. edulis Lour.	Senegal	Shrub
E. heterophylla L.	Indochina	Herb
E. hirta L.	New World Tropics	Herb
E. intisy Drake	Indonesia	Herb
E. nerifolia L.	Madagascar	Herb
E. pulcherrima Willd.	Malaysia	Shrub
E. trigyna Haw.	Pantropical	Shrub
Glochidion blancoi Lowe	Java	Tree
G. borneense Boerl.	Tropical Asia	Tree
G. llanosa Muell. Arg.	Southeast Asia, Indonesia, Philippines	Tree
G. ramiflorum Forst.	Indonesia, Pacific Islands	
G. rubrum Bl.	Southeast Asia	Tree
Hymenocardia acida Tul.	Congo	Tree
H. ulmoides Oliv.	Congo	Shrub
Jatropha curcas L.	Pantropical	Shrub
J. multifida L.	Pantropical	Herb
J. urens L.	Philippines	Shrub
Maesobotrya bertramiana Butn.	Congo	Tree
M. floribunda Benth.	Africa	Shrub
M. hirtella Pax	Africa	Shrub
Manihot esculenta Crantz	South America	Shrub
Maprounea africana Muell. Arg.	Tropical Africa	Shrub
M. membranacea Pax et Hoffm.	Tropical Africa	Shrub
Micrococca mercurialis (L.) Benth.	Tropical Africa	Shrub
Microdesmis pentandra Hook. f.	Tropical Africa	Tree
M. puberula Planchon	Tropical Africa	Tree
M. zenkeri Pax	Tropical Africa	Tree
Phyllanthus acidus Skeels	Tropical Asia	Tree
P. emblica L.	Tropical Asia	Tree
P. muellerianus Excell	West Africa	Tree
Plukentia corniculata Paina Smith	Tropical Asia	Shrub
P. volabilis L.	Tropical America	Shrub
Pterococcus corniculatus Pax. et Hoffm.	Southeast Asia	Vine
Ricinus communis L.	Pantropical	Shrub
Sauropus androgynus Merr.	India	Shrub
Tetracarpidium conophorum Muell. Arg.	Tropical Africa	Shrub
FLACOURTIACEAE		
Flacourtia jangomas Roeusch.	Indonesia	Tree
F. rukam Zoll. et Mor.	Tropical Asia	Tree
Pangium edule Reinw.	Tropical Asia, Pacific Islands	Tree
GENTIANACEAE		
Limnanthemum cristatum Griseb.	Malaysia	Aquat.
L. indicum Thw.	India	Herb
GERANIACEAE		
Erodium circutarium Herit.	Pansubtropical	Herb
E. moschatum l'Her	Near East	Herb
Impatiens balsamina L.	Indonesia	Herb
I. dichiva Hook. f.	Congo	Herb
I. flaceida Arn.	Sri Lanka	Herb
Tropaeolum majus L.	South America	Herb
GESNERIACEAE		
Cyrtandra decurrens de Vr.	Indonesia	Herb
Klugia notoniana A. D.C	Southeast Asia	Herb
K. zeylanica Gardn.	Sri Lanka	Herb
GNETACEAE		
Gnetum africanum Welv.	Central Africa	Tree
G. buchholzianum Engl.	Central Africa	Tree
G. gnemon L. Bagu.	Indomalaysia	Tree
G. indicum Merr.	Africa	Tree
G. tisserantii	Southeast Asia	Tree
GOODENIACEAE		
Scaevola frutescens Krause	Tropical Asia	Shrub
GRAMINEAE		
Acrocers amplectans Stapf.	Gambia	Grass
Aristida graciiior Pilg.	Africa	Grass
A. plumosa L.	Africa	Grass
A. stipoides R. Br.	Africa	Grass

Species	Region	Habit
Bambusa arundinacea Willd.	Tropical Asia	Bamb
B. atra Lindl.	Tropical Asia	Bamb
B. bambos Backer	Tropical Asia	Bamb
B. multiplex Raensch	Tropical Asia	Bamb
B. spinosa Bl.	Tropical Asia	Bamb
B. vulgaris Schrad.	Pantropical	Bamb
Cymbopogoncitratus Stapf.	Pantropical	Herb
Dendrocalamus asper Backer	Tropical Asia	Bamb
D. hamiltonii Ness. et Arn.	Southeast Asia	Bamb
Digitaria gayana A. Chev.	Africa	Herb
Echinochloa colona Link	Africa, India	Grass
E. crus-galli Beauv.	Indonesia	Grass
Eleusine coracana Gaerth.	Africa	Grass
E. indica Gaertn.	Old World Tropics	Grass
Gigantochloa verticillata Munro	Southeast Asia	Bamb
Hyparrhenia spp.	Africa	Herb
Isachne albens Trin.	Tropical Asia	Bamb
I. globosa O. Ktze.	Southeast Asia	Herb
Oxytinanthera abyssinica Munro	Uganda	Grass
Panicum barbatum Lam.	Southeast Asia	Grass
P. chamaeraphioides Hack	Southeast Asia	Grass
P. colonum L.	Indonesia	Grass
P. crus-galli L.	Indonesia	Grass
P. palmifolium Koenig	Indonesia	Grass
Pennisetum purpureum Schum.	West Africa	Grass
Rhynchelythrumrepens C.E. Hubb	Africa	Herb
Saccharum officinarum L.	Southeast Asia	Herb
Schizostachyum brachycladum Kurz.	Indomalaysia	Bamb
Setaria palmaefolia Stapf.	Tropical Asia	Herb
Themeda gigantea liack.	Indonesia	Grass
Zea mays L. var. rugosa	Madagascar	Herb
Zizania latifolia Turcz.	Singapore, China, Hong Kong	Grass

GUTTIFERAE

Garcinia amboinensis Spreng.	Southeast Asia	Tree
G. atrovirides Griff.	Southeast Asia	Tree
G. cowa Roxb.	Southeast Asia	Tree
G. dioica Bl.	Southeast Asia	Tree
Garcinia microstigma Kurz.	Southeast Asia	Tree
G. sizygifolia Pierre	Southeast Asia	Tree
Psorospermum quineense Legunoko	West Africa	Tree

HAMAMELIDACEAE

Altingia excelsa Nor.	Southeast Asia	Tree

HYDROCHARITACEAE

Hydrella sp.	India	Aquat.
Hydrocharis dubia Backer	Southeast Asia	Herb
Otelia alismoides Pers.	Philippines	Aquat.
Vallianeria gigantea Gaern.	Philippines	Herb

HYDROPHYLLACEAE

Hydrolea zeylanica Vahl	Tropical Asia	Shrub

HYPERICACEAE

Cratoxylon polyanthus Korth.	Thailand	Tree
Psorospermum tenuifolium D.C.	Congo	Shrub

LABIATAE

Aeollanthus frutescens Benth.	Nigeria	Herb
A. heteropioides Oliver	West Africa	Herb
A. pubescens Benth.	West Africa	Herb
Coleus amboinicus Lour.	Indomalaysia	Herb
C. aromaticus Benth.	Africa	Herb
C. parviflorus Benth.	Subtropical Asia	Herb
C. rotundifolius Chev. et Perr.	Africa	Herb
Hausmaniastrum lilacinum J.K. Morton	Africa	Herb
Hoglundia oppositifolia Vahl.	Congo	Herb
Hyptis brevipes Poit.	Tropical Asia	Herb
H. pectinata Poit.	Tropical Africa	Herb
H. spicigera Lam.	Tropical Africa	Herb
H. suaveolens Poir.	Southern Asia	Herb
Leucas aspera Link.	Tropical Asia	Herb
L. cephalates Spreng.	India	Herb
L. clarkii Hook. f.	India	Herb
L. lanata Benth.	India	Herb
L. lavandula Smith	Indonesia	Herb
L. martinicensis R. Br.	India	Herb
L. mollissima Wall.	Southern Asia	Herb
L. zeylanica R. Br.	Southern Asia	Herb
Mentha arvensis L.	Pantropical	Herb
M. citrata Ehrhart	Central America	Herb
M. javanica Span.	Pantropical	Herb
M. merdinah Backer	Indonesia	Herb
M. piperita L.	Pantropical	Herb
M. spicata L.	Pantropical	Herb
M. umbellata Hall. f.	Sudan	Herb
Ocimum arborescens Boj.	Congo	Shrub
O. americanum L.	New World Tropics	Herb
O. arborescens Boj.	Congo	Herb
O. basilicum L.	Pantropical	Herb

Species	Region	Habit
O. canum Sims.	Indonesia	Shrub
O. sanctum L.	Southeast Asia	Herb
O. viride Willd.	West Africa	Herb
Origanum majorana L.	Mediterranean	Herb
O. onites L.	Mediterranean	Herb
O. vulgare L.	Mediterranean	Herb
Perilla frutescens Britt	Tropical Asia	Herb
Platystoma africanum P. Beauv.	Congo	Herb
Plectranthus kamerunensis Gurke	Central Africa	Herb
Podostemon cablin Benth.	Tropical Asia	Herb
Rosmarinus officinalis L.	Tropical Asia	Herb
Salvia hispanica	Spain	Herb
S. officinalis L.	Worldwide	Herb
S. verbenaca L.	Africa	Herb
Solenostemon monostachus Beauv.	West Africa	Herb
Thymus vulgaris L.	Pansubtropical	Herb

LAURACEAE

Species	Region	Habit
Litsea firma Hook. f.	Thailand	Tree
L. glaucescens HBK	Central America	Tree
L. guatemalensis Mez.	Guatemala	Tree
L. novoleontis Bart.	Mexico	Tree
Persea borbonia Spreng	South Florida	Shrub

LECYTHIDACEAE

Species	Region	Habit
Barringtonia acutangula Gaertn.	Southeast Asia	Tree
B. asiatica Kurz.	Thailand	Tree
B. fusiformis King	Africa	Tree
B. insignis Miq.	Malaysia	Tree
B. racemosa Roxb.	Southeast Asia	Tree
B. spicata Bl.	Malaysia	Tree
Planchonia grandis Ridl.	Southeast Asia	Tree
P. valida Bl.	Indomalaysia	Tree

LEEACEAE

Species	Region	Habit
Leea macrophylla Roxb.	India	Tree
L. manillensis Walp.	Philippines	Tree

LEGUMINOSAE

Species	Region	Habit
Abrus precatorius L.	Pantropical	Vine
Acacia albida Del.	Zimbabwe	Tree
A. arabica Willd.	Africa	Shrub
A. concinna D.C.	India, Burma	Tree
A. farnesiana Wild.	Pantropical	Tree
A. drepanolobium Harms, ex Sjosted	East Africa	Tree
A. insuavis Laco.	Thailand	Vine
A. macrothyrsa Harms.	Malawi	Shrub
A. nigrescens Oliv.	Tropical Africa	Tree
A. nilotica (L.) Del.	Tropical Africa, India	Tree
A. socotrana Balf. f.	Somalia	Shrub
A. zygia L.	Africa	Shrub
Adenanthera atropsperma F. Muell.	Australia	Tree
A. pavonia (L.) Roxb.	Tropical Asia, Pacific Islands	Tree
Aeschynomene africana Smith	Africa	Tree
Afzelia africana Smith	Africa	Tree
A. bella Harms.	West Africa	Tree
A. bijugar A. Gray.	Thailand	Tree
A. quanzensis Welw.	Africa	Tree
A. xylocarpa Craib	Thailand	Tree
Albizia adianthifolia (Schum.) W.F. Wight	Congo	Tree
A. chevalieri Harnes.	Nigeria	Tree
A. falcataria (L.) Fosb.	Southeast Asia	Tree
A. gemmifera C.A. Smith	Africa	Tree
A. procera Benth.	Southeast Asia	Tree
A. zygia (D.C.) Macbr.	West Africa	Tree
Arachis hypogaea L.	Paraguay, Argentina	Herb
Astragalus abyssinicus A. Rich	Africa	Herb
Bauhinia esculenta Burch.	South Africa	Tree
B. malabarica Roxb.	Southeast Asia	Tree
B. nonandra	Guiana	Tree
B. purpurea L.	Tropical Asia	Tree
B. racemosa Lam.	Burma, India	Tree
B. reticulata D.C.	Tropical Africa	Tree
B. tomentosa L.	Tropical Asia	Tree
B. variegata L.	Tropical Asia	Herb
Cajanus cajan (L.) Hutch.	Africa	Tree
Calopogonium mucunoides Desv.	Tropical America	Vine
Canavalia ensiformis (L.) D.C.	Central America	Herb
C. maritima Piper.	Pantropical	Vine
Cassia alata L.	Pantropical	Tree
C. angustifolia Vahl	India	Tree
C. auriculata L.	Tropical Asia	Shrub
C. fistula L.	India	Tree
C. floribunda Cav.	Tropical Asia	Tree
C. garrettiana Craib.	Indonesia	Tree
C. hirsuta L.	New World Tropics	Herb
C. javanica L.	Pantropical	Tree
C. laevigata Willd.	Pantropical	Herb
C. mimosoides L.	Southeast Asia	Herb
C. obtusifolia L.	South America	Herb
C. occidentalis L.	Tropical Asia	Tree
C. siamea Lam.	Southeast Asia	Tree
C. singueana Del.	Southeast Asia	Tree
C. surattensis Burm. F.	India	Tree
C. tomentosa L.	Mexico	Tree
C. tora L.	Tropical Asia	Shrub
Ceratonia siliqua L.	North Africa	Tree

Species	Distribution	Habit
Cicer arietinum L.	Mediterranean region	Herb
Clitoria ternatea L.	Asia, Molucca Islands	Vine
Crotalaria falcata Vahl. ex D.C.	Nigeria	Herb
C. glauca Willd.	Tropical Africa	Herb
C. guatemalensis Benth.	Central America	Herb
C. juncea L.	India	Herb
C. longirostrata Hook. et Arn.	Tropical America	Herb.
C. microcarpa Hochst. ex Benth.	Tanzania	Herb
C. ochroleuca G. Don.	Central Africa	Herb
C. retusa L.	Central Africa	Herb
C. sessiliflora L.	India	Herb
Cyamopsis psoraloides C.C.	India	Herb
C. senegalensis Guill. et Perr.	Africa	Herb
Cynometra reniflora L.	Thailand	Tree
Daniella olivieri Hutch. et Dalz.	Africa	Tree
Delonix alata Gawile	India	Tree
Derris elliptica Benth.	Thailand	Vine
D. heptaphylla Merr.	Thailand	Vine
D. heterophylla Merr.	Malaysia	Herb
D. oliginosa Benth.	Thailand	Vine
Desmodium cinereum D.C.	Tropical America	Herb
D. parviflorum D.C.	India	Herb
D. umbellatum D.C.	Tropical Asia	Shrub
Dewevrea bilabiata M. Micheli	Congo	Tree
Dolichos bracteatus Baker	India	Vine
D. lablab L.	Pantropical	Vine
Dysoxylumeuphlebium Merr.	Indonesia	Vine
Entada phaseoloides		
…Merr.	Indonesia	Vine
E. scandens Benth	Congo	Vine
Eriosema glomeratum (Guill. et Perr.) Hook. f.	Congo	Herb
Erythrina berteroana Urb.	Tropical America	Tree
E. fusca Lour.	Tropical America	Tree
E. herbacea L.	Florida	Shrub
E. subumbrans Merr.	Tropical Asia	Tree
E. variegata L.	Tropical Asia	Tree
Flemingia macrophylla O. Kze.	India	Herb
Gliricidia maculata H.B.K.	Pantropical	Tree
G. sepium (Jacq.) Steud.	Pantropical	Tree
Glycine japonicum L.	Japan	Herb
G. laurentii de Wild.	Pantropical	Herb
G. max (L.) Merr.	Pantropical	Herb
Gourliea decoticans Gillies	Chile	Tree
Indigofera arrecta Hochst. ex A. Rich.	East Africa	Shrub
I. pulchella Roxb.	India	Shrub
Lathyrus sativus L.	Pansubtropical	Herb
Lens culinaris Medik.	Southwest Asia	Herb
Leucaena esculenta Benth	Mexico	Tree
L. leucocephala de Wild.	Tropical America	Tree
Lolium rigidum Gaud.	Algeria	Herb
Lotus edulis L.	India	Tree
Medicago denticulata Willd.	India	Herb
M. sativa L.	India	Herb
Mezoneurum latisiliquum Merr.	Philippines	Herb
Milletia sericea Wight et Arn.	Indomalaysia	Tree
Mucuna aterrima Holland	Indonesia	Vine
M. pruriens (L.) D.C.	Pantropical	Vine
M. utilis Wall ex Wight	Worldwide	Herb
Nepuina oleracea Lour.	Thailand	Aquat.
N. prostrata Baill.	Southeast Asia, Madagascar	Aquat.
Parkia speciosa Hort. ex Hassk.	Southeast Asia	Tree
Parochetus communis Buch. Ham. ex D. Don	East Africa	Vine
Phaseolus aureus Roxb.	Worldwide	Herb
P. calcaratus Roxb.	Worldwide	Herb
P. coccineus L.	Central, South Amer. Highlands	Herb
P. limensis Maef.	Worldwide	Herb
P. lunatus L.	Tropical America	Herb
P. vulgaris L.	Mexico	Herb
Piliostigma malabaricum Benth.	Thailand	Shrub
Pisum arvense L.	Worldwide	Herb
P. sativum L.	Worldwide Highlands	Herb
Pithecellobium kunstleri Prain	Malaysia	Tree
P. lobatum Benth.	Southeast Asia	Tree
Psophocarpus palustris Desv.	Zaire, Madagascar	Vine
P. tetragonolobus(L.) D.C.	Southeast Asia	Herb
Pterocarpus angolensis D.C.	Angola	Tree
P. erinaceus Poir	Africa	Tree
P. indicus Willd.	Pantropical	Tree
P. lucens Lepr.	Africa	Tree
P. osun Craib.	West Africa	Tree
P. santalinus L.f.	West Africa	Tree
P. santaloides l'Her	Africa	Tree
P. soyauxii Taub.	West Africa	Tree
Pueraria thunbergiana Benth.	China, Japan	Vine
Rhynchosia manobotya Harms.	Tropical Africa	Tree
Rothia trifoliata D.C.	India, Sri Lanka	Tree
Saraca indica L.	Thailand	Tree

Species	Distribution	Habit
Sesbania aegyptiaca Poir.	Pantropical	Shrub
S. grandiflora (L.) Pers.	Southeast Asia	Tree
S. roxburghii Merr.	India, Thailand	Tree
S. teraptera Hochst. ex Baker	Sudan	Herb
Sesuvium portulacastrum (L.) L.	Tropical Africa	Herb
Smitnia ellioti Bak. f.	Africa	Shrub
S. sensitiva Ait.	Tropical Asia	Herb
Sphenostylis briartii (deWild.) Bak. f.	Tropical Africa	Vine
S. erecta Hutch	Tropical Africa	Vine
S. schweinfurthii Harms.	Tropical Africa	Vine
S. stenocarpa (Hochst. ex A. Rich.) Harms.	West Africa	Vine
Tamarindus indica L.	Tropical Asia	Tree
Tephrosia elegans Schum.	Tropical Africa	Herb
Tephrosia linearis Pers.	Tropical Africa	Herb
T. purpurea Pers.	Pantropical	Herb
T. vogelii Hook. f.	Pantropical	Herb
Teramnus labialis Spreng.	Indomalaysia	Vine
Tetrapleura tetraptera Taub.	Africa	Tree
Trigonella corniculata L.	Africa	Herb
T. foenum-graecum L.	India	Herb
T. occuita Del.	Africa, India	Herb
T. polycerata L.	Tropical Africa	Herb
Tylosma fassogiensis Torre et Hill.	Africa	Tree
Uraria crinata Desv.	Tropical Asia	Herb
Vicia abyssinica	East Africa	Herb
V. faba L.	Worldwide	Herb
Vigna hosei Backer	Southeast Asia	Herb
V. marginata Benth.	Pantropical	Herb
V. marina Merr.	Tropical Asia	Herb
V. mungo (L.) Hepper	India	Herb
V. phaseoloides Baker	Africa, Asia	Herb
V. reticulata Hook. f.	Malawi, Zaire	Herb
V. sinensis Savi ex Hook;	Asia	Herb
V. triloba Walp.	Pantropical	Herb
V. umbellata (Thunb.) Ohwi et Ohashi	Asia	Vine
V. unguiculata subsp. cylindrica (L.) Verdc.	Tropical Asia	Vine
Virecta procumbens Sm.	Congo	Herb
Voandzeia subterranea (L.) D.C.	West Africa	Herb
Whitfordiodendron atropurpureum Donn.	Thailand, Burma	Tree
W. erianthum Donn.	Malaysia	Tree
W. pubescens Burk.	Thailand	Tree
LEMNACEAE		
Lemna minor L.	Pantropical	Aquat.
Wolffia arrhiza Wimm.	Southeast Asia, Japan	Herb
LILIACEAE		
Allium ampeloprasum L.	Europe, Asia	Herb
A. angolense Baker	Zaire	Herb
A. ascalonicum L.	West Asia	Herb
A. cepa L.	Central Asia	Herb
A. fistulosum L.	North China	Herb
A. kurrat Schweinf. ex K. Krause	Near East	Herb
A. nigritanum A. Chev.	Central America	Herb
A. odorum L.	Siberia, Japan	Herb
A. porrum L.	Asia Minor	Herb
A. sativum L.	Central Asia	Herb
A. schoenoprasum L.	Eurasia	Herb
A. triquetrum L.	North Africa	Herb
A. tuberosum Rotl. ex Spreng	Asia	Herb
Aloe barteri Baker	West Africa	Herb
A. baumii Engl. et Gilg.	Southwest Africa	Herb
A. saponaria Haw.	South Africa	Herb
A. vaombe Dec. et Poisson	West Africa	Herb
A. vera L. var. chinensis (Haw.) Berger	Tropical Asia	Herb
A. vera L. var. officinalis Forsk	Pantropical	Herb
Anthericum subpetiolatum Baker	Africa	Herb
Asparagus acutifolius L.	Libya	Herb
A. africanus Lam.	South Africa	Herb
A. albus L.	North Africa	Herb
A. aphyllus L.	Libya	Herb
A. capensis L.	South Africa	Herb
A. declinatus L.	South Africa	Herb
A. laricinus Burch.	South Africa	Herb
A. officinalis L.	Eastern Europe	Herb
A. paule-guilielmi Solms-Caub.	Tropical Africa	Herb
A. racemosus Wildd.	Sudan	Herb
A. stipularis Forsk.	Libya	Herb
A. suaveolens Burch.	South Africa	Herb
Asphodelus fistulosus L.	North Africa	Herb
A. tenuifolius Cor.	North Africa	Herb
Cordyline fruticosa A. Goepp	Pantropical	Shrub
Dracaena angustifolia L.	Tropical Africa, Madagascar	Shrub
D. mannii Baker	West Africa	Shrub
D. reflexa Lam.	Africa	Shrub
D. thalioides Makay ex E. Mort.	Africa	Shrub
Gloriosa virenseens Lindl.	Congo	Vine
Muscari comosum Mill.	Liberia	Herb
Pleomele angustifolia N.E. Brown	India to Pacific Islands	Shrub

Species	Distribution	Habit
P. elliptica N.E. Brown	Indonesia	Shrub
Smilax bona-nox	Florida	Shrub
S. leucophylla Blume	Malaysia	Vine
Tulbaghia camerooni Baker	Africa	Herb
Yucca aloifolia L.	Central America	Herb
Y. elefantopes Hort.	Central America	Herb
LOGANIACEAE		
Strychnos spinosa Lam.	Tropical Africa	Shrub
S. suberosa de Wild	Congo	Shrub
LORANTHACEAE		
Globimetula braunii (Engl.) van Tiegh.	Tropical Africa	Herb
Loranthus discolor Engl.	Nigeria	Herb
L. exocarpi Behr.	Australia	Herb
LYTHRACEAE		
Lagerstroemia macrocarpa	Thailand	Tree
Pemphis acidula Forst.	Indonesia, Polynesia	Tree
MALVACEAE		
Abelmoschus esculentus Moench.	Africa	Herb
A. manihot Med.	Southeast Asia	Shrub
A. moschatus Moench.	Middle East, India	Herb
Abutilon cabrae de Wild. et Th. Dur.	Congo	Shrub
A. indicum (L.) G. Don	India	Shrub
Gossypium arboreum L.	Thailand	Shrub
G. brasiliense Macf.	Thailand	Shrub
G. herbaceum L.	Thailand	Shrub
Hibiscus abelmoschus L.	Southeast Asia, West Africa	Shrub
H. acetosella Welw. ex Hiern.	East Africa	Shrub
H. articulatus Hochst ex A. Rich	Cameroon	Shrub
H. aspera Hook. f.	Volta, Cameroon	Herb
H. bifurcatus Cav.	Brazil	Shrub
H. cancellatus Roxb.	India	Herb
H. cannabinus L.	Pantropical	Shrub
H. digitatus Cav.	Brazil	Shrub
H. eetveldianus de Wild. et Th. Dur.	Africa	Shrub
H. ficulneus Cav.	Southeast Asia	Herb
H. furcatus Wild.	Sri Lanka	Herb
H. gilletii de Wild.	Congo	Shrub
H. lancibracteatus de Wild. et Th. Dur.		Herb
H. physaloides Guill. et Perr.	Congo, Malawi	Herb
H. radiatus Cav.	India, Malaysia	Shrub
H. rosa-sinensis L.	Pantropical	Shrub
H. roselloides Guill.	Pantropical	Shrub
H. rostellatus Guill. et Perr.	Tropical Africa	Shrub
H. sabdariffa L.	Angola	Herb
H. surattensis L.	Tropical Asia	Shrub
H. tiliaceus L.	Pantropical	Tree
Hilleria latifolia (Lam.) Walter	Congo	Herb
Malva capitata Cav.	Africa	Herb
M. nicaeensis All.	India, Near East	Herb
M. parviflora L.	India, Near East	Herb
M. rotundifolia L.	India, Near East	Herb
M. niacensis All.	India, Near East	Herb
M. rotundifolia L.	India, Near East	Herb
M. sylvestris L.	India, Near East	Herb
M. verticillata L.	India, Near East	Herb
Sida alba L.	Chad, Malawi	Herb
S. humilis Willd. var. moriflora	India	Herb
S. rhombifolia L.	Pantropical	Herb
Thespesia populnea Soland.	Pantropical	Tree
Urena lobata L.	Madagascar	Herb
MARANTACEAE		
Calathea macrosepala K. Schum.	Central America	Herb
Phrynium confertum (Benth.) K. Schum.	Tropical Africa	Herb
Sarcophrynium arnoldianum de Wild.	Congo	Herb
MARSILEACEAE		
Marsilea crenata Presl.	Madagascar, Indonesia	Herb
MELASTOMATACEAE		
Amphiblemma wildemanium Cogn.	Congo	Shrub
Astromia papetaria Blume	Polynesia, Indonesia	Tree
Dicellandra barteri Hook.	Congo	
Dichaetanthera corymbosa (Cogn.) Jac. Fel.	Congo	Herb
Dinophora spenneroides Benth.	Gabon	Herb
Dissotis decumbens Triana	Congo	Herb
D. grandiflora Benth.	Guinea	Herb
D. hassii Cogn.	Congo	Herb
D. multiflora Triana	Southeast Asia	Herb

Species	Distribution	Habit
D. prostrata Triana	Southeast Asia, Africa	Herb
D. sylvestris Jacq-Fel.	Tropical Africa	Herb
Marumia muscosa By.	Indomalaysia	Shrub
Medinilla hasseltii Blume	Malaysia, Southeast Asia	Shrub
M. rubicunda Blume	India	Shrub
Melastoma malabathricum L.	Tropical Asia, India	Shrub
Memecylon caeruleum Jack.	Tropical Asia	Shrub
Ochthocharis borneensis Blume	Malaysia	Shrub
Phaeoneuron dicellandroides Gilg.	Congo	Shrub
Takersia laurenti Cogn.	Congo	
Tristema grandiflorum de Wild.	Congo	

MELIACEAE

Species	Distribution	Habit
Aglaia boillonii Pierre Santul	Vietnam, Cambodia	Tree
Azadirachta indica Juss.	India	Tree
Cedrela sinensis Juss.	Southeast Asia	Tree
Melia excelsa Jack.	Malaysia	Tree
M. indica Brand.	Malaysia	Tree
Turraea vogelii Hook. f.	Congo	Tree

MELIOSMACEAE

Species	Distribution	Habit
Meliosma pinnata Roxb.	India	Tree

MENISPERMACEAE

Species	Distribution	Habit
Cocculus villosus D.C.	Africa, India	Vine
Limaciopsis loangensis Engl.	Africa	Vine

MORACEAE

Species	Distribution	Habit
Allaenthus luzonicus Benth. et Hook. f.	Philippines	Tree
A. glabra Warb.	Philippines	Tree
Artocarpus champeden Spreng.	Southeast Asia	Tree
A. integra Merr.	Southeast Asia	Tree
Brosimum alicastrum Sw.	Tropical America	Tree
Broussonetia alicastrum Sw.	Pacific Islands	Tree
B. papyrifera (L.) Vent.	Indonesia	Tree
Cecropia peltata L.	Pantropical	Tree
Chlorophora excelsa Benth.	Africa	Tree
Craterogyne kameruniana (Engl.) Lanjouw		
Cudrania cochinchinensis Kudu et Masam	Tropical Asia	Tree
C. gavensis Trec.	Indonesia	Shrub
Dammaropsis kingiana Warb.	Polynesia	Tree
Ficus alba Reinw.	Pantropical	Shrub
F. annulata Bl.	Pantropical	Tree
F. asperifolia Miq.	Cameroon	Tree
F. capensis Thunb.	Tropical Africa	Tree
F. dammaropsis Diels.	Indonesia	Tree
F. elastica Thunb.	Pantropical	Tree
F. fistulosa Reinw.	Pantropical	Tree
F. glabella Bl.	Tropical Asia	Tree
F. glomerata Roxb.	Tropical Asia	Tree
F. gnaphalocarpa Steud. ex Miq.	East Africa	Tree
F. hirta Vahl.	West Africa	Tree
F. infectoria Roxb.	Pantropical	Tree
F. ingens Miq.	India	Tree
F. lepicarpa Bl.	Africa	Tree
F. mucosa Welw.	West Africa	Tree
F. neohebridarum Guil.	Pacific Islands	Tree
F. polita Vahl.	Tropical Africa	Tree
F. pseudopalma Blanco	Southeast Asia	Tree
F. quercifolia Roxb.	Tropical Asia	Vine
F. religiosa L.	Pantropical	Tree
F. rumphii Bl.	Tropical Asia	Tree
F. stenocarpa F. Muell.	Pacific Islands	Tree
F. variegata Bl.	Southeast Asia	Tree
Morus alba L.	China	Tree
M. celtidifolia H.B.K.	Central America	Tree
M. corylifolia H.B.K.	South America	Tree
M. indica L.	Tropical Asia	Tree
M. nigra L.	Pantropical	Tree
Myrianthus achoreus P. Beauv.	West Africa	Tree
M. arboreus P. Beauv.	Tropical Africa	Tree
M. libericus Rendle	West Africa	Shrub
Paratrophis tahitiensis Drace	Pacific Islands	Shrub

MORINGACEAE

Species	Distribution	Habit
Moringa bracteata Roxb.	India	Tree
M. oleifera Lam.	India	Tree
M. peregrina (Forsk.) Fiori	Uganda	Tree
M. stenopetala	Ethiopia	Tree

MUSACEAE

Species	Distribution	Habit
Ensete vetricosum (Welw.) E. E. Cheesman	Ethiopian highlands	herb
Ravenala madagascariensis Sonn.	Madagascar	Tree

MYRSINACEAE

Species	Distribution	Habit
Aegiceras		

Species	Distribution	Habit
corniculatum Blanco	Southeast Asia	Shrub
Ardisia boisieri A. D.C.	Indonesia	Shrub
A. crispa A. DC.	Worldwide	Shrub
A. humilis Vahl.	Sri Lanka	Shrub
A. laevigata	Indonesia	Shrub
A. littoralis Andr.	Malaysia	Shrub
A. polycephala Wall.	Burma, India	Shrub
A. solanacea Roxb.	India	Shrub
Embelia philippinensis A. D.C.	Philippines	Vine
E. ribes Burm. f.	Southeast Asia	Vine
E. schimperi Vatke	East Africa	Vine
Maesa blumei D. Don.	Indomalaysia	Shrub
M. chista Al. Don	India	Tree
M. indica Wall.	India	Tree

MYRTACEAE

Species	Distribution	Habit
Decapermum fruticosum Forst,	Southeast Asia	Shrub
Eugenia duthieana King	Thailand	Tree
E. grata Wight	Thailand	Tree
E. lineata Duthie	Indonesia	Tree
E. longiflora Fisch.	Worldwide	Tree
Melaleuca leucadendron L.	Australia	Tree
Pimenta acris Kostel	Africa	Tree
P. dioica Merr.	Pantropical	Tree
Syzygium lineatum Merr. et Perry	Malaysia	Tree
S. malaccensis L.	Southeast Asia	Tree
S. oblatum Wall.	Tropical Asia	Tree
S. polyanthus Walp.	Indonesia	Tree
S. polycephalum Merr. et Perry	Tropical Asia	Tree

NELUMBONACEAE

Species	Distribution	Habit
Nelumbo nucifera Gaertn.	Iran	Aquat.

NYCTAGINACEAE

Species	Distribution	Habit
Boerhavia diffusa L.	Pantropical	Herb
B. plumbaginea Cav.	Africa	Herb
B. repens L.	West Africa	Herb
Mirabilis jalapa L.	Worldwide	Herb
Pisonia grandis R. Br.	Tropical Asia	Tree
P. alba Span.	Southeast Asia	Shrub
P. sylvestris Teijsm et Binnend	Indonesia	Shrub

OCHNACEAE

Species	Distribution	Habit
Ourateae affinis (Hook. f.) Eng.	Tropical Africa	Tree
O. arnoldiana de Wild. et Th. Dur.	Congo	Shrub
O. calophylla (Hook. f.) Eng.	Tropical Africa	Tree
O. crocea Bark.	Malaysia	Tree
O. hookeri Bark.	Indomalaysia	Tree
O. leptoneura Giiq.	Africa	Shrub
Sauvagesia erecta L.	Tropical Asia, Africa	Herb

OLACACEAE

Species	Distribution	Habit
Meliantha suavis Pierre	Thailand	Shrub
Olax acumenata Wall.	India	Tree
O. ibmricata Roxb.	Southeast Asia	Shrub
O. scandens Roxb.	Tropical Asia	Shrub
O. zeylancia L.	India, Sri Lanka	Shrub
Ptychopetalum alliaceum de Wild.	Congo	Shrub
Sclorodocarpus borneensis Becc.	Malaysia	Tree
Strombosia javanica	Southeast Asia	Tree
Blume	Indonesia	Tree
S. philippinensis Vidal.	Philippines	Shrub
Ximenia americana L.	Indonesia	Shrub

OLEACEAE

Species	Distribution	Habit
Schrebera swietenioides Roxb.	India, Burma	Shrub

ONAGRACEAE

Species	Distribution	Habit
Jussieua abyssinica Dandy et Bren.	Africa	Herb
J. repens L.	Pantropical	Aquat.
Ludwigia peploides Flerov.	Southeast Asia	Herb
L. repens L.	Africa, Indochina	Herb

OPILIACEAE

Species	Distribution	Habit
Champereya griffithii Hook. f.	Southeast Asia	Shrub

ORCHIDACEAE

Species	Distribution	Habit
Anaectochilus albolinineatus Par. et Reichenb.	Malaysia	Herb
A. reinwardtii Blume	Malaysia	Herb
Habenaria sp.	Indonesia	Herb
Renanthera moluccana Bl.	Indonesia	Herb

OROBANCHACEAE

Species	Distribution	Habit
Cistanche phelypaea L. Cout.	Africa	Herb

OXALIDACEAE

Species	Distribution	Habit
Averrhoa bilimbe L.	Southeast Asia	Tree

Species	Distribution	Form
Oxalis acetosella L.	South Africa	Herb
O. bahiensis Prog.	Brazil	Herb
O. cernua Thunb.	Africa	Herb
O. corniculata L.	Pantropical	Herb
O. corymbosa A. D.C.	Southeast Asia	Herb
O. deppei Lodd.	Mexico, Japan	Herb
O. gigantea	Andes	Herb
O. hirsutissima Zucc.	Brazil	Herb
O. obliquifolia Steud. ex A. Rich.	East Africa	Herb
O. repens Thumb.	Philippines	Herb
O. sepium St. Hill.	West Indies to Peru	Herb
O. tuberosa Mol. Oca.	Andes	Herb

PALMAE

Acanthophoenix crinieta Wendl.	Reunion Island	Palm
A. rubra Wendl.	Reunion Island	Palm
Acrocomia sclerocarpa Mart.	Caribbean	Palm
Ancistrophyllum secundiflorum Mann et Wendl.	Tropical Africa	Palm
Areca borneensis Becc.	Indonesia	Palm
A. catechu L.	Tropical Asia	Palm
Arenga ambong	Philippines	Palm
A. engleri Beee.	Taiwan	Palm
A. pinnata Merr.	Tropical Asia	Palm
A. sacharifera Labill.	Malaysia	Palm
Borassus aethiopium Mart.	East Africa	Palm
B. flabellifer L.	Southeast Asia	Palm
B. sundaica Becc.	Tropical Asia	Palm
B. tunicata Lour.	China, India	Palm
Calamus ovoideus Thw.	Sri Lanka	Vine
Caryota eumingii Lodd.	Philippines	Palm
C. mitis Lour.	Tropical Asia	Palm
Chamaedorea sp.	Warm America	Palm
Chamaerops humilis L.	North Africa, Argentina	Palm
Cocos nucifera L.	Malaysia	Palm
C. oleracea Mart.	Brazil	Palm
C. yatay Mart.	Argentine	Palm
Copernica cerifera Wendl.	Madagascar	Palm
Corypha elata (L.) Roxb.	Southeast Asia	Palm
Daemonorhops periacanthes Miq.	Indonesia	Palm
Dictyosperma alba Wendl.	Reunion Island	Palm
Diplothernium caudescens Mart.	Brazil	Palm
Dypsis gracilis Borj.	Madagascar	Palm
Elaeis guineensis Jacq.	Tropical Africa	Palm
Euterpe edulis Mart.	Brazil, Guyana	Palm
E. oleracea Engelm.	Brazil	Palm
Hyphaene thebaica Mart.	Tropical Africa	Palm
Kentia sapida Mart.	New Caledonia	Palm
Martinezia eorallina Mart.	Martinique	Palm
Maximiliana martiana	Brazil, Guyana, Surinam	Palm
Metroxylon sagu Roth.	Tropical Asia	Palm
Nonnorhopsritchieana H.	India	Palm
Oenocarpus bacaba Mart.	South America	Palm
Oneosperma filamentosa Hume	Iles de la Sonde	Palm
Oreodoxa oleracea Mart.	Barbados, Antilles	Palm
O. regia Kunth	Cuba	Palm
Phoenix daetylifera L.	North Africa, South Africa, Middle East	Palm
P. reclinata Jacq.	Tropical Africa, India	Palm
Phytelephas macrocarpa Ruiz	Colombia, Peru	Palm
Raphia vinifera Beauv.	Tropical Africa, Asia	Palm
Rhopalostylis sp.	Norfolk Islands, New Zealand	Palm
Sabal palmetto Lodd.	West Indies	Palm
Sagus laevi Rumph	Tropical Asia	Palm
Salacca edulis Reinre	Southeast Asia	Palm
Serenoa repens Small	South Florida	Palm
Thrinax argentea Millsp.	Panama	Palm

PANDANACEAE

Pandanus latifolius	Sri Lanka	Shrub
P. odorus Ridley	Malaysia, Southeast Asia	Shrub
P. polycephalus Lam.	Moluccas	Shrub
P. tectorius Soland. ex Balf. f.	Southeast Asia	Shrub

PAPAVERACEAE

Argemone mexicana L.	Mexico	Herb
Papaver syriacum Boiss. et Blanch	Near East	Hert

PARKERIACEAE

Species	Distribution	Form
Ceratopteris sp.		Herb

PASSIFLORACEAE

Adenia cissampeloides Harms.	Africa	Vine
A. venenata Forsk.	Tropical Africa	Vine
Passiflora foetida L.	Pantropical	Vine
P. lunata Willd.	Pantropical	Vine

PEDALIACEAE

Species	Distribution	Form
Ceratotheca sesamioides Endl.	Tropical Africa	Herb

Species	Distribution	Habit
Pedalium murex L.	Tropical Asia, Africa	Herb
Sesamum alatum Thonn.	Subtropical Africa	Herb
S. angolense Welw.	Tropical Africa	Herb
S. angustifolium Engl.	Tropical Africa	Herb
S. calicynum Welw.	Tropical Africa	Herb
S. indicum L.	Worldwide	Herb
S. orientale L.	Pantropical	Herb
S. radiatum Schum. et Thonn.	West Africa	Herb

PERIPLOCACEAE

Species	Distribution	Habit
Mondia whitei (Hook. f.) Skeels	Congo	Vine

PHYTOLACACEAE

Species	Distribution	Habit
Gisekia pharmaceoides L.	Sri Lanka	Herb
Mohlana latifolia Miq.	Congo	Herb
Phytolacca abyssinica Hoffm.	East Africa	Herb
P. acinosa Roxb.	Subtropical Asia	Herb
P. brachystachys Miq.	Hawaii	Herb
P. decandra L.	India	Herb
P. dioica L.	South America	Herb
P. dodecandra l'Her.	Tropical America, West Africa	Herb
P. esculenta Van Houte	Guinea Coast	Herb
P. octandra L.	Central America, Brazil	Herb
P. rivinoides Kunth. et Bouche	Central, South America	Herb

PIPERACEAE

Species	Distribution	Habit
Heckeria peltata Kunth.	Pantropical	Shrub
H. umbellata Kunth.	Southeast Asia	Shrub
Houttuynia cordata Thumb.	India	Herb
Peperomia pellucida (L.) H.B.K.	Pantropical	Herb
P. vividispica Trel.	Central, South America	Herb
Piper auritium H.B.K.	Central America	Herb
P. betle L.	Southeast Asia	Herb
P. sormentosum Roxb.	Thailand, Southeast Asia	Vine
P. stylosum Miq.	Indomalaysia	Vine
P. umbellatum L.	Tropical Africa	Herb

PLANTAGINACEAE

Species	Distribution	Habit
Plantago asiatica L.	Pantemperate	Herb

PLUMBAGINACEAE

Species	Distribution	Habit
Statice thonini Viv.	Liberia	Herb

PODOSTEMONACEAE

Species	Distribution	Habit
Leddermanniella minutiflora	Tropical Africa	Aquat.
L. sehlechteri Engl.	Tropical Africa	Aquat.
Podostemum minutiflorus Benth. et Hook.	Africa	Aquat.
Sphaerothylax heteromorphe Baill.	Tropical Africa	Aquat.

POLYGALACEAE

Species	Distribution	Habit
Carpolobia alba Don	Tropical Africa	Herb
C. glabrescens Hutch.	Tropical Africa	Herb
C. lutea Don	Zaire	Herb
Polygala persirariifolia D.C.	Tanzania	Herb
Securidaca longipedunculata Fres.	Tropical Africa	Vine

POLYGONACEAE

Species	Distribution	Habit
Ampelygonumchinensi Lindl.	Malaysia, India	Herb
Emex spinosus Campd.	Liberia	Herb
Fagopyrum tataricum Gaertn.	India	Herb
Oxygonum atriplicifolium Mart.	Africa	Herb
Polygonum barbatum L.	Africa, Madagascar	Herb
P. crespidatum Sieb. et Succ.	Africa, Madagascar	Herb
P. cuspidatum Sieb. et Zucc.	Madagascar	Herb
P. glabrum Willd.	Tropical Africa	Herb
P. guineense Sch. et Th.	Tropical Africa	Herb
P. hydropiper L.	Africa	Herb
P. maximowiczii Regel.	Southeast Asia	Herb
P. minus Huds.	Japan	Herb
P. odoratum Lour.	Africa	Herb
P. orientate L.	Southeast Asia	Herb
P. perfoliatum L.	Southeast Asia	Herb
P. plebeium R. Br.	Southeast Asia	Herb
P. pubescens Blume	India	Herb
P. pulchrum Blume	Africa	Herb
P. salicifolium Brouss.	Tropical Asia, Africa	Herb
P. senegalense DeWild. et Meninga	Tropical Africa	Herb
P. serrulatum Lag.	Tropical Africa	Herb
P. setosulum A. Rich.	Zaire	Herb
P. tomentosum Willd.	East Africa	Herb
Rheum hybridum L.	Tropical Africa	Herb
Rumex abyssinicus Jacq.	Worldwide	Herb
R. acetosa L.	Tropical Africa	Herb
R. ambigius Gren.	Europe	Herb
R. bequaertii De Wild	Tropical Asia	Herb
R. crispus L.	East Africa	Herb
	Brazil	Herb

Species / Authority	Distribution	Habit
R. dentatus L.		Herb
R. glormeratus Murr.	Venezuela	Herb
R. hydrolapathum Huds.	Philippines	Herb
R. nepalensis Spreng.	Nepal	Herb
R. patientia L.	Senegal	Herb
R. sagittatus Thunb.	Indonesia	Herb
R. vesicarius L.	Sahara	Herb
PONTEDERIACEAE		
Eichhornia crassipes Solm.	Pantropical	Aquat.
Heteranthera reniformis Ruiz et Pav.	Tropical America	Herb
Monochoria hastaefolia Presl	Sri Lanka	Aquat.
M. hastata (L.) Solms et Laub.	Indomalaysia	Aquat.
M. vaginalis Presl.	Southeast Asia	Aquat.
PORTULACEAE		
Calandrina micrantha Schlecht.	Mexico	Herb
Claytonia exigua Torr. et Gray	Chile	Herb
C. perfoliata Doon. ex Willd.	East Siberia, North America	Herb
Portulaca afra Jacq.	South Africa	Herb
P. grandiflora Hook.	Pantropical	Herb
P. johnnii Poelm.	Pacific Islands	Herb
P. lutea Soland.	Pacific Islands	Herb
P. oleracea L.	South Africa	Herb
P. pachyrriza Gagnep.	Indochina	Herb
P. pilosa L.	Tropical America	Herb
P. quadrifida L.	Tropical Asia	Herb
P. samoensis V. Poulin.	Pacific Islands	Herb
P. tuberosa Roxb.	India	Herb
Hook. f.	South America	Herb
T. caffrum Eck. et Zeiyh	South America	Herb
T. crassifolium Willd.	Tropical America	Herb
T. cuneifolium (Vahl.) Willd.	East Africa	Herb
T. patens Willd.	Brazil	Herb
T. portulacifolium Aschers	Tropical Asia, Africa	Herb
T. triangulare (Jacq.) Wild.	South America	Herb
PRIMULACEAE		
Lysimachia candida Lindl.	Tropical Asia	Shrub
L. clethroides Duby	Indonesia	Herb
PROTEACEAE		
Helicia javanica Blume	Tropical Asia	Shrub
H. serrata Blume	Indonesia	Shrub
RANUNCULACEAE		
Ranunculus multifidus Forsk.	Africa	Herb
Thalictrum minus L.	South Africa	Herb
RHAMNACEAE		
Colubrina asiatica Brongn.	Tropical Asia	Shrub
Rhamnus prinoides l'Her.	Ethiopia	Shrub
Ziziphus mauritania Lam.	India	Tree
RHIZOPHORACEAE		
Bruguiera [...] Blume	Tropical Asia	Tree
B. conjugata Merr.	Tropical Africa, Asia	Tree
B. gymnorhiza Lam.	Tropical Asia	Tree
Rhizophora mangle L.	Pantropical	Tree
R. mucronata Lam.	Pantropical	Tree
ROSACEAE		
Rosa damascena Mill.	Indonesia	Shrub
R. moschata Mill.	Indonesia	Shrub
R. multiflora Thunb.	Tropical Asia	Shrub
Rubus rosaefolius Sm.	Southeast Asia	Shrub
RUBIACEAE		
Amaralia calicyna K. Schum.	Tropical Africa	Herb
Anotis hirsuta Miq.	Indonesia	Herb
Borreria hispida K. Schum.	Tropical Africa	Herb
Canthium monstrosum Merr.	Africa	Tree
Coffea arabica L.	Ethiopia	Shrub
Cuviera angolensis Walw.	Tropical Africa	Herb
C. longiflora Hiern.	Tropical Africa	Herb
Dentella repens Forst.	Southeast Asia, India	Herb
Fadogia cienkowskii Schweinf.	Tropical Africa	Shrub
Feretia podanthera Del.	Nigeria	Tree
Geophila obvallata T. Didr.	Africa	Herb
Grumilea ungoniensis K. Schum. et Krause	Africa	Herb
Hedyotis auricularia L.	Malaysia, India	Herb
H. nitida Wight et Arn.	India, Sri Lanka	Herb
H. scandens Roxb.	Central Africa	Herb
Heinsia crinita G. Tayl.	Africa	Tree
H. pulchella K. Schum	Tropical Africa	Shrub

Species	Distribution	Habit
Morinda citrifolia L.	India, Malaysia	Tree
M. elliptica Ridl.	India	Shrub
Mussaenda arcuata Poir	Africa	Shrub
M. cambodiana Pierre et Pitard.	Indochina	Shrub
M. frondosa L.	Tropical Asia	Shrub
M. glabra Vah.	Malaysia	Shrub
M. roxburghii Hook. f.	India	Shrub
M. stenocarpa Hiern.	Congo	Shrub
M. villosa Wall.	Malaysia	Shrub
Oldenlandia lancifolia D. C.	Zaire	Herb
O. macrophylla D. C.	Tropical Africa	Herb
O. scandens K. Schum.	India	Vine
Paederia foetida L.	Indomalaysia	Shrub
P. scandens Merr.	Philippines	Shrub
P. verticiliata Blume	Indomalaysia	Shrub
Pavetta crassipes K. Schum.	Tropical Africa	Shrub
P. esculenta de Wild.	Congo	Shrub
P. odorata Willd.	Tropical Asia, Africa	Shrub
Pentanisia schweinfurthii Hiern.	Africa	Tree
Petunga microcarpa D.C.	Indonesia	Shrub
Pseudomussaenda stenocarpa (Hiern.) Petit.	Congo	Shrub
Pseudospondiasmicrocarpa (A. Rich) Engl.	Congo	Tree
Psychotria kisantuensis de Wild.	Congo	Tree
Randia octomera Benth. et Hook	Congo	Shrub
Ravenia robustior Jum. et Perr.	Africa	Tree
R. uliginosa Poir.	India, Malaysia	Shrub
Rothmannia octomera (Hooker) Fagenrind	Congo	Shrub
Rubia cordifolia L.	Asia	Shrub
Sarcocephalus esculentus Afzel.	Africa	Tree
S. orientalis Merr.	Southeast Asia	Tree
S. russeggeri Kotschy	Africa	Tree
S. undulatus Miq.	Indomalaysia	Tree
Spermacoce hispida L.	Southeast Asia	Herb
Tricalysia longestipulata de Wild. et Th. Dur.	Congo	Shrub
Vangueria spinosa Roxb.	Tropical Asia	Tree

RUTACEAE

Species	Distribution	Habit
Aegle marmelos L.	Indomalaysia	Tree
Afraegle paniculatum (Schum. et Thonn.) Engl.	West Africa	Tree
Acronychia paniculata Miq.	Southeast Asia	Tree
Citrus amblycarpa Ochse	Southeast Asia	Tree
C. hystrix D. C.	Southeast Asia	Tree
Erioglossum rubiginosum L.	Southeast Asia	Shrub
Evodia lucida Miq.	Indonesia	Shrub
Fagara chalybea Engl.	Tropical Africa	Tree
F. leprieurii Engl.	Africa	Tree
F. olitoria Engl.	Africa	Tree
F. paracantha Milldbr.	Tanzania	Shrub
Glycosmis pentaphylla (Retz.) Correa	Tropical Asia	Shrub
Murraya koenigii Spreng.	India	Tree
Ruta graveolens L.	Worldwide	Herb
Toddalia aculeata Pers.	Sri Lanka	Tree
T. asiatica Lam.	Madagascar, Philippines	Tree
Zanthoxylumoxyphyllum Edgw.	India	Tree

SALVADORACEAE

Species	Distribution	Habit
Dobera roxburghii Planch	Africa	Shrub
Salvadora persica L.	Africa, India	Tree

SAPINDACEAE

Species	Distribution	Habit
Allophylus olnifolius Radlk.	Africa	Tree
Cardiospermum grandiflorumSwartz.	Tropical America,	Vine
C. halicacabum L.	Tropical Africa	Vine
Cubilia blancoi Blume	Tropical America	Tree
Mischocarpus sundaicus Bl.	Philippines, Indonesia	Tree
Paullinia pinnata L.	India	Shrub
Schleichera oleosa Merr.	Congo	Tree
S. trijuga Willd.	Southeast Asia	Tree

SAPOTACEAE

Species	Distribution	Habit
Bassia longifolia L.	India	Tree
Madhuka indica Roxb.	Mediterranean to Australia	Tree
Manilkara zapata L.P. Royen	Tropical America	Tree

SCROPHULARIACEAE

Species	Distribution	Habit
Artanema angustifolium Benth.	Tropical Asia	Shrub
Limnophila aromatica Merr.	India	Tree
L. conferta Benth.	Worldwide	Herb
L. erecta Benth.	Sri Lanka	Tree
L. indica Merr.	Madagascar, Philippines	Herb
L. roxburghii G. Don	India	Herb
L. rugosa Merr.	Tropical Asia	Herb
Striga macrantha Benth.	Sierra Leone	Herb
Torania parviflora Benth.	Tropical Africa	Herb

SMILACACEAE

Species	Habit	Distribution
Smilax macrophylla Roxb.	Vine	India
SOLANACEAE		
Capsicum annuum L.	Shrub	South America
C. baccatum L.	Shrub	South America
C. frutescens L.	Shrub	Worldwide
C. pendulum Willd.	Herb	South America
Cestrum latifolium Lam.	Shrub	South America
Cyphomandrahartwegi Sendt.	Shrub	South America
Lycium chinense Mill.	Shrub	China
Nicotiana tabacum L.	Herb	South America
Physalis angulata L.	Herb	Pantropical
P. minima L.	Herb	Zaire
P. peruviana L.	Herb	Peru, Chile
Schwenkia americana L.	Herb	Africa
Solanum aethiopicum L.	Herb	Tropical Africa
S. bansoense Damm.	Herb	Tropical Africa
S. blumei Nees.	Herb	Tropical Asia
S. crassipetalum Wall.	Herb	Himalayas
S. dasyphyllum Schum. et Thonn.	Herb	Tropical Africa
S. dewerevrei Damm.	Herb	Tropical Africa
S. distichum Thonn.	Herb	Tropical Africa
S. duplosinuatum Klotzsch.	Herb	Tropical Africa
S. erythracanthum Dun.	Herb	Madagascar
S. giorgi de Wild.	Herb	Tropical Africa
S. incanum L.	Herb	Africa, Tropical Asia
S. indicum L.	Herb	Africa, Tropical Asia
S. lescrauwaerti de Wild.	Herb	India
S. lyratum Thunb.	Herb	Japan to Indonesia
S. macrocarpon L.	Herb	West Africa
S. melongena L.	Shrub	India
S. nigrum L.	Herb	Africa
S. nigrum var guineense		
S. nodiflorum Jacq,	Herb	West Africa, U.S.
S. olivare Paill. etBouiss. P.	Herb	Pantropical
S. radiatum Sendt.	Herb	West Africa
S. sessiliflorum Dun,	Herb	Brazil
S. snoussi A. Chev.	Herb	Central Africa
S. spirale Roxb.	Herb	Tropical Asia
S. subsessilis de Wild.	Herb	Africa
S. terminale Forsk.	Herb	Africa
S. torvum Schwartz.	Herb	Southeast Asia
S. tuberosum L.	Herb	South America
S. uporo Dun.	Herb	Andes
S. wildemannii Damm.	Herb	Pacific Islands
S. xanthocarpum Sch. et Wendl.	Herb	Tropical Asia, Africa, India
SONNERATIACEAE		
Sonneratia acida L. f.	Tree	Southeast Asia
S. alba Smith	Tree	Southeast Asia
STERCULIACEAE		
Cola diversifolia de Wild. et Th. Dur.	Tree	Congo
C. gilletii de Wild.	Tree	Congo
Heritiera minor L.	Tree	India
Kleinhovia hospita L.	Tree	Tropical Asia to Australia
Melochia corchorifolia L.	Herb	Pantropical
M. umbellata Stapf.	Herb	Pantropical
Sterculia appendiculata Engl.		
S. tragacantha Lindl.	Tree	Africa
Triplochiton sclerozylon K. Schum.	Tree	Tropical Africa / Africa
SYMPLOCACEAE		
Symplocos odoratissima Choisy	Tree	Southeast Asia
TILIACEAE		
Corchorus acutangulus Lam.	Herb	Pantropical
C. aestuana L.	Herb	Tropical Africa, Asia
C. capsularis L.	Herb	India
C. olitorius L.	Herb	West Africa
C. procumbens Boj.	Herb	Mauritius
C. tridens L.	Herb	Tropical Africa
C. trilocularis L.	Herb	Tropical Africa, Asia
Glyphaea laterifolia Monach	Shrub	Africa
Grewia carpinoifolia Juss.	Shrub	Tropical Africa
G. corylifolia A. Rich	Tree	Africa
G. mollis Juss.	Shrub	Tropical Africa
G. retusa Chiov.	Tree	Africa
G. villosa Willd.	Tree	Africa
Triumfetta annua L.	Herb	Africa
T. cordifolia A. Rich	Shrub	Tropical Africa
T. gartramia L.	Herb	Malaysia
T. rhomboideaJacq.	Shrub	Tropical Africa, Asia
TROPAEOLACEAE		
Tropaeolum brasiliense Casar.	Herb	Brazil
T. majus L.	Herb	Worldwide
T. pentaphyllum Lam.	Herb	South America

TYPHACEAE

Species	Distribution	Habit
Typha angustifolia L.	Africa	Herb
T. capensis Roxb.	Africa	Herb
T. elefantina Roxb.	North Africa, India	Herb

ULMACEAE

Species	Distribution	Habit
Celtis integrifolia Lam.	Tropical Africa	Tree
C. luzonica Warb.	Philippines	Tree
C. sinensis Pers.	Subtropical Asia	Tree
Holoptelea integrifolia Planch.	Subtropical Asia	Tree
Trema guineensis Ficalho	Africa	Tree
T. orientalis Bl.	Tropical Asia	Tree

UMBELLIFERAE

Species	Distribution	Habit
Alepidea sp.	Africa	Herb
Anethum graveolens L.	Worldwide	Herb
A. sowa Roxb. ex Fleming	India	Herb
Annesorhiza flagellifer Berth. Davy	Africa	Herb
Apium graveolens L.	Worldwide	Herb
Carum carvi L.	Europe	Herb
C. involucratum Baill.	North Africa	Herb
Centella asiatica (L.) Urb.	Southeast Asia	Herb
Chaerophyllum bulbosum L.	Europe	Herb
Coriandrum sativum L.	Worldwide	Herb
Cryptotaenia canadensis A. D.C.	Pantropical	Herb
C. japonica Hassk.	Orient	Herb
Daucus carota L.	Europe	Herb
Eryngium creticum Lam.	Near East	Herb
E. floridanum Coult.	Central America	Herb
E. foetidum L.	Pantropical	Herb
Ferula communis L.	North Africa	Herb
Foeniculum vulgare Mill.	Mediterranean	Herb
Hydrocotyle javanica Thunb.	Indonesia	Herb
H. sibthorpioidea Lam.	Tropical Asia	Herb
Oenanthe anomala Dur. et Coss.	North Africa	Herb
Petroselinum crispum (Mill.) Nym.	Worldwide	Herb
Peucedanum capense Sond. Cf. Apium	Africa	Herb
P. japonicum Thunb.	Philippines	Herb
Scandix iberica Biel.	Near East	Herb
Sium sp.	South Africa, East Asia	Herb
Smyrnium olusatrum L.	North Africa, Europe	Herb
Trachyspermum roxburghianum Craib.	Indonesia	Herb

URTICACEAE

Species	Distribution	Habit
Boehmeria nivea (L.) Gaud.	Tropical Asia	Shrub
B. platyphylla D. Don	Africa	Shrub
Conocephalus suaveolena Blume	Malaysia	Vine
Cudrania javensis Trecul	Southeast Asia, Moluccas	Shrub
Dorstenia sp.	Africa	Herb
Elatostema edule C.B. Rob.	Philippines	Herb
Fleurya aestuans (L.) Gaud.	Sri Lanka	Herb
F. interrupta (L.) Gaud.	Philippines	Herb
F. ovalifolia (Schum.) Dandy	Tropical Africa	Herb
F. podocarpa Wedd.	Tropical Africa	Herb
Girardinia heterophyllas Decne.	India, Sri Lanka	Herb
G. palmata Gaud.	India	Herb
Laportea stimulans Miq.	Indomalaysia	Herb
L. terminalis Wight.	India	Herb
Pilea glaberrima Bl.	Indonesia	Herb
P. melastomoides By.	Southeast Asia	Herb
Pipturus arborescens C. B. Rob.	Philippines	Shrub
Pouzolzia guineensis Benth.	Sri Lanka	Herb
P. tuberosa Wight.	India	Herb
P. viminea Wedd.	India	Herb
P. zeylanica Benn.	Tropical Asia	Herb
Urera cameroonensis Wedd.	West Africa	Vine
U. mannii Wedd.	West Africa	Vine
U. obovata Benth.	West Africa	Vine
U. oblongifolia Benth.	West Africa	Shrub
Urtica dioica L.	North Africa, North America	Herb
U. massaica Mildbr	Tropical Africa	Herb
U. pilulifera L.	North Africa, North America	Herb
U. urens L.	Africa	Herb
Villebrunea rubescens Bl.	Southeast Asia	Herb
V. sylvatica Blume	Indomalaysia	Herb

VALERIANACEAE

Species	Distribution	Habit
Fedia cornucopiae Gaertn.	North Africa	Herb
Valerianella eriocarpa Desv.	Worldwide	Herb
V. olitoria Poll.	Mediterranean	Herb

VERBENACEAE

Species	Distribution	Habit
Avicennia officinalis L.		Tree
Clerodendron inerme Gaertn.	India	Shrub
C. minahassae T. et B.	Indonesia	Shrub
C. serratum Spreng.	Southeast Asia	Shrub
C. siphonanthus R. Br.	Tropical Asia	Shrub
Lantana camara L.	Pantropical	Shrub
L. salvifolia Jacq.	India	Herb

Species	Distribution	Habit
Lippia adoensis Hochst.	West Africa	Herb
L. geminata H.B.K.	Brazil	Herb
L. graveolens H.B.K.	Tropical America, Africa	Herb
L. helleri	Tropical America, Africa	Shrub
L. micromera Schau.	Hawaii	Herb
L. nodiflora Michx.	Tropical Asia	Herb
L. pseudothea Schauv.	Brazil	Herb
Premna divaricata Wall.	Malay Peninsula	Shrub
P. esculenta Roxb.	India	Herb
P. foetida Reinw.	Indomalaysia	Herb
P. glabra A. Gray	Pacific Islands	Herb
P. integrifolia L.	India, Sri Lanka	Herb
P. latifolia Roxb.	India	Herb
P. odorata Blanco	Philippines	Tree
Stachytarpheta indica Vahl.	Pantropical	Herb
S. jamaicensis Vahl.	South America	Herb
Vitex cienkowski Kotsch	West Africa	Tree
V. diversifolia Baker	West Africa	Tree
V. doniana Sweet	Tropical Africa	Tree
V. negundo L.	Pantropical	Shrub

VIOLACEAE

Species	Distribution	Habit
Alsodeia bengalensis Wall.	India	Shrub
A. castanaefolia Spreng.	Brazil	Shrub
A. physiphora Mart.	Brazil	Shrub
Viola abyssinica Oliv.	Africa	Herb

VITACEAE

Species	Distribution	Habit
Cissus adnata Roxb.	Tropical Asia	Vine
C. barteri Blume	Congo	Vine
C. capensis Willd.	South Africa	Vine
C. dinklagei	Gabon	Vine
C. discolor Blume	Southeast Asia	Vine
C. palmatifolia Planch.	West Africa	Vine
C. petiolata Hook.	Congo	Vine
C. populnea Guill. et Perr.	West Africa	Vine
C. producta Afzel.	Gabon	Vine
Cissus pseudocaesia Gild. et Br.	Africa	Vine
C. quadrangularis L.	Africa, Tropical Asia	Vine
C. repens Lam.	Tropical Asia	Vine
Leea aspera Edgew.	India	Vine
L. macrophylla Roxb.	India	Vine
L. quineensis	West Africa	Tree
Tetrastigma harmandii Pl.	Tropical Asia	Vine
T. lanceolarium Planch.	Tropical Asia	Vine
T. loheri Gagnep.	Philippines	Vine
T. thomsonianum Planch.	Tropical Asia	Vine
Vitis vinifera L.	Worldwide	Vine

ZINGIBERACEAE

Species	Distribution	Habit
Aframomum granum-paradisi K. Schum.	Africa	Herb
A. citratum Pers.	Africa	Herb
A. giganteum K. Schum.	China	Herb
Alpinia galanga Sw.	China	Herb
A. officinarum L.		
Amomum cardamomum Willd.	Malaysia	Herb
A. citratum Pers.	Pantropical	Herb
A. maximum Roxb.	Indonesia	Herb
A. officinarum Hance	Tropical Asia	Herb
A. uliginosum Koenig ex Retz.	Malaysia	Herb
Costus phyllocephalus K. Schum.	Congo	Herb
C. speciosus Smith	Southeast Asia	Herb
Curcuma amada Rosb.	Southeast Asia	Herb
C. aurantiaca van Zijp.	India	Herb
C. longa L.	Southeast Asia	Herb
C. manga Val. et van Zijp.	Southeast Asia	Herb
C. xanthorrhiza Roxb.	Southeast Asia	Herb
C. zedoaria Rosc.	Southeast Asia	Herb
Kaempferia galanga L.	Southeast Asia	Herb
K. pandurata Roxb.	Southeast Asia	Herb
K. rotunda L.	Southeast Asia	Herb
Languas pyramidata Merr.	Tropical Asia	Herb
L. uviformis Burk.	Tropical Asia	Herb
Phaeomeria atropurpurea Schum.	Tropical Asia	Herb
P. speciosa Koord	Tropical Asia	Herb
Zingiber officinale Rosc.	Pantropical	Herb

ZYGOPHYLLACEAE

Species	Distribution	Habit
Balanites aegyptiaca (L.) Del.	North Africa to Mediterranean	Tree
Fagonia sp.	Sahara	Herb
Kallastroemia maxima Torr. et Gray	Central America	Herb
Tribulus alatus Delile	India	Herb
T. terrestris L.	India, East Africa	Herb

Index to Genera and Common Names Mentioned in the Text